Studies in Rhetorics and Feminisms

Series Editors, Cheryl Glenn and Shirley Wilson Logan

FOOD,
FEMINISMS,
RHETORICS

EDITED BY MELISSA A. GOLDTHWAITE

Southern Illinois University Press
Carbondale

Southern Illinois University Press
www.siupress.com

Cover illustration: *Women Are Like That* (detail),
    video still by Rachelle Beaudoin, 2014

Library of Congress Cataloging-in-Publication Data

Names: Goldthwaite, Melissa A., 1972– editor.
Title: Food, feminisms, rhetorics / edited by Melissa A. Goldthwaite.
Description: Carbondale : Southern Illinois University Press, [2017] | Series: Studies
    in rhetorics and feminisms | Includes bibliographical references and index.
Identifiers: LCCN 2016044017 | ISBN 9780809335909 (pbk.) | ISBN 9780809335916
    (e-book)
Subjects: LCSH: Food writing. | Food in literature. | Feminist literature. | Food
    writers—Biography.
Classification: LCC TX644 .F66 2017 | DDC 808.06/6641—dc23
LC record available at https://lccn.loc.gov/2016044017

One of the pleasantest of all emotions is to know that I, I with my brain and my hands, have nourished my beloved few, that I have concocted a stew or a story, a rarity or a plain dish, to sustain them truly against the hungers of the world.

—M. F. K. Fisher, *The Gastronomical Me*

CONTENTS

Acknowledgments   xi   / *vii*

Preparation and Ingredients: An Introduction to *Food, Feminisms, Rhetorics*   1
Melissa A. Goldthwaite

Part I. Purposeful Cooking: Recipes for Historiography, Thrift, and Peace

1. Writing Recipes, Telling Histories: Cookbooks as Feminist Historiography   15
Carrie Helms Tippen

2. The Embodied Rhetoric of Recipes   30
Jennifer Cognard-Black

3. Understanding the Significance of "Kitchen Thrift" in Prescriptive Texts about Food   48
Jennifer E. Courtney

4. Promoting Peace, Subverting Domesticity: Cookbooks against War, 1968–83   60
Abby Dubisar

Part II. Defining Feminist Food Writing

5. The Meaning of a Meal: M. F. K. Fisher and Gastronomical
    Kairos   77
    Erin Branch

6. Feminist Culinary Autobiographies: *Batterie de Cuisine* to Peaceable
    Kingdom   89
    Lynn Z. Bloom

7. From Street Food to Digital Kitchens: Toward a Feminist Rhetoric
    of Culinary Tourism (or, How Not to Devour Paris and Eat Your
    Way through Asia)   100
    Kristin Winet

Part III. Rhetorical Representations of Food-Related Practices

8. Not Your Father's Family Farm: Toward Transformative Rhetorics
    of Food and Agriculture   119
    Abby Wilkerson

9. Baklava as Home: Exile and Arab Cooking in Diana Abu-Jaber's
    Novel *Crescent*   132
    Arlene Voski Avakian

10. Feeling Good and Eating Well: Race, Gender, and Affect in Ruth
    Ozeki's *My Year of Meats*   142
    Winona Landis

11. Sugar and Spice: Cooking with the Girl Poisoner   155
    Sylvia A. Pamboukian

12. Boxed Wine Feminisms: The Rhetoric of Women's Wine Drinking
    in *The Good Wife*   171
    Tammie M. Kennedy

Part IV. Rhetorical Representations of Bodies and Cultures

13. The Commodification of Mexican Women on Mexican Food
    Packaging   189
    Consuelo Carr Salas

14. Feeding the Self: Representations of Nourishment and Female
    Bodies in Holocaust Art   200
    Alexis Baker

15. Evolving Ana: Inviting Recovery   212
    Morgan Gresham

16. Reconstructing the Female Food-Body: Profanity, Purity, and the Bakhtinian Grotesque in *Skinny Bitch*   222
Rebecca Ingalls

17. Gusto and Grace: *Two Fat Ladies* and the Rhetorical Construction of a Fat Culinary Ethos   237
Sara Hillin

18. Deconstructing the Plus-Size Female Sleuth: Fat Positive Discourse, Rhetorical Excess, and Cultural Constructions of Femininity in Cozy Crime Fiction   251
Elizabeth Lowry

Contributors   265
Index   269

ACKNOWLEDGMENTS

Ideas often come from conversations around tables. The idea for this book /xi came in October 2012 on a day of celebration with a house full of friends, family, food, and drink. I'm grateful to Cheryl Glenn and Jennifer Cognard-Black, who were both there to celebrate with me that day, and who both had a hand in shaping this project. My thanks to Jennifer, again, and the other contributors who wrote, revised, and helped turn an idea into a book.

Many others contributed, too: Cheryl, again, and Shirley Wilson Logan, the editors of the Studies in Rhetorics and Feminisms series, provided support and helpful suggestions. Kristine Priddy and Judy Verdich, at Southern Illinois University Press, guided this project with attention to detail. The outside reviewer's comments led to important additions and revisions. Mary Goldthwaite-Gagne introduced me to Rachelle Beaudoin's art. An image from Rachelle's performance piece *Women Are Like That* appears on the cover; if you go to her website, you can view the full performance. In addition, a sabbatical granted by Saint Joseph's University gave me time to focus.

At home, two beings nourished me. I spent much of my adult life wanting to be alone in *my* kitchen. Even when I cooked for loved ones or guests, I didn't want help. I didn't desire conversation or collaboration while I cooked. With Howard Dinin, that changed—I changed. Now, we share kitchens. *Ours.* For the first time in my adult life, someone else does the majority of the food shopping and cooking, freeing me to spend more time on my work.

Additionally, Howard helps with that work, preparing images and offering assistance and ideas. And then there's Artemis; for nearly fourteen years, she has been my most constant and sweetest companion. When work requires long hours and deep focus, she curls up next to me and sleeps; she also gets me outside at least twice a day, and she makes sharing food a true pleasure.

To all who contributed to this project: thank you.

FOOD, FEMINISMS, RHETORICS

PREPARATION AND INGREDIENTS: AN INTRODUCTION TO *FOOD, FEMINISMS, RHETORICS*

Melissa A. Goldthwaite

EXAMINING FOOD-RELATED PRACTICES

> A focus on food practices can help to bring specificity to examinations of cultures as well as revealing the power dynamics within them. Close attention to who is cooking what, for whom, and under what conditions can break down totalizing notions of gender, race, and class.
> —Arlene Avakian, "Cooking Up Lives: Feminist Food Memoirs"

Observe, examine—so many messages ripe for interpretation. In a local department store, the spatula sold as a grill tool has a built-in bottle opener and is twice as large and sturdy as any sold near kitchen utensils. Walk the aisles of a local grocery store. Are there Hungry-Man frozen dinners, Manwiches, an entire line of Skinnygirl products? How is the store organized? Are there sections for "ethnic" foods, particular diets, organic foods? What foods or products are most prominent? Which ones are absent? At home, unwrap a Dove chocolate to find three words printed on the foil wrapper: "chocolate loves unconditionally."

Keep looking. Look back. What foods were forbidden when you were a child? What were you fed? Where did it come from? Who prepared it? What did you refuse? What did you not know existed? What material conditions shaped your relationship to food?[1] What food-related messages about bodies,

culture, religion, region, economics, and gender roles did you receive—
and from whom?

Messages surrounding food—its availability, its preparation, its consumption, its role in the lives of individuals, families, and cultures—are multiple
and conflicting. Food is sustenance and poison, fuel and temptation, home
culture and one of the most memorable introductions to new cultures and
places. Preparing food is drudgery and joy, duty and delight. In her introduction to *Kitchen Culture in America*, Sherrie A. Inness writes that "eating
is an activity that *always* has cultural reverberations. Food is *never* a simple
matter of sustenance. How we eat, what we eat, and who prepares and serves
our meals are all issues that shape society" (5). Such shaping messages come
not just from food marketers, advertisers, and designers but from a range
of sources—mundane and literary, ethnic and economic (family practices,
cultural taboos, where one lives, what one watches and reads).

With reflection and analysis, understanding of such messages can shift
and change and be critiqued. In the essay "Boiled Chicken Feet and Hundred-Year-Old Eggs: Poor Chinese Feasting," for example, Shirley Geok-
lin Lim writes that in her family, chicken feet were only to be enjoyed by
married women. Lim's aunts warned that if she ate them before she was
married, she'd grow up to run away from her husband (217), a poignant
warning since her mother had left. She further explains, "The chickens were
divided according to gender, the father receiving the white breast meat,
the sons the dark drumsticks, and the daughters the skinny backs, while
the women ate the feet and wings" (218). In the first section of her essay,
she critiques the gendered taboos of her childhood in Malaysia, yet as she
continues, Lim considers other factors that helped create such taboos. She
reflects on poverty, class differences, and the distinctions between American
and Chinese cultures.

When she and her brother share soy-boiled chicken feet as adults later in
the essay, Lim's nuanced understanding of the complex social and economic
forces that have shaped her comes through clearly. She writes that "even after
decades of American fast foods and the rich diet of the middle class, my
deprived childhood had indelibly fixed as gastronomic fantasies those dishes
impoverished Chinese had produced out of the paltry ingredients they could
afford" (224). Instead of earlier images of chickens' feet that had stepped on
"duck and dog and their own shit" (217), Lim gives readers a transformed
understanding of this food both withheld from her and rejected by her in
childhood. She provides a context for the gendered taboos and ends with the
image of her brother sharing "the best of [their] childhood together" (224).

She then presents readers with a recipe for soy-boiled chicken feet, a dish that—for Lim—represents complex and conflicting messages.

Lim's essay provides just one example of the ways the messages we receive can shape how we view, define, and feel about food, ourselves, and others. Food-related practices can affect personal choices, purchases, relationships, traditions, and political actions. But those messages can also be reflected on, questioned, viewed differently, and sometimes changed.

In response to Sherrie A. Inness's call for "more critical attention to cooking culture in general, whether it be books, television shows, Internet sites, or magazine articles," this collection on food, feminisms, and rhetorics includes rhetorical analyses of a range of texts, gendered roles, and expectations in relation to food (*Secret Ingredients* 15). The authors in this collection use forms of feminist rhetorical theory to reflect on food-related texts, practices, and—in some cases—the role of food and cooking in their own lives and cultures.

EMPLOYING FEMINIST RHETORICS

Feminist scholarship isn't intended to be used only for the recovery and recuperation of female rhetorical figures. We can use feminist questions to rethink traditional topics (argument and ethos, for instance), people (private and public), and time periods (past and present).

— Cheryl Glenn, quoted in "Feminist Rhetorical Studies—Past, Present, Future"

In the past two decades, feminist scholars have demonstrated an increased interest in the study of gender and food. As Arlene Avakian observes, there was a time when "other than addressing food disorders, feminists were reluctant to explore cooking and eating, linking these activities only with women's oppression"; however, she points to a shift in focus, "a veritable flood of feminist analyses of all the various aspects of food" ("Cooking Up" 277). Avakian's contributions, among others, include *Through the Kitchen Window: Women Writers Explore the Intimate Meanings of Food and Cooking* and a collection she edited with Barbara Haber, *From Betty Crocker to Feminist Food Studies*. Sherrie Inness's work has also been significant and prolific, as the following titles attest: *Cooking Lessons: The Politics of Gender and Food*; *Dinner Roles: American Women and Culinary Culture*; *Kitchen Culture in America: Popular Representations of Food, Gender, and Race*; *Pilaf, Pozole, and Pad Thai: American Women and Ethnic Food*; and *Secret Ingredients:*

Race, Gender, and Class at the Dinner Table. From collections on women, food, and globalization (Barndt) to analyses of particular foods and cultures (Abarca, Bower, Williams-Forson), the breadth and depth of feminist food studies continues to grow.

With these and other examples of feminist food studies already available, why choose rhetoric as an analytical lens? In the introduction to their collection *The Rhetoric of Food: Discourse, Materiality, and Power,* Joshua J. Frye and Michael S. Bruner claim rhetoric as a means "to help explain the dynamics and the consequences" of food, material, and power (1). They draw on Kenneth Burke's work to point to the persuasive power of rhetoric in forming attitudes and inducing action, and they also argue for the importance of rhetoric to illuminate and critique injustices. I see the same potential in rhetorical analysis and believe, further, that feminist rhetorical analysis can offer approaches to topics, people, ideas, and positions left out of other studies. One approach that illustrates the potential of bringing rhetorical and feminist theories together is what Krista Ratcliffe calls "rhetorical listening," a "stance of openness that a person may choose to assume in relation to any person, text, or culture" with the purpose of cultivating conscious identifications (25). Through this collection, I wish to value the contributions of both feminist and rhetorical theories, bringing them together in productive ways and providing a forum for many voices—including both new and established scholars.

Several questions helped guide the selection of chapters for this book. What does a particular approach to or representation of food, body, self, others, or cultures allow one to do? What are the effects? When should those approaches or representations be critiqued—and on what grounds? How does the author take rhetorical concerns—such as speaker/writer, audience, purpose, genre, and context—into account?

In a feminist rhetorical context, attention to who is speaking or writing involves consideration of the ethics of representation: representations of both self and others. Jacqueline Jones Royster and Gesa E. Kirsch, in *Feminist Rhetorical Practices: New Horizons for Rhetoric, Composition, and Literacy Studies*, seek to "pay attention, not just to ethics and representation but specifically to ethos, to the ethical self" both in texts studied and ones created (14). In working with the writers and scholars whose chapters are in *Food, Feminisms, Rhetorics*, I have been interested in and attentive to the ways they present themselves and their subjects—to their attention to ethos as both a scholarly lens (Bloom, Branch, Baker, Hillin) and a personal position (Tippen, Cognard-Black, Courtney, Winet, Salas, Baker, Gresham).

Even as contributors analyze the purpose of the texts and practices they study, they reveal their own purposes—whether to claim the importance of understudied or undervalued genres, to critique social injustices, or to help readers see familiar texts and practices in a new way. The subjects and objects they study are varied—from cookbooks to genre fiction, from blogs to food systems, from product packaging to paintings—but the overall message is the same: food is worthy of scholarly attention.

Just as the purposes, contexts, and genres analyzed in this collection are varied, so are the rhetorical theories used. Some scholars illuminate traditional—often Aristotelian—concepts such as ethos, pathos, logos, and kairos, claiming their subjects use such rhetorical strategies for feminist ends. Others use more current feminist rhetorical theories, such as invitational rhetoric (Foss and Griffin) or rhetorical listening (Ratcliffe) or social circulation (Royster and Kirsch), applying these theories to practices as diverse as peace activism, pro-ana and fat positive rhetoric, and alcohol consumption. Other scholars pay attention to identity formation and the importance of self-naming, recognizing the complexity of such processes and practices and how they might be shaped and used rhetorically.

/ 5

PART I. PURPOSEFUL COOKING: RECIPES FOR HISTORIOGRAPHY, THRIFT, AND PEACE

Feminist rhetoric often prompts researchers to question what rhetorical subjects are "deemed worthy of attention and study" (Royster and Kirsch 51). Although cookbooks and recipes have not, in the past, been popular subjects of research in the field of rhetoric and composition, feminist scholars increasingly claim them as worthy of study. As Inness observes, cookbooks have been "more than a place to record recipes"; they have also been "sites to discuss political issues," and they also often include "lessons for social change" (*Secret Ingredients* 7).

Many of the chapters included in *Food, Feminisms, Rhetorics* illustrate Inness's observation. Carrie Helms Tippen, in "Writing Recipes, Telling Histories: Cookbooks as Feminist Historiography," claims cookbooks as feminist historiography, arguing that cookbook writers can be seen as rhetoricians. She values the use of narrative in cookbooks and shows how recipes can have both historical and rhetorical significance. In "The Embodied Rhetoric of Recipes," Jennifer Cognard-Black uses both narrative and rhetorical analysis in a way that exemplifies and furthers Tippen's argument. Cognard-Black analyzes recipes as a generic form, one with personal, historical, and rhetorical import, showing the "embodied rhetoric" of recipes handed down generationally as simultaneously empowering and limiting—but fully worthy of academic attention.

Food-related texts often do more than provide instructions for cooking and eating; several contributors to this collection analyze other rhetorical purposes. In "Understanding the Significance of 'Kitchen Thrift' in Prescriptive Texts about Food," Jennifer E. Courtney analyzes the meaning of *thrift* in its historical and rhetorical context and in relation to thriving, arguing that domestic guides can offer "readers not only practical information but powerful alternatives to mainstream discourses of gendered consumption." While Courtney locates her study in domestic spheres, Abby Dubisar, in "Promoting Peace, Subverting Domesticity: Cookbooks against War, 1968–83," considers texts that encourage women to perform both domestic and public roles. She studies antiwar and peace activist cookbooks that "teach feminist rhetoricians the potential of domestic genres to promote activist causes and frame political identities." Although the chapters included in this section analyze cookbooks and recipes in different contexts, they all show the ways personal, cultural, and political identities are connected and can have historical import and rhetorical effects.

PART II. DEFINING FEMINIST FOOD WRITING

Food writing, of course, is not limited to recipes, cookbooks, or domestic guides; it also includes food-related essays, memoirs, autobiographies, blogs, and other genres. From M. F. K. Fisher's 1937 publication *Serve It Forth* to more recent autobiographies by female chefs, much of this writing is by women and might be claimed as "feminist." It's worth asking, though, what rhetorical elements make food writing feminist? Erin Branch offers a case study for feminist rhetorical practice in her analysis of Fisher's food writing. Branch shows "how Fisher employs what rhetorical scholars have described as a 'feminine style' to argue that the pleasures food can provide are as important as any of its other benefits." She praises Fisher's "welcoming ethos." Though both Branch and Lynn Z. Bloom share an admiration for Fisher's writing, Bloom—in "Feminist Culinary Autobiographies: *Batterie de Cuisine* to Peaceable Kingdom"—complicates the definition of "feminist food writing" by considering the differing rhetorical strategies employed by three feminist autobiographers who write about food. She argues that they "subvert (and sometimes expand) the default feminine model of effortless succor and succulence," offering different models for feminist food writing.

Kristin Winet, too, analyzes nonfiction food writing, turning her attention to culinary tourism as represented by those who write about themselves and others in blogs that encourage food-related travel. Before defining strategies of feminist food writing, Winet critiques certain forms of "cosmopolitanism, decontextualization, devouring, and escapism" often used by travel writers who focus on food. Like other writers in this section, Winet turns to Fisher's work to help define "a more self-reflective, careful, and compassionate relationship to food" both at home and abroad. Together, these essays and the ones that follow in part 3 show that feminist food writing is neither monolithic nor beyond critique—and that definitions of what it means to be feminist change over time.[2]

PART III. RHETORICAL REPRESENTATIONS OF FOOD-RELATED PRACTICES

What are the effects of representing food-related practices in particular ways? What representations reinforce traditional gender roles, racial inequality, or other social hierarchies? What are the possibilities for representations that might lead to positive transformation? What complexities and ambiguities need to be acknowledged? From analyzing the rhetoric of sustainable food movements to exploring the complex relationships among national, ethic, and gendered identities to interrogating the rhetoric of wine consumption as represented in a popular television show, authors included in this section consider the social, cultural, and political effects of particular representations of food-related practices.

Several essays in this section consider social justice/injustice, gender, and race and ethnicity. In "Not Your Father's Family Farm: Toward Transformative Rhetorics of Food and Agriculture," Abby Wilkerson looks at "the potential of family rhetoric in movements for food justice and sustainability to reinforce existing social hierarchies and inequalities" and offers alternative approaches to sustainable food that take "racial justice and socioeconomic inequality" into account. Arlene Voski Avakian argues that Diana Abu-Jaber's deployment of food and cooking in the novel *Crescent* "creates a cultural space for the characters to explore national, ethnic, and gender identities both in diaspora and exile" and helps counter Arab American stereotypes. Winona Landis's analysis of Ruth Ozeki's use of pathos in the novel *My Year of Meats* also considers issues of food justice, racial inequality, and family rhetoric; Landis shows both the possibilities and limitations of positive feeling as a rhetorical strategy, illuminating the complexity of the issues about which Ozeki writes.

Other fictional texts, especially those written for children, also use pathos to shape reader response, often making clear the opposition between "good" and "bad" characters, separating those who poison and from those who nourish. In "Sugar and Spice: Cooking with the Girl Poisoner," Sylvia A. Pamboukian examines the figure of the girl poisoner in children's literature, noting how this character differs from representations of adult female poisoners (presented mainly as unfeminine and unlikeable witches). Her analysis reveals the ways both girl poisoners and representations of women in such stories "enact a variety of rhetorical purposes, thereby transgressing conventions of both age and gender."

The line between poison and nourishment can become especially blurry when considering representations of adult women drinking. In "Boxed Wine Feminisms: The Rhetoric of Women's Wine Drinking in *The Good Wife*," Tammie M. Kennedy considers how wine drinking is represented in contemporary popular culture as a necessary means for women to do "emotion work" in balancing their professional and personal responsibilities and needs. Rather than taking a firm position on whether drinking wine is good for women, she uses her analysis to help "feminist rhetoricians better locate both potential spaces of transformation and potentially dangerous consequences" of women drinking to cope with pressures.

PART IV. RHETORICAL REPRESENTATIONS OF BODIES AND CULTURES

Like the chapters in the previous section, those in this section also analyze food-related practices and representations, but this section's pieces focus on bodies and culture—both self-representation and representations of others for particular rhetorical purposes. These essays consider questions such as: What are the effects of representing and naming oneself and others in particular ways? How do such representations serve rhetorical purposes that have personal, cultural, and political effects?

Consuelo Carr Salas, in "The Commodification of Mexican Women on Mexican Food Packaging," considers the purpose and audience for stereotypical representations of Mexican women on food packaging, arguing that some images seek to persuade consumers of a product's "authenticity," even as those images reinforce an essentialized image of Mexican women and culture. Alexis Baker, too, examines visual rhetoric, analyzing representations (both self-representations and representations by other artists) of women's bodies in Holocaust art. She sees the prevalence of "healthy, well-nourished, fully functioning female bodies" as evidence of a "cultural and spiritual sense of self" determined not by physical reality but by a gendered cultural identity. Baker argues that such representations "operate as visual metaphors about the survival of women's cultural and spiritual identity—despite the horrors of the Holocaust."

In "Evolving Ana: Inviting Recovery," Morgan Gresham, too, writes about the importance of identity construction and seeks to understand rather than denounce controversial websites that play a role in shaping the identities of many young women. In particular, Gresham analyzes the pro-ana site House of Thin and recognizes its potential to invite (but not demand) recovery through a form of invitational rhetoric and an acceptance of (and perhaps redefinition of) the label "pro-ana." Of course, not all rhetoric used by women is invitational or accepting of a range of relationships to food, as Rebecca Ingalls shows in her Bakhtinian analysis of Rory Freedman and Kim Barnouin's *Skinny Bitch*. Ingalls claims that the *Skinny Bitch* authors use "grotesque realism" as a rhetorical strategy, seeking to shame women into adopting a vegan diet (and avoiding caffeine, alcohol, refined sugar, white flour, and other foods).

The two remaining essays in this collection study approaches to foods / 9 and bodies far different from the ones exalted in *Skinny Bitch*. Sara Hillin considers the work of Jennifer Paterson and Clarissa Dickson Wright, known as the "Two Fat Ladies" on their television show and as writers of cookbooks, showing how they exploit "negative cultural connotations of fatness" to create a positive ethos and platform for their own personal and political concerns: celebrating a love for food, advocating for food (especially meat) safety, and critiquing trends in cooking that call for substitution or deprivation.

Elizabeth Lowry also considers cultural associations with fatness in her study of "feminism, fat positive discourse, and the detective novel"—specifically, dessert-themed books that feature a fat female protagonist whose "fondness for food" helps her solve crimes. Lowry claims that such narratives and protagonists provide examples of women who accept their bodies as they are and give "a rhetorical space to challenge harmful assumptions about fat people." Yet Lowry also acknowledges the range of representations in such novels—that some of these books fail to take into account the complexities of the protagonist's embodied reality or sometimes perpetuate gender stereotypes.

As Lowry seeks to answer the question of whether fat positive detective novels should be considered feminist, she makes clear that feminism is not "a monolithic discourse," which is, perhaps, the main message of this collection. Food, gender, identity, culture—and the language, strategies, and representations used to talk and write about these aspects of living and being—are complex and often full of irony. A "transsexual escort model" who calls herself Mandi Faux can create a pro-ana website that invites an audience of mainly young women to recover from disordered eating. Vegan "skinny bitches" and meat-loving "fat ladies" can use similar rhetorical strategies (hyperbole, reappropriating disparaging terms) to create arguments about what it means to have a "healthy" relationship to food and to one's body. Those who are starving can be represented as nourished; hunger can be both physical and emotional; images used to represent "authenticity" may have little connection to a complex reality; cookbooks can teach more than how to cook. And even though there exists no perfect recipe for dismantling unjust social, political, and economic hierarchies; no language that communicates with every audience; no food that can satisfy every hunger—there are, each day, opportunities to nourish, to learn better methods for preparing food and for analyzing it, to critique and to be more generous in sharing foods, practices, ideas, and ourselves.

Notes

1. In *Vibration Cooking: or, The Travel Notes of a Geechee Girl*, Vertamae Smart-Grosvenor writes, "You won't find any heavy baking recipes in this book cause I'm not a good baker. I have never lived in a place that has a decent oven" (24). In the same chapter, she offers a recipe for cooking brains and another for "possum and taters" (19, 28). Her recipes show that what is available—from appliances to ingredients—shapes one's relationship to food and cooking.

2. The scholars in this section focus on the writing of white women. For an article that further expands the definition of feminist food writing, see Avakian's "Cooking Up Lives: Feminist Food Memoirs." Avakian provides an intersectional feminist reading of food memoirs by Diana Abu-Jaber, Annia Ciezadlo, Linda Furiya, and Judith Newton, showing that while

> differences in training, profession, race/ethnicity, and age exist among these authors, cooking and eating are critical to their understanding of their lives, and they all use the daily material practices around food to explore relations of domination within shifting cultures and identities. (280)

Works Cited

Abarca, Meredith E. *Voices in the Kitchen: Views of Food and the World from Working-Class Mexican and Mexican American Women*. Texas A&M UP, 2006.

Avakian, Arlene. "Cooking Up Lives: Feminist Food Memoirs." *Feminist Studies* 40.2 (2014): 277–303.

———, ed. *Through the Kitchen Window: Women Writers Explore the Intimate Meanings of Food and Cooking.* Beacon P, 1997.

Avakian, Arlene Voski, and Barbara Haber, eds. *From Betty Crocker to Feminist Food Studies: Critical Perspectives on Women and Food.* U of Massachusetts P, 2005.

Barndt, Deborah, ed. *Women Working the NAFTA Food Chain: Women, Food, and Globalization.* Sumach P, 1999.

Bower, Anne L., ed. *African American Foodways: Explorations of History and Culture.* U of Illinois P, 2007.

Enoch, Jessica. "Feminist Rhetorical Studies—Past, Present, Future: An Interview with Cheryl Glenn." *Composition Forum* 29 (2014): n. pag. Accessed 31 January 2016.

Foss, Sonja K., and Cindy L. Griffin. "Beyond Persuasion: A Proposal for an Invitational Rhetoric." *Communication Monographs* (March 1995): 2–18.

Frye, Joshua J., and Michael S. Bruner, eds. *The Rhetoric of Food: Discourse, Materiality, and Power.* Routledge, 2012.

Inness, Sherrie A. *Cooking Lessons: The Politics of Gender and Food.* Rowman and Littlefield, 2001.

———. *Dinner Roles: American Women and Culinary Culture.* U of Iowa P, 2001.

———, ed. *Kitchen Culture in America: Popular Representations of Food, Gender, and Race.* U of Pennsylvania P, 2001.

———, ed. *Pilaf, Pozole, and Pad Thai: American Women and Ethnic Food.* U of Massachusetts P, 2001.

———. *Secret Ingredients: Race, Gender, and Class at the Dinner Table.* Palgrave Macmillan, 2006.

Lim, Shirley Geok-lin. "Boiled Chicken Feet and Hundred-Year-Old Eggs: Poor Chinese Feasting." *Through the Kitchen Window: Women Writers Explore the Intimate Meanings of Food and Cooking.* Ed. Arlene Voski Avakian. Beacon P, 1997. 217–25.

Ratcliffe, Krista. *Rhetorical Listening: Identification, Gender, Whiteness.* Southern Illinois UP, 2005.

Royster, Jacqueline Jones, and Gesa E. Kirsch. *Feminist Rhetorical Practices: New Horizons for Rhetoric, Composition, and Literacy Studies.* Southern Illinois UP, 2012.

Smart-Grosvenor, Vertamae. *Vibration Cooking: or, The Travel Notes of a Geechee Girl.* 1970. Ballantine Books, 1992.

Williams-Forson, Psyche A. *Building Houses Out of Chicken Legs: Black Women, Food, and Power.* U of North Carolina P, 2006.

PART I

PURPOSEFUL COOKING: RECIPES FOR HISTORIOGRAPHY, THRIFT, AND PEACE

1. WRITING RECIPES, TELLING HISTORIES: COOKBOOKS AS FEMINIST HISTORIOGRAPHY

Carrie Helms Tippen

In *Reclaiming Rhetorica*, Andrea Lunsford explains that the mission of her collection is to recover the presence of women in the rhetorical tradition in order "to open up possibilities for multiple rhetorics" (6). The title of this present collection, *Food, Feminisms, Rhetorics*, likewise acknowledges a need for multiple rhetorics, for multiple definitions of what rhetoric is and with what texts it is concerned. This chapter aims to do what the contributors of *Reclaiming Rhetorica* have done, what Cheryl Glenn continued to do in *Rhetoric Retold*, what Anne Bower did in *Recipes for Reading*, what Elizabeth Engelhardt did in *A Mess of Greens*, and what Psyche Williams-Forson did in *Building Houses Out of Chicken Legs*: all have looked into the narratives of the historical past to identify voices silenced because of their gender, race, or class and have written a narrative that offers a challenge to the received metanarrative. Lunsford and Glenn challenge the exclusivity of "canonical rhetorical history [that] has represented the experience of males, powerful males, with no provision or allowance for females" (Glenn, *Rhetoric* 2). Bower asks in the introduction to *Recipes for Reading*, can one "value . . . [a cookbook] not just as a fun source of recipes but as a literary text whose authors constructed meaningful representations of themselves and their world?" (2). The essays in that collection bear out the answer in a resounding *yes*; the ordinary women who give their names and recipes to community cookbooks are, indeed, talented users of language and savvy rhetoricians. Engelhardt adds the voices of rural women and girls to the story of southern foodways by asking "how the South gets defined, by whom, at what time, and why it matters" (4), arguing that the picture is incomplete without these voices. Through an examination of representations of chicken and African Americans, Williams-Forson contends that the narratives and stories left by black women contradict stereotyped images imposed from the outside, and that the "story of feminist consciousness, community building, cultural work, and personal identity" in that text (1–2) presents an alternative to received metanarratives. In all these cases, feminist historiography is the method employed for opening up definitions and adding complicating narrative threads to the fabric of history.

Feminist historiography emphasizes absences in narratives, recovering voices, facts, or events that had previously been unknown or unacknowledged and offering an alternative narrative. In *Rhetoric Retold*, Glenn identifies her methodology as a three-pronged approach through the "angles" of historiography, feminism, and gender studies (4). The intersection of these three angles is feminist historiography, a process that requires a *redefinition of rhetoric* in order to renarrate the *history of rhetoric* to include women as *practitioners of rhetoric*. As Glenn explains in "Truth, Lies, and Method: Revisiting Feminist Historiography,"

> writing women (or any other traditionally disenfranchised group) into the history of rhetoric, then, can be an ethically and intellectually responsible gesture that disrupts those frozen memories in order to address silences, challenge absences, and assert women's contributions to public life. (389)

At its core, feminist historiography is about recovering women's accomplishments, experiences, and voices in order to disrupt the received "paternal narrative" of history (Glenn, *Rhetoric* 5). Glenn describes the product of historiography as a story and a map. The story is a reordering of events in a narrative. The map is a reimagination of connections between individuals. The "feminist" in feminist historiography, then, accomplishes three goals: (*1*) producing a story of women that resists the received paternal narrative, (*2*) reimagining of the nature of history itself as a network of interrelated people, and (*3*) reimagining the work of writing history in defiance of an understanding of narrative as teleological. A feminist historiography might not look like a linear timeline of events; rather, it might resemble an atlas with overlapping zones of influence. Or it might look like a cookbook.

Cookbooks are the perfect antidote to a rhetoric that would "name and valorize one traditional, competitive, agonistic, and linear mode of rhetorical discourse" (Lunsford 6). Instead, cookbooks embody a rhetoric that does precisely what Lunsford calls for "a reclaimed Rhetorica" to do: "Its characteristic and principal aim is not deception or conquest . . . but understanding, exploration, connection, and conversation" (6). Cookbooks are similarly antithetical to traditional historical narratives. Though a cookbook is made up of narratives—including introductions, headnotes, and recipe paratext—the cookbook itself suggests that the story of a time and place could just as easily be told through the chronology of a meal (soup to nuts) as it could through the chronology of public events.

Cookbook writers make their rhetorical purposes most explicitly clear in narrative elements. In these brief but ubiquitous passages of text, cookbook authors articulate their agendas. This chapter looks at the narrative text of one cookbook in particular, *Sweets: Soul Food Desserts and Memories*, to make two points about feminist historiography. First, I argue that *Sweets* itself is an example of how a cookbook can accomplish a kind of feminist historiography by telling a story and drawing a map of a time and place that highlights the accomplishments of women as culinary innovators and disrupts linear paternal narratives of that time and place. Secondly, my reading of *Sweets* is not unlike *Rhetoric Retold* or *Reclaiming Rhetorica*: I, too, am uncovering women rhetors (in the form of the author Patty Pinner and the women she cites in her book) and defining everyday acts of writing as rhetorical. Reading cookbook narratives through the lens of feminist historiography gives a language for identifying, naming, and describing the rhetorical choices of cookbook authors.

Lynne Ireland argued in 1981 that compiled cookbooks serve as "in a sense, an autobiography" (108), a narrative of the social, ethnic, and religious identity of a group. In *Eat My Words: Reading Women's Lives through the Cookbooks They Wrote*, Janet Theophano reads cookbooks as both autobiographies (stories about individual women) and sources of evidence for historicizing women's lives more generally. Theophano suggests that the traditional sources that historians have used to understand historical times and places ("newspapers, journals, diaries, manuscripts, biographies, autobiographies, and memoirs") underrepresent ordinary women. These women were generally less "able to write their own accounts of domestic life" in those expected genres than men were, and unless they were connected to famous men, their contributions were rarely valued as historical documents worth saving (2). Theophano found that cookbooks were among the few documents authored by and for women that were protected and "passed down" as heirlooms (2). She argues that these "intimate stories reveal individual women telling their own life stories, their versions of their communities, and the visions they have of society and culture" (3). Like feminist historiographies, cookbooks tell an alternative narrative about the world of women in the past through an alternative narrative form.

Susan Leonardi also emphasizes the "gendered nature" of the recipe as a form of narrative. When historical narratives are repeated, their effects can be measured in abstract ways; when a recipe is repeated, it has "a literal result, the dish itself." As Leonardi explains, "this kinship to the literality of human reproducibility, along with the social context of the recipe, contributes to the gendered nature of this form of embedded discourse" (344). Indeed, the very nature of the recipe as a "visceral" and domestic product "makes recipes a feminine discourse" (343). Like Theophano, Leonardi suggests that a recipe, and by extension a book of recipes, is a particularly feminine way of knowing and sharing knowledge. Though contemporary cookbooks are as likely to be written by men or for men as by or for women, the recipe as a form remains bound in traditionally feminine spheres of domestic economy and executed in narrative forms counter to traditionally masculine ways of telling history. In this way, the cookbook, in its many configurations, has a tendency to complicate boundaries between masculine and feminine, the public and the private, high and low culture, and history and memory.

When we combine Leonardi's picture of the cookbook as feminine with Theophano's understanding of the cookbook as historical narrative, we can see more clearly how many cookbook writers are engaged in feminist historiography and feminist rhetoric. Rien Fertel argues that "cookbooks can and do mirror history," urging historians to look at cookbooks as valid primary sources for historical study (14). While I certainly agree with this validation of cookbooks, I would further suggest that cookbooks are actively writing and rewriting history with a rhetorical agenda. In her article "'Revising the Menu to Fit the Budget': Grocery Lists and Other Rhetorical Heirlooms," Jamie White-Farnham contends that texts are rhetorical if "they make social and material effects, reflecting and creating the realities of the people who use them" (213). The rest of this chapter demonstrates how one cookbook in particular uses narratives of the past to reflect and create social networks of cooking women and employs recipes to reflect and create material realities. In other words, cookbooks, like the one examined here, represent kinds of feminist historiographies: narratives that focus on silenced women and challenge phallocentric methods of writing history.

Cookbook writers are historiographers as well as rhetors, innovators of culinary knowledge, and agents of cultural power. As Patty Pinner traces the origins of a recipe through female cooks and innovators in *Sweets*, she is writing women not only into the history of a single dish but also into the history of a cuisine and, by extension, a culture. Women as recipe innovators are women as cultural arbiters. I argue that the narratives in *Sweets* have a rhetorical function similar to feminist historiography; they offer a critique, a challenge, or an alternative to the received history. *Sweets* consistently uses narratives to trace the history of a recipe through the hands of women, giving them credit as innovators and focusing on women and women's roles.

(RE)WRITING THE GREAT MIGRATION IN RECIPES

Sweets is a dessert cookbook, divided into sections for cakes, pies and cobblers, puddings, cookies and candies, and ice creams. Each section begins with an extended memory, a two-to-three-page narrative tangentially related to the section. With only a few exceptions, the recipes are named for a female relative or friend; for example, "Aint [*sic*] Millie's Graham Cracker Cake" and "Miss Essie Brazil's Three-Layer Coconut Cake" are typical titles. Most named recipes are preceded by a half-page narrative about the recipe's namesake, explaining that the namesake innovated the recipe, or that the woman   / 19
was otherwise associated with the recipe in Pinner's memory as someone who regularly prepared or preferred to eat this recipe.

The narrative that follows for "My My's Pound Cake," a recipe Pinner associates with her grandmother, provides an example of Pinner's narrative style and rhetorical purpose:

> Pound cakes are a truly Southern dessert. They acquired their name because typically they were made from a pound each of butter, sugar, and flour. My My made the best pound cakes in the world. Her cakes were moist and fragrant concoctions that rose to delightful heights in the same baking tins that she had used when she lived down South. My My declared that a so-called pound cake that called for anything less than a pound each of the aforementioned was just that—so-called. (11)

Most of the recipe narratives describe the character of the eponymous woman and a specific memory, often unrelated to the dish. The last few lines identify the woman as the contributor of the recipe.

Sweets is a hybrid text, memoir and cookbook, chock-full of black-and-white family photographs and family stories. Most of the narratives focus on the matriarch of Pinner's family, her grandmother whom the family called My My. Pinner explains in the introduction to *Sweets* that her grandparents

(My My and Pop) and some of their friends moved from Mississippi to Michigan in 1948 to find work with General Motors. They settled in Saginaw in a neighborhood Pinner describes as "the heart of the black community" (1). The circumstances of the family's move to Michigan place their narrative within that of the Great Migration, the movement of six million African Americans from the rural South to the urban centers of the North and West (Wilkerson 9). Though Pinner never uses the phrase "Great Migration," *Sweets* offers an alternative history of this movement, one that focuses on the experiences of women of the Midwest and South in the mid-twentieth century.

In the early pages of *The Warmth of Other Suns: The Epic Story of America's Great Migration*, Isabel Wilkerson describes the forces that caused African American families in the early twentieth-century to consider leaving the South:

> There were sharecroppers losing at settlement. Typists wanting to work in an office. Yard boys scared that a single gesture near the planter's wife could leave them hanging in an oak tree. They were all stuck in a caste system as hard and unyielding as the red Georgia clay, and they each had a decision before them. (8)

In this short passage, the central themes of the Great Migration metanarrative are represented. The South was a place of violence and economic stagnation. The move north was for security, opportunity, stability, and mobility. Editor Alferdteen Harrison makes a similar assessment in the preface to the collection *Black Exodus: The Great Migration from the American South*:

> Older African-Americans generally remember when an aunt, uncle, cousin, or close friend left the South to go to school or to find a job in northern industries. Some remember or have heard of a person who had to leave because of violence in the segregated society. (vii)

Harrison outlines the specific forces that "encouraged" the Great Migration as follows:

> The use of the myth of white racial superiority to justify and enforce segregation through overt hostility and lynchings; the idling African-American labor in the South because of increasing white job competition as industrialization and agricultural mechanization came to the South; the work opportunities in the war industries in the north; and the relocation of large numbers of African-Americans from areas where they had lost hope of bettering their conditions. (viii)

According to these two narratives, violence and work are the twin engines of the movement. It would be difficult for a historian to deny that these were powerful influences; however, the result is a male-centered narrative. Wilkerson and Harrison both suggest that young males were the targets of racial violence, and that males stood to benefit most from industrial jobs.

Farah Jasmine Griffin's examination of Great Migration narratives, *"Who Set You Flowin'?,"* describes the anatomy of twentieth-century migration narratives in many genres, including fiction, music, photography, and painting. Her analysis of the conventions of the migration narrative is more balanced in its representations of women's and men's experiences than Wilkerson or Harrison, but like those two historians, Griffin, as artistic critic, also focuses on violence as the motivation for migration. According to Griffin, the inciting moment for migration in these artistic representations is almost always violence or the "fear of the violence," including scenes of "lynching, beating, and rape" (5). Though Griffin acknowledges that there are great variations in the pattern of the migration narrative, she claims, "In all cases, the South is portrayed as an immediate, identifiable, and oppressive power" (4). In other words, the migration narrative is one of escape from an oppressive South toward a "'freer' North" (3).

/ 21

Pinner's twenty-first-century migration narrative greatly differs from the outlines drawn by Wilkerson, Harrison, and Griffin. While Pinner's narrative of the Great Migration begins with African American men moving to urban manufacturing centers to find work, the greater balance of her narrative focuses on the experience of women. Pinner's account differs most significantly from those described above in the marked absence of violence and in its focus on the recreation of southern identity and traditions in the North through women's cultural activities. By focusing on women, the domestic space, and cooking as cultural work, Pinner is doing feminist historiography: writing women into the Great Migration narrative in a way that emphasizes their experiences and their contributions to community identity. In her reflective history, violence is completely absent and women's work for pay is given primacy.

Pinner's version of the Great Migration narrative returns often to a few themes that contradict the familiar metanarrative represented by Wilkerson and Harrison. First, Pinner's account suggests that the women in her family were anxious to maintain their southern identity and ties to the South. Through sharing food and recipes with women still "down home," they performed and preserved their identities as southerners. Second, and related to the first theme, Pinner describes an unobstructed freedom to travel to and from the South. Pinner portrays many instances of friends and relatives traveling across regional lines unchallenged by racial violence and unchecked by the indignities of segregation that so often characterize narratives of twentieth-century African American travel and migration. Finally, Pinner's narratives redraw the lines between public and private spheres, suggesting that the domestic space of the kitchen is truly a public space, an important social hub where women participate in public debate and enter the marketplace as entrepreneurs, employers, artists, and consumers.

The narratives in *Sweets* suggest that the women in Pinner's family are anxious to identify themselves as "authentic" southerners outside of the South. Foodways scholars disagree about the meaning and value of authenticity (for more, see Lisa Heldke's *Exotic Appetites* and Josée Johnston and Shyon Baumann's *Foodies*). This project takes on the issue of "authenticity" from a rhetorical position. Authenticity is a socially constructed category of identity that offers privileges to its members, and membership is "proven" rhetorically through purposeful arguments. As migrants and "displaced Southerners," Pinner's family has much invested in claiming their southern identity; claiming membership in southern authenticity is one way that the family finds belonging and the privileges of community. Even though Pinner was born and raised in Saginaw, Michigan, the family's southern identity was carefully protected and performed through food and cooking. The narrative of "My My's Pound Cake" provided above is the first recipe in the book, and it is identified explicitly as "truly a Southern dessert" (11). Baking a "truly" southern pound cake in "the same baking tins that she had used when she lived down South" is My My's performance of authentic southernness in Detroit. Southern identity was not something the family attempted to escape or forget.

Baking is presented as an activity for maintaining southern identity and, to use Griffin's terminology, for making connection to "the ancestor." Griffin explains that twentieth-century migration narratives are characterized by the figures of "the ancestor" and "the stranger": the one representing connection to a continuous community and the other representing isolation in the urban landscape. Griffin argues that in migration narratives that "stress the significance of an ancestor," as *Sweets* does, "the South becomes a place where black blood earns a black birthright to the land, a locus of history, culture, and possible redemption" (5). In *Sweets*, the South is not a place to escape, but a source of culture; southernness is not an identity marker to be removed, but a source of community. In the introduction to *Sweets*, Pinner writes that baking was an integral part of My My's personal identity and her experience of southern culture in public life: "An important part of My My's social life back home [in Mississippi] had been centered around her reputation as a wonderful cook (her food baskets, and especially her dessert baskets, were highly coveted items at church socials and community events)" (1). My My does not settle easily into life in "the *Great Up North*" (2), but once My My and Pop move out of a boardinghouse into their own home, My My sets out immediately to recreate her kitchen "the way it had been down South" (1) and to reenter public life in the kinds of communities familiar to her. Pinner says, "As it had been in the South, church soon became an important part of My My's social life. And just as quickly, her food baskets—especially those holding her desserts—became as popular as they had been in Mississippi" (2). The rituals of baking seem to be as fundamental to the performance of authentic southern identity as the recipes themselves. Cooking for the church socials is a transplanted ritual that makes practicing southern foodways in the North a method for maintaining connection with "the ancestor" through a continuous regional identity, community, and culture.

Pinner describes recipe and food sharing between the relatives who remained in the South and those who moved north as another means of preserving and performing southernness outside of the South. In a two-paragraph narrative titled "Cakes of My Childhood," Pinner depicts the exchange of recipes between relatives. Though My My had a store of southern recipes "in her head," she often called family members in the South to send recipes for something "new and different" (16). In this case, it appears that "authentic" southern food does not necessarily mean old and familiar. A new recipe, if practiced and approved by the southern relatives, could work just as well in the performance of southern identity. By virtue of living in the South, the southern relatives were authorized as authentic sources of culinary capital. The continuous communication and sharing of food and food knowledge maintained the southern identity of Pinner's family.

/ 23

Pinner's narrative suggests that there was fairly regular travel between the relatives in the North and in the South. Pinner describes this travel as unproblematic and unmarked by violence or the threat of violence. In this way, Pinner's narrative is distinct from Griffin, Wilkerson, and Harrison, who all emphasize violence as an essential Great Migration experience. Pinner's choice to tell about the pleasant and frequent movement between North and South and to erase violence is deliberate and conforms to the rhetorical situation of the cookbook genre. Cookbooks, as a genre, have a decided "lean" towards epideictic rhetoric, praising the cooks who have gone before and convincing audiences that the recipes therein are delicious. In effect, *Sweets* does what a lot of white-authored southern cookbooks and magazines do: it erases a history of violence in the South in favor of a more pleasing narrative.

Pinner describes visiting her cousin in Mississippi, and she uses language that suggests this trip happened more than once. For example, Cud'n Flossie was obsessive about cleanliness and insisted that everyone who came to her home take a bath as soon as they arrived. They were ordered to bathe "whenever [they] went to visit Cud'n Flossie" so often that they "knew that no matter what time of the morning or night [they] arrived," they would be ordered to the tub (24). Uncle Sam, who also lived in Detroit, visited the South more than once as well. Once he stayed with Flossie, but when she caught him only pretending to take a bath, "the next time he went South" he stayed with Cud'n Minnie (24). Pinner continues to use past progressive verb tenses to describe past actions that happened more than once: "When we took trips to Mississippi to visit our relatives, Cud'n Ebelle would make us the most fabulous dinners" (60). Pinner suggests that the Michigan family traveled to Mississippi quite frequently and easily and visited several families.

Further, Pinner indicates that travel went both ways. Miss Drucilla, My My's best friend from childhood, made an annual visit from Springfield, Mississippi, to Saginaw, Michigan. Though the trip seems to have been physically taxing on Miss Drucilla's swollen feet, it also seems to have been a regular part of the Great Migration experience (48). When the southern relatives came north, they still ate the southern foods they were used to. Miss Drucilla preferred a "Lemon Rum Cake" served with "a down-home seafood dinner" (48). Cud'n Sue, who was also apparently a moonshiner, was another frequent visitor from Mississippi: "Whenever Cud'n Sue came North for a visit, we'd ask her to make a batch of her delicious fudge," and "her joyful and loving essence remained in our homes long after she left" (128). In this woman-centered narrative of interstate travel, there is a marked absence of violence and an emphasis on family love and connections.

Pinner's narrative of the Great Migration effectively erases any trace of racial discrimination or violence—or at the very least, anxiety—that must have been a part of interstate travel in the 1950s and 1960s. She certainly eliminates racial tension in the South as a motivation for migration. But this absence of violence does not necessarily mean that the narrative is inaccurate or disingenuous. To the contrary, Paul Gilroy suggests in *Against Race* that this kind of erasure (especially when done by an African American writer for an African American audience) can be a positive force. Gilroy suggests that "action against racial hierarchies can proceed more effectively when it has been purged of any lingering respect for the idea of race" (13), including "antiracist" language that upholds race as a category despite its good intentions (53). Writing a history of African Americans that does not include racially motivated violence can suggest a rejection of victimhood. Pinner's decision to focus on the experiences of her family in particular—rather than her whole ethnic group—resists the absorption of the individual experience into the collective narrative, disrupting racial hierarchies by denying race as an overarching category of identity. Similarly, Psyche Williams-Forson suggests that women's narratives about food and its meanings provide a method for exercising power in culture:

> In their ability to control the "symbolic language of food," and to dictate what foods say about them and their families, women often negotiate the dialectical relationship between the internal identity formation of their families and the externally influenced medium of popular culture. In this way, they protect their families against social and cultural assault as well as assist in the formation and protection of identity. (92)

Pinner's choice to emphasize women's creativity and to eliminate men's violence in her narrative suggests that she is using the "internal identity" of her family to resist the "externally influenced" metanarrative. Whether or not it was her intention to do so, Pinner offers a narrative that presents an alternative to the metanarrative of the Great Migration: one that highlights solidarity and community over victimhood.

/ 25

Though Great Migration narratives tend to focus on men's industrial work and cooking narratives tend to focus on private kitchen experiences, Pinner figures the kitchens of her childhood as public forums and marketplaces where women are active members of an economy. Early in *Sweets*, Pinner explicitly connects cooking with the public display of knowledge and skill, earning women cultural capital. The women in her family "used every meal as an opportunity to flaunt their culinary skills, as an opportunity for prestige and to be noticed, and a chance to further establish themselves as the queens of soul food" (2). Food was central to community gatherings and establishing social relationships and hierarchies. Pinner repeats that cooking, and especially baking, was a form of public competition, and the women in her family were winning. A public reputation for culinary skill extends back to Grandma Annie Loston, Pinner's maternal great-great-great-grandmother who "was a slave on a Mississippi plantation" (3). According to the family "legend," "Grandma Annie was known throughout the community as the best cook. Folks are said to have come far and wide for her cakes, pies, and homemade breads because her confections were as beautifully crafted as they were delicious" (3). In these examples, it is clear that kitchen work is conducted in a complex public network and that the women participate in the exchange of cultural capital.

Cooking earned more than just acclaim though. In some cases, Pinner suggests that activities in the kitchen were money-making ventures. Pinner describes at least two female relatives who were licensed beauticians that used their kitchens as salons, bringing the public marketplace into the domestic sphere. Pinner says that Aint Marjell (3) and Aint Laura used their kitchens as "beauty parlor[s]" (42). By opening up business in the kitchen, Marjell and Laura opened their homes to the public. Pinner describes the movement of "chatty, ruby-lipped neighborhood women in and out of [Marjell's] kitchen" (3). In almost all of her descriptions of kitchen spaces, Pinner emphasizes conversation and the sharing of women's knowledge in that public space. It was in the kitchen that "My My preached her womanly sermons to her girls at her kitchen-table pulpit. There were always sermons of domestic power, not ones of kitchen drudgery" (111). Working with other women in the kitchen—whether it was a beauty salon or a place to prepare food—is most often depicted as talking and teaching time when Pinner's female relatives attempted to "prepare" the younger girls "for the art of womanhood" (56).

Outside the home kitchen, women in Pinner's family used their skills to add to the family economy. Marjell "worked as a hairdresser to supplement the money she earned as a waitress and a cook at a neighborhood restaurant" (3). Pinner describes Aint Bulah as "truly a Renaissance woman of the 1930s and 1940s. She was college educated, an entrepreneur, well traveled, and a staunch supporter of the advancement of women" (88). Bulah, who contributed a recipe for "Cream Cheese Pound Cake," owned "Community Grocery Store on Louisa Street in New Orleans" (13). Bulah shared her prosperity as an employer, hiring Pinner's mother as a young girl:

> By the age of ten, my mama was spending her summers working in Aint Bulah's grocery store, where Mama got to be quite a little businesswoman—keeping the store stocked, sweeping and cleaning, making sure that folks paid their bills by the last Friday of every month. (13)

This hiring within in the family is a common theme. Aint Laura (one of the kitchen hairdressers) also hired Pinner's mother as a child to sweep the kitchen-salon floor (42). Pinner's mother hired Pinner to hunt for wild strawberry plants, dig them up, and transplant them in front of the house. Her mother paid her a nickel per plant (151). These stories suggest that there were opportunities for women to work as entrepreneurs and employers, empowering the community of women from the inside. (See Williams-Forson for a more thorough examination of African American women as kitchen entrepreneurs.)

Even a cursory reading of *Sweets*, however, presents some complications to my presentation of the book as *feminist* historiography. In a lot of ways, *Sweets* is a very conventional book, advancing conservative notions of femininity and domesticity, compulsory heterosexual marriage, essentialist definitions of women as caregivers, and fantasy themes of food as spiritual nourishment. Pinner praises her relatives for teaching her "life lessons" from the front porch that amount to gender policing: shaming women for their appearances and blaming women for provoking men into harassing them in the streets (156). Though on the whole cooking is presented as an empowering act, feminist readers may find the focus on cooking for men's pleasure to be troublesome. My My eagerly shares her culinary knowledge with her daughters, "believing that if they acquired good kitchen skills[,] it would help them find their way into the hearts of some fine young men" (2). Pinner writes about "a pretend cousin" named Daisy whose advice for keeping a man is hard to swallow:

> If you have a house dog, don't let it outdo you when it comes to showin' the man how glad you are to see him come home. When the doggie hears his car pull up and comes runnin' through the house like a fool, be waiting at the door beside the dog. (119)

/ 27

In addition to the troubling comparison of wife to dog, the advice reinforces the division and the hierarchy of the masculine public world over and apart from the feminine domestic one.

Perhaps *Sweets* advances conservative notions of compulsory heterosexual marriage too often to satisfy some definitions of a *feminist* text for some readers; nevertheless, I contend that the method of narration is still *feminist historiography.* Pinner provides a woman-centered historical narrative of midcentury African Americans in the midst of the Great Migration through a woman-centered genre that challenges prior narratives by presenting alternative experiences. As historiography, *Sweets* is feminist both in what is told (a narrative about domestic life outside of the typical narrative of political violence) and how it is told (achronologically, without respect to linear time). What makes *Sweets* an especially subversive historiography is its disguise as a cookbook and a family memoir. Rather than a chronological, linear narrative of historical events, Pinner presents her narrative achronologically. Her narrative is prompted by the recipe, suggesting that a history of a people can be told just as effectively by dividing it into cakes and pies as by dividing it into epochs and wars.

I promised a second level of interpretation, my own feminist historiography, an inclusion of Pinner and the women of her cookbook into the history of rhetoric. Like Glenn and Lunsford, I, too, am redefining rhetoric to include texts and contexts where women's voices have been marginalized. By arguing that cookbooks and recipes are as rhetorically constructed for public audiences as political speeches, I am adding women's voices to that canon. The narrative of the Great Migration as a male-dominated flight from a violent South toward an industrial North obscures women's experiences. Pinner shows the women of her narrative as entrepreneurs, employers, artists, and social engines of the black community. By focusing on women as historical innovators of culinary knowledge and founders of cultural traditions, Pinner's stories make even broader claims about who can produce and authenticate cultural knowledge. For example, the most powerful figure at the center of Pinner's cultural life, the holder of all cultural knowledge, is her grandmother who never attended school past the third grade (48).

Luce Giard's "The Nourishing Arts" from *The Practice of Everyday Life* convinced me of the need for new definitions of rhetoric that would include

kitchen writing. I could agree with Giard that there were, in my own life, "women ceaselessly doomed to both housework and creation of life," but I could not so easily agree that they were also "women excluded from public life and the communication of knowledge. . . . Women bereft of writing" (Giard 153–54). If anything, the men in my family were the ones "bereft of writing." They left no traces of themselves on paper, but the women left behind piles and piles of writing on three-by-five-inch index cards in neat plastic sleeves.

Of course, Giard is talking about a different kind of writing. She meant *literature*, not recipe cards. And she was probably talking about a different kind of public life. She meant *politics*, not church socials. And she was thinking of a different kind of knowledge—academic capital, not culinary knowledge. There are, indeed, definitions of literature that cannot contain a handwritten recipe. There are definitions of rhetoric that cannot find a place for a cookbook. And yet, to really honor the "Innumerable Anonymous Women" of the Kitchen Women Nation (Giard 154), the "Shiva goddesses with a hundred arms who are both clever and thrifty" (157), and the bearers of "a subtle intelligence full of nuances and strokes of genius" (158), the first step is to crack open the definitions of *writing, literature, public, rhetoric, knowledge,* and *power* until they will admit kitchen women as authors, rhetors, and cultural agents.

Works Cited

Bower, Anne L., ed. *Recipes for Reading: Community Cookbooks, Stories, Histories.* U of Massachusetts P, 1997.

Engelhardt, Elizabeth S. D. *A Mess of Greens: Southern Gender and Southern Food.* U of Georgia P, 2011.

Fertel, Rien T. "'Everybody Seemed Willing to Help': The *Picayune Creole Cook Book* as Battleground, 1900–2008." *The Larder: Food Studies Methods from the American South.* Ed. John T. Edge, Elizabeth Engelhardt, and Ted Ownby. U of Georgia P, 2013. 10–31.

Giard, Luce. "The Nourishing Arts." *The Practice of Everyday Life.* Vol 2. *Living and Cooking.* By Michel de Certeau, Giard, and Pierre Mayol. Trans. Timothy J. Tomasik. U of Minnesota P, 1998. 151–69.

Gilroy, Paul. *Against Race: Imagining Political Culture beyond the Color Line.* Harvard UP, 2002.

Glenn, Cheryl. *Rhetoric Retold: Regendering the Tradition from Antiquity through the Renaissance.* Southern Illinois UP, 1997.

———. "Truth, Lies, and Method: Revisiting Feminist Historiography." *College English* 62.3 (2000): 387–89.

Griffin, Farah Jasmine. *"Who Set You Flowin'?": The African-American Migration Narrative.* Oxford UP, 1995.

Harrison, Alferdteen, ed. *Black Exodus: The Great Migration from the American South.* UP of Mississippi, 1991.

Heldke, Lisa. *Exotic Appetites: Ruminations of a Food Adventurer.* Routledge, 2003.

Ireland, Lynne. "The Compiled Cookbook as Foodways Autobiography." *Western Folklore* 40 (1981): 107–14.

Johnston, Josée, and Shyon Baumann. *Foodies: Democracy and Distinction in the Gourmet Foodscape.* Routledge, 2010.

Leonardi, Susan J. "Recipes for Reading: Summer Pasta, Lobster à la Riseholme, and Key Lime Pie." *PMLA* 104.3 (May 1989): 340–47.

Lunsford, Andrea A., ed. *Reclaiming Rhetorica: Women in the Rhetorical Tradition.* U of Pittsburgh P, 1995.

Pinner, Patty. *Sweets: Soul Food Desserts and Memories.* Ten Speed P, 2006.

Theophano, Janet. *Eat My Words: Reading Women's Lives through the Cookbooks They Wrote.* Palgrave Macmillan, 2002.

White-Farnham, Jamie. "'Revising the Menu to Fit the Budget': Grocery Lists and Other Rhetorical Heirlooms." *College English* 76.3 (January 2014): 208–26.

Wilkerson, Isabel. *The Warmth of Other Suns: The Epic Story of America's Great Migration.* Random House, 2010.

Williams-Forson, Psyche A. *Building Houses Out of Chicken Legs: Black Women, Food, and Power.* U of North Carolina P, 2006.

2. THE EMBODIED RHETORIC OF RECIPES

Jennifer Cognard-Black

INTRODUCTION

When I got married in 1992, I received a few cookbooks as wedding gifts: from my mom, Anne Cognard, the now infamous 1975 "new edition" of the mother-and-daughter Rombauers' *Joy of Cooking*; from my paternal grandmother, Peg Cognard, the *"Reader's Digest" Great Recipes for Good Health*; and from my best friend, Kristi Frahm, a copy of *The Enchanted Broccoli Forest* by Mollie Katzen. As a twenty-three-year-old, newly zealous vegetarian, I mostly turned to Katzen, especially for my first, anxious dinner parties—bright yellow turmeric still marking recipes I used for my initial attempts at hippie hostessing. Mom had told me that *Joy* was a book containing "every answer to any cooking question you'll ever have," and so I treated it as an encyclopedia: how to freeze fresh tomatoes or what to substitute for missing buttermilk. The *Reader's Digest* book I ignored. I wasn't tempted by a book boasting recipes low in calories, cholesterol, and salt: a kind of abstemiousness and absence of flavor that I didn't associate with my grandmother, a woman of abundance. Within my first year of housekeeping, I donated *Great Recipes* to a book sale at the university where I was a graduate student.

Yet I still retained my grandmother's culinary influence in that early, efficiency-apartment kitchen, for I'd also received another cooking text from my mother the night before my wedding: a plastic, mauve-colored recipe box, organized with hand-drawn alphabetic dividers and filled with handwritten index cards containing all the best dishes and baked goods that my mom had learned. A few of the recipes were from my mother's youth in Scotland ("Flora's Rich Cream Scones" and "Joan's Shortbread" testify to this heritage), but mostly, Mom was given these recipes by her mother-in-law. The "B" section alone, chiefly for "Breads," is an archive of some of Peg Cognard's best baking: "Canned Bread," "Banana Bread," "Southern Cornbread," "Perfect White Bread," "Orange Xmas Bread," "Sticky Pull Apart Rolls," "Butterhorn Rolls," and one recipe actually handed up to Grandma from my mom for "Gruyere Herb Bread." While each of these recipe cards is fairly utilitarian in its form and style—my mother wrote all of them in pencil or pen, with a title at the top, a list of ingredients below, and then a few short sentences of efficiently worded instructions—as feminist scholars have shown studying cookbooks of all kinds, these texts remain potent pieces of writing. They contain the intertwined stories of my mother's and my grandmother's foodways and thus evoke their respective kitchens, cooking communities, national and ethnic affiliations, place in history, and culinary identities.[1]

But allow me to return for a moment to the unusual fact that my mother gave me a handwritten copy, on note cards, of a compendium of my grand- mother's recipes in the early 1990s—at a time, it's true, when the Internet wasn't widely used (no e-mail, no food blogs, no BigOven or Epicurious websites), but yet it was still easy to take personal documents, such as old recipe cards, to Kinko's and have them photocopied and spiral-bound into a makeshift book. Instead, my recipe box is a one-of-a-kind manuscript of an altogether different sort: a boxed-bound book, with index-card pages that may be reordered at a reader's will and yet are organized broadly according to alphabetic chapter headings. And that my mother spent not just mental time but bodily time in the making is significant. These texts are tactile, homespun. The cursive is an extension of my mother's personality, open yet tidy, and a trace of her skin cells remain across each card. Indeed, a strong appeal of my recipe box is its closeness to the body, how it represents and even contains it: my mother's, mine, and even my grandmother's. The collaboratively voiced narrator of these recipes establishes its ethos, in part, by this corporeal fingerprint, this intimacy. My recipe box is a text I trust.

With this corporeality in mind, I want to suggest that what persuades a reader most in such recipe cards is that they constitute what I'm calling an "embodied rhetoric." This essay, then, seeks to delineate how recipes create and sustain this embodied rhetoric in the United States, particularly among recipe-sharing cultures of letters among women.[2]

Jennifer Cognard-Black

THE RHETORIC OF RECIPES

Before I discuss what I mean by the embodied rhetoric of recipes, I want to explain more closely the highly specific and atypical form of the recipe itself—as both a particular and a peculiar rhetorical genre. Built around a stable organizational structure and adopting a strategic voice, a recipe seeks both to inform and to persuade its audience on how to prepare a certain dish and how best to go about doing so. Though a recipe may appear seemingly simple or even simplistic, or as merely an ingredient list followed by a set of instructions, it is actually a highly complex form, one containing discrete parts and serving multiple functions within a wide range of rhetorical contexts: ordinary and exceptional, popular and erudite, private and public, practical and literary. Moreover, though a form determined by its logos—a didactic genre meant to instruct a reader on how to assemble a specific foodstuff—a recipe is simultaneously pathos-driven. It's a synthesis of collective memories from a community of cooks who share and extend these memories with their readership. And, perhaps surprisingly, it's also a narrative in its own right.

32 /

The Logos of Recipes

Sociologists and linguists, along with feminist historians and literary theorists, have long contended that the recipe should be valued as sui generis, a unique piece of discourse.[3] Sociologist Graham Tomlinson, writing about thirty years ago, selected the recipe as his exemplar for studying the characteristics of written instructions, analyzing its structure in minute detail. Tomlinson begins by noting that a recipe must have what he calls the "standard two-part format," meaning a list of ingredients followed by a paragraph or more of instructions (203). A recipe's form, then, is determined by its logos for it is arranged rationally, chronologically, and even spatially on the page as a series of if/then statements. This if/then structure, Tomlinson asserts, serves as a set of "scientific hypotheses or promises. If one takes a particular action, then predicted consequences will follow" (202). Such simplicity is what makes the recipe form so useful—and so ubiquitous. If a reader gathers these ingredients in this list, then she or he may follow the subsequent directions, resulting in something (hopefully delicious) to eat.

These precise, stable, and logical qualities of the if/then disposition of recipes have enabled the form to function as a scientific genre within the realm of cooking. Indeed, this format became prototypical in North America as a direct result of the professionalization of homemaking into an academic discipline at the end of the nineteenth century, first termed "domestic sciences" and then, later, "home economics." The intent of the curriculum for this new discipline was to apply empirical approaches and principles to domestic situations, including the chemistry of cooking and the nutritional value of foods. In 1896, when Fannie Merritt Farmer produced her widely influential *Boston Cooking-School Cook Book* for use at the school where she served as principal, she thought of her volume as a manual meant to teach "scientific cookery."[4] Prior to this publication, recipes in America had been presented in published cookbooks and personal manuscripts via a range of rhetorical forms, from long paragraphs to mere outlines. But Farmer self-consciously standardized her recipes, organizing them like formulas and, thereby, investing them with a scientific ethos. Additionally, Farmer codified the use of distinct and replicable measurements within her ingredient lists, rejecting terms such as "dash" and "handful" in favor of level "tablespoons," "teaspoons," and "cups." This precise and consistent diction, echoing the specialized language of the laboratory, further strengthened the integrity of her recipes.

Thus the modern form of the recipe is rational and highly reproducible. / 33 And yet even this seemingly straightforward format is modified in almost every case by numerous elements that mediate the recipe's structure, such as inserting a title, crediting an author or authors, evoking a region or nation, giving evaluative and informational comments, providing notes on presentation, suggesting advice on how and when to serve, extending cultural or personal comments on the dish itself, adding illustrations, and noting components that may be considered optional. Also, while the ingredients of a recipe are certainly conveyed through the precise diction of measurement, such as "teaspoon" and "¼ cup," adjectives, adverbs, and verbs that further refine and treat these ingredients are often imprecise.

For instance, from ingredients on a recipe card owned by my grandmother Peg Cognard for "Orange-Pecan Loaf," what might "finely-snipped" dates, "coarsely chopped" pecans, or even "grated" orange peel mean, exactly? How does a cook "snip" a date? How "coarse" is coarse? And just how fine should the grated orange peel be? Moreover, even though the subsequent instructions usually follow a clear sequence, that sequence may or may not convey the necessary kitchen equipment, recommended setup, complete cooking process, and serving advice—again, all in ambiguous diction necessitating assumptions about what certain words mean (for example, "thick" or "sprinkle"). As linguist Cornelia Gerhardt points out, recipes are not simple, straight-forward . . . instructions that can be successfully used by any novice[;] they represent a register containing presuppositions on many levels, necessary incompleteness in the steps of preparations or sets of instructions, [and] assumptions about cultural knowledge, practical skills, and technical equipments evoking a complex set of practices. (43)

In other words, recipes are as varied as the dishes they attempt to convey, and readers must develop a kind of recipe literacy in order to understand fully the meaning within these texts.

The Pathos of Recipes

It is within the many modifications of the if/then recipe form that pathos resides: where recipe writers elicit historical, personal, communal, narrative, symbolic, and imagistic associations to appeal to their readers' emotions—appeals that are often gendered. To illustrate this point more fully, let me turn to a recipe that predates the ones my mother gave me on the eve of my wedding. This recipe card is for "Date Puffed Rice Balls" (figure 2.1), and as a document, it is at least sixty years old. It comes from a personal archive: an impressive collection of fourteen hundred handwritten recipes, all contained in a single, long recipe box that I inherited from Peg Cognard, my grandmother, when she died.

"Date Puffed Rice Balls" recipe card

By the time I knew my grandmother the best (in her sixties, seventies, and eighties), Peg was a highly skilled seamstress, maker, cleaner, gardener, decorator, and cook. To be more precise, she was a consummate cook, a virtuoso in the kitchen. Wearing aprons she embroidered herself, she pitted and canned cherries that grew from the tree in her backyard; baked her own white and brown bread each week; kept dozens of homemade oatmeal chocolate-chip cookies in her freezer for whatever occasion might crop up (including a visit from her grandchildren); made thirty different kinds of cookies and candies for her "Christmas baking"; cleaned and prepared the pheasant and trout my grandfather shot and caught; and participated in dedicated cooking circles, including supper clubs and various ladies clubs—particularly the Women's Society of Christian Service. In addition, for Sunday supper each week after church, she cooked ample and delectable meals: rich meats, complicated potato and vegetable dishes, salads with such imagistic names as "Cherry Mincemeat" and "Copper Pennies," homemade breads or rolls served with her own preserves, and at least one made-from-scratch dessert, such as "Thumb-Print Cookies," "Lemon Freeze," "Chocolate Scotcheroos," "Waldorf Astoria Red Cake," or simply a latticed cherry pie made with her own cherries and a homemade crust (a personal favorite).   / 35

In other words, Cognard didn't just view herself as a good cook or a good housekeeper. She also identified as a domestic aesthete, demonstrating beauty through making and serving attractive food. She wasn't merely a maker; she was also a teacher. And recipes facilitated this dual position, their form predicated on both making (art) and didacticism (craft).

The section of Grandma Cognard's box that contains the most cards is "Desserts," and of these, many are instructions for making cookies, bars, brownies, or balls. A particular recipe for Date Puffed Rice Balls is one that Cognard apparently received from a friend, but it's recorded in her own handwriting.

Certainly, this particular text is recognizable as a "recipe" because it starts with the requisite list of ingredients ("1 stick oleo—½ c sugar / 1 c finely chopped dates"), followed by instructions that begin, "Heat over low heat + stir till well mixed." Yet almost immediately, the traditions of this genre are compromised, with Cognard embedding additional ingredients in the subsequent instructions—a "beaten egg," "2 c Rice Krispies," and "Angel flake or shredded cocoanut [sic]." From the get-go, then, Cognard—as writer—is already modifying this text from what might be called its cookie-cutter formula, imbuing it with a more idiosyncratic structure and voice.

The recipe's title and credit line in the upper-right-hand corner further modify its fundamental form, providing more than just subject matter and signature. Indeed, I argue that all recipe titles and attributions potentially convey a food's ethnicity, class origin, historical period, authorship, and connection to a specific discourse community. In this case, in order to understand what "Puffed Rice" and "Balls" refer to, a reader needs to be an informed member of a group of consumers who can afford, and who know where to buy, Rice Krispies. These readers also recognize the then-current fashion for ball-shaped desserts and consider them worth making. In addition, this dessert is attributed to a creator named "Florence Anderson," whose name alone gives information about her gender, her probable race, and her likely locale. With the surname "Anderson" (or "son of Ander / Andrew"), she is almost certainly an Anglo-American woman from a family who probably emigrated at some point from England to the United States. She's probably someone, too, growing up during a time in which "Florence" was a relatively common female name, which means somewhere between 1880 and 1940.[5] Importantly, too, this attribution actually constructs a dual authorship since the recipe itself is in Cognard's handwriting but is ascribed to someone else. As such, this text is clearly collaborative, gesturing to the practice of midcentury, middle-class female cooks sharing their creations with each other: a practice that is part and parcel of the recipe form itself. Let me note, too, that Cognard's own annotation above the title, "good," signals an assessment tool at work, where certain recipes receive positive interpretations (for example, "good!" or "very good!"), while others do not (for instance, "not worth the trouble" or "so-so"). So here is evidence that the voice of a recipe is not merely informative and collaborative: it is also evaluative.

Looking beyond the title and credit line to the ingredient list, this recipe for Date Puffed Rice Balls reveals even more about the text's historical period, in part by the quantification language of "cups," "teaspoons," and "tablespoons" (thereby signaling a post–Fannie Farmer era), as well as Cognard's use of the term "oleo," from the Latin *oleum* meaning "oil," an abbreviation of "oleomargarine"—a butter substitute made from purified beef fat mixed with milk. First patented in 1873 in the United States, this foodstuff became more widespread when real butter was rationed during wartime.[6] Thus Cognard wields the language of her particular kitchen.

Yet it's also worth noting that hers is a 1950s middle-class American kitchen. According to feminist culinary critic Sherrie Inness, by the middle of the twentieth century, such a kitchen was represented in cookbooks, advertisements, and women's magazines as "an up-to-date room overflowing with innovative technology and new convenience foods" (156). It's not an exaggeration to say that these new technologies and foods revolutionized cooking, allowing results to be more consistent and cooking more expedient: the wood-burning stove was replaced by gas and then electric ranges; the apple-parer came to be a universal kitchen tool; both frozen and canned foods became widely available; and measuring cups were now commonplace kitchenware.[7]

Five years before her death, Cognard wrote a memoir, "Incidents in My Life." In this memoir, Cognard explains that, when she herself was a newlywed, she lived for a time in a small apartment in Rock Port, Missouri. She laments, "We [had] an old-fashioned range. . . . I recall having such a time trying to bake as I had to stick my hand into the oven to guess at its temperature. . . . I never liked Rockport [sic]" (32). Later on, however, moving to Auburn, Nebraska, she and her husband rented a small house, which was "unfurnished, except for a davenport," and yet they had enough money to purchase some furniture and a "good gas stove." As Cognard notes, the new stove "served us well, through all our moves, and was still in use in the basement of our last home in Omaha . . . many years later" (32).

In owning such an up-to-date and well-made appliance, Cognard achieved status—her workshop stylish, her tools advanced. Moreover, what she made /37 in this workshop equally bespoke her position as a homemaker on the rise: her pantry now included more than the jams and jellies she made herself or the tomatoes she grew, harvested, and "put up" back when she lived on an acreage. Rather, it now boasted such name brands as Rice Krispies cereal and Angel Flake coconut—brands that, by the 1950s, signaled a mass-produced American cuisine sold as "healthful" and "contemporary" due to their uniformity and secure packaging.[8] In the memorable words of Inness, "the well-stocked kitchen became a signifier of the American dream" (144).

Touching on just the title, attribution, ingredients, and necessary tools alone, then, a reader already understands that Date Puffed Rice Balls is an emotional text as well as an informative one. A whole world has been evoked, one in which writers and readers—as well as cooks and eaters— find themselves at an American table during the 1950s or early 1960s, with the resources to enjoy desserts made from ingredients produced by an industrialized food economy and imagined within an "American dream" kitchen. Furthermore, the collaborative authorship and artistry that's happening as women swap, record, and edit these texts brings to mind a feminized form of exchange that's both vibrant and precise. As such, the rhetoric of recipes is complex in its appeal and nuanced in both its voice and structure.

The Embodied Rhetoric of Recipes

Beyond invoking a historical period and a community of cooking women, perhaps the most pathos-based elements of any recipe are its narrative qualities, which are also crucial to the recipe's uniqueness as an embodied text. Feminist literary critic Anne Bower has argued convincingly that community cookbooks are a form of American storytelling—and, as such, a kind of literature. Breaking down the codes and conventions of these cookbooks into detailed discussions of their settings, characters, plots, and themes, Bower maintains that such books have all the basic elements of a story—elements that, in turn, their readers recognize as literary. As Bower insists, "professional novelists are not the only ones who use the language of domesticity to consider our history, our present lives, and our future" (49).

While this reasoning is convincing, Bower also believes that recipes themselves are not narrative but merely functional. "The only sequence of events a [recipe] reader desires is the linear process of the recipe," she contends.

> For a beginning—take these ingredients; for a middle—go through these processes; and of course, for an ending, voilà!—a dish to please the tummy and the tongue. But reading for *more* than a recipe, reading the full cookbook as a text, can yield inklings of different beginnings-middles-ends and a new sense of plot. (37)

Literary critic Susan Leonardi concurs, insisting that "like a story, a recipe needs a recommendation, a context, a point, a reason to be. A recipe is, then, an embedded discourse"—meaning a discourse that's completely reliant on the cookbook or novel or memoir in which it is contained (340).

I disagree. I contend that recipes are stories unto themselves. Certainly a recipe changes if it's the basis of a poem or the centerpiece of an essay. And yet a recipe's title, ingredient list, annotations, illustrations, and directions conjure the power of imagery and tell a story.

Consider that an opening ingredient list constructs a three-dimensional space, one initiating a narrative through which a reader-cook will move from A to B to C—from beginning to middle to end—first in reading but then, even more importantly, in enacting the text when she or he puts it in motion. In order to enter this particular Date Puffed Rice Ball story, the reader-cook will need, first, to set out one stick of oleo, a half cup of sugar, and one cup of finely chopped dates on her or his kitchen counter. In a sense, then, a scene is set: this list is akin to "Once upon a Time," told in the third-person point of view, that tried-and-true perspective signaling an omniscient narrator.

But instead of introducing a cottage in the woods or a castle on a hill, the reader is asked to imagine that idyllic 1950s American kitchen—a sugary, fruity, buttery scene in which ball desserts are all the rage. On this particular recipe card, this scene is underscored by the illustration of hanging hot pads in cheerful primary colors, dangling from a wooden spoon in the left-hand corner, a visual that's purposefully nostalgic and tidy, with a gingham design on the hot pads and each one placed precisely in a row on the spoon.

After evoking this setting, the recipe then moves into that expected set of directions: a series of imperative phrases beginning with verbs in the present tense. Heat. Add. Cook. Mix. Roll. This storyteller is confident, telling a reader exactly what she or he must do through a series of precise verbs—how to move through the space and time of this setting (in other words, the plot) to arrive at a successful dish (the "just deserts" or denouement). Yet this narrator isn't merely assured. In starting each task with a verb, the narrator also invites a reader to cocreate meaning by participating directly and actively in the unfolding of this narrative, always in the now, the eternal present tense. For the reader-cook is also a reader-character.

And here's where a recipe sharply differs from other kinds of storytelling texts. When Date Puffed Rice Balls are actually cooked and not just read about, the material world beyond the text is changed—fiction becomes fact. The fantasy so often played out in short stories, children's books, novels, and films in which a reader gets to walk into a piece of fiction is realized in the flesh-and-blood world of actual experience. A reader doesn't just imagine herself or himself as a cooking character within this setting, doing these kitcheny things. A reader actually becomes that character.[9]

/ 39

Thus the reading experience of recipes is distinct. In this case, Peg Cognard's audience comes to contain sugar, dates, and puffed-rice cereal, changing not just sense but substance. And Cognard, as author, will have the privilege of maintaining her connection to her reader-cooks by sustaining them, literally, long after the recipe is back in its box. They will carry her writing with them for the rest of their lives. As rhetorician Jamie White-Farnham has said of domestic writings she terms "rhetorical heirlooms"—including shopping lists and recipes—they are significant not so much for their physical forms but "in their rhetorical forms, in their ability to be adapted for use according to circumstances, and *in their ability to affect circumstances*" (211, emphasis mine).[10]

As I've tried to make clear through this extended example, then, both the recipes my mother gave me for my wedding and, too, the profusion of cards I inherited from my grandmother's own master recipe box are examples of embodied rhetoric in a number of ways. First, they inscribe a specific authorial body: that of the recipe writer, holding the pencil or pen, translating a literal dish into the symbolic of language. Yet such cards also inscribe other bodies as well, both the quick and the dead. There are the bodies of the past—the women (and a few men) who originally created and shared these recipes with the writer of the current moment, scribbling on a card. Then there are also the bodies of the future and those of the future-present. For one, there's the figure of the imagined cook, the recipient of this card, when she or he eventually gathers ingredients and moves through a kitchen, animating this text, this story. And, too, there are those bodies that will be (and then are) in the process of sustaining themselves, literally: those lucky few who sit down to a plate of sugary Date Puffed Rice Balls, thereby turning the words of a recipe into a living legacy. An embodied rhetoric.

CONCLUSION

My own readerly and eaterly body is built from Grandma Cognard's culinary construction of the past. This means that my body carries the optimism (the ideal) but also the limitations (the real) of her embodied rhetoric. To conclude my thoughts on the embodied nature of recipes, I will expand a bit on both: my real and my ideal inheritance, especially as a woman writer and a home cook in my own right.

The Real

As a cook, recipe writer, and member of the body culinary, my grandmother was also judgmental, a racist, a sexist, and sometimes small-minded about other people's looks.

BRIEF EXAMPLES. Grandma Cognard once tried to make a joke by wondering aloud what a "grasshopper" drink could possibly be. I told her. As a college student, my body was, in part, a drinking body. She gave me a withering look and said, "I'm sorry you know that." She called Brazil nuts "nigger toes" for her entire life; she often commented on working-class women's "slovenly" appearance when we were at the store or the mall together; and though heavy herself, she maintained a fierce competition with her daughter, my aunt Shirley, who was a thinner version of fat. As a feminist myself and someone who works hard to articulate the intersectionality of racism, sexism, classism, and homophobia in my classrooms, this part of my embodied inheritance is difficult to recognize and to admit.

EXTENDED EXAMPLE. Grandma Cognard was also vain about her cooking abilities. There is but one instance in her memoir in which Cognard compliments her own culinary and entertaining skills, but the moment is telling. At the last reunion ever planned for her own side of the family—which, traditionally, had been held close to her mother's birthday and ceased after "Mommie" died—my grandparents were in charge of organizing the event: renting the hall, providing the drinks, and bringing the main course (the rest was potluck). Cognard decided to bake "a huge ham loaf with pineapple slices" (20). At the time, she was feuding with a sister named Laura—who Cognard represents in her memoir as a jealous woman. Cognard goes into detail about how one of her brothers reacts to her supper:

> Buster (Walter) was home from the Air Force, and after eating dinner he said, "That's the best meal I've ever eaten in my life." Laura looked mad as a bulldog. The dinner was good. I doubt if Buster had ever had such a ham loaf before. I also had made Mommie's table decorations with rabbits sitting, joined at the top. On one side I had printed "Happy Birthday, Mommie" and "Happy Easter" on the other. I had taken birthday napkins and used a tall single rabbit for the middle of the table. This was the only family reunion for which table decorations had been used. (20)

That Cognard records Buster's hyperbolic compliment in direct dialogue, as a quotation, as "evidence," goes on to make a comparison between a bulldog and Laura, and then states simply, "The dinner was good," speaks to Cognard's self-congratulatory attitude over the success of her ham loaf and, more broadly, her meal. That the scene is one of family—not church members or neighbors or friends—highlights the reputational stakes. Cognard's abilities would be judged by sisters and brothers as well as by the cook she admired most, her own mother. So to further her status not only as a cook extraordinaire but as a decorous and decorative hostess, Cognard synthesizes her piety (observing Easter) with her filiality (commemorating Mommie's birthday) with her sense of taste—displayed in her homemade centerpieces and holiday-themed trimmings.

Here, then, the ham loaf recipe, in its realized form, comes to embody Cognard's pride: pride in it being *her* dish and in it representing her brother's "best meal." And as Buster, Laura, Cognard herself, and the reader consume this pride, each comes to embody Cognard's sense of self, for better or for ill. For Laura, this consumption is for ill, furthering her unhappiness. For Buster, it's for better: a happy repast. For Cognard and for me—a reader who is also the inheritor of her recipes, raised on her writing (figuratively, literally)—that prized ham loaf is a vexed identity. It's an identity both profound and petty, a story that pushes and pulls.

The Ideal

Feminist critic Sarah Sceats, writing about the incorporation of recipes within certain novels, comes to the conclusion that such food literature—primarily written for and "consumed" by women—is both potent and powerful, despite its resistance to rejecting traditionally defined femininity. "From a feminist point of view," Sceats admits, "this may seem a limiting conclusion, entrapping women in a retrograde domesticity" (185). Yet she continues, "On the other hand, the combination of networking, mutual support, shared knowledge, creative experiment and the creation of a specific discourse may be viewed by anyone as an empowerment greatly to be desired" (185).

When my mother, with a doctorate in Renaissance literature and a lifelong vocation as a teacher, gave to her daughter—then working on a master's degree in English—a recipe box full of handwritten recipe cards the night before her white-dress wedding, this act bespoke a tension between the professional and the domestic that clearly persists to this day. Even now, twenty-five years later, my own expert literacies are still ones that are recognized as a legitimate part of the meritocracy that is academia: the work I do as an editor, an English professor, and a published writer. Yet I believe that engaging the embodied rhetoric of my grandmother's recipes makes me a more complex woman reader and writer than those other ways achieved solely through established authorial means. Moreover, in being one among the body culinary of this particular community, I honor the world it memorializes while, at the same time, I can critique it. I can change it.

Every Christmas, my mom and I bake Peg Cognard's Butterhorn Rolls—it's a ritual at least as old as I am. In doing so, we revive my grandmother (dead for a decade) but also a woman neither of us ever knew named Delza from Auburn, Nebraska, from whom Cognard first received this recipe. We also turn Cognard's flat, figurative, and historical recipe card into something organic, material, extant, and real. And, too, we incorporate Cognard's past into our now. Redolent with the smell of yeast and lightly browned from the oven, we unwrap the horn-shaped rolls like presents perpetuating our own present—the experience of our own bodies.

Thus this Butterhorn Rolls recipe (figure 2.2) is a form of writing unlike any other, informing and persuading its audience in singular ways. For one, this recipe is simultaneously figurative and literal: metaphoric and yet insistently material, both the method for making butterhorn rolls and also its inviting result, ready for butter. In addition, this recipe records the past, inhabits the now, and imagines what's to come—a palimpsest of previous

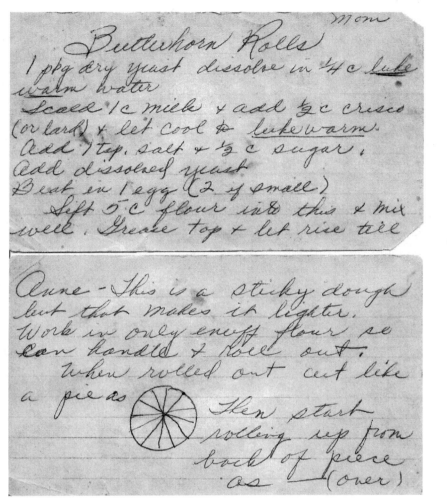

"Butterhorn Rolls" recipe card

butterhorn-roll recipes, an articulation of the present outcome of the current recipe, and a vehicle for visualizing future rolls that may or may not be baked and served. Perhaps most importantly, this recipe is also an inherently collaborative form, a perpetual revision of past versions of butterhorn rolls but also a form that must be incarnated in the actions, and eating, of its current audience in order to be realized completely.

Finally, however, is what happens when this recipe moves on, beyond my mother's and my own bodies. For Grandma Cognard is also remembered and remade in the next generation when my own daughter, Katharine—only four years old when her great-grandmother died—helps to make, and then enjoys, the fruits of this Butterhorn Rolls recipe. Katharine didn't know her great-grandmother in a conscious way: the only real inheritance she has from her and her body culinary is in consuming her recipes.

This, then, is potentially a way to see the embodied rhetoric of recipes as endless transformation, to keep these texts from being essentialized into a past body, a retrograde body, a singular body. For just as novels often reflect back to readers their prejudices and limitations, their meanness and violence, and thereby teach humanity to strive to be better, recipes have the power to inspire endless optimism because they endlessly create and sustain new bodies.

Rhetorician Lynn Bloom's idea that the readers and authors of food writing are "allies" is provocative here. As she puts it, "they share a passion for both the text and the subtext, a zestful appetite for life, which they expect to be satisfying—if not in the living, then in the writing, the retelling and interpreting" (354). For unlike the author of a novel or a poem—and yet akin to the sensuous or sardonic food commentator—a recipe writer cocreates meaning with a reader most fully when the text is consumed by the reader's mind and body with a passion for both the writing and the living. Recipes are remarkable insofar as authors become passionate, zestful allies with their readers to produce texts meant to take on the literal weight and heft of the living people who read and use them. The word forever made flesh.

All cooking and reading women, the dead and the living, cocreate such texts. This is a radical kind of authorship, close to the wonder of childbirth, to that other miracle of making bodies. I suggest, then, that a recipe demands an adaptation of the rhetorical triangle, with the "dish" becoming a sensuous and sensory "text" mediating between writer and reader—not a metonymic substitute for the text but, rather, an organic, three-dimensional version of that text, scooped from the stovetop or, in the case of butterhorn rolls, pulled from the oven, now waiting on the kitchen counter to be "read."

Notes

I wish to extend a special thanks to "the two Sues" (Sue Bobek and Sue Bacon) at St. Paul United Methodist Church in Omaha, Nebraska, who gave me access to their only copy of the *Golden Jubilee Cookbook* that my grandmother helped write, and who also assisted me with finding other information about Peg Cognard's involvement in their church. I also wish to thank Roger Cognard for his invaluable patience in helping me get the details right about his mother's life, as well as Anne Cognard for making me, and then giving me, the living text that is my mauve-colored recipe box. This essay would have been all the poorer without the support and advice of these individuals.

1. As a number of feminist historians and literary critics have noted, both recipes themselves along with compilations in manuscripts and cookbooks serve as archives of individual and community memory, as well as a history of women's literacy. In her groundbreaking study of American cookbooks as repositories of women's writing, *Eat My Words: Reading Women's Lives through the Cookbooks They Wrote*, folklorist Janet Theophano claims that, from the seventeenth century through the late nineteenth century,

> cookbooks and recipe collections were a "place" where [women] could engage in compiling, editing, categorizing, composing, and responding to written texts. Women wrote letters to request recipes, compiled cookbooks for publications, and submitted their own creations to newspapers and magazines. Likewise, they read and wrote in the margins of the published works that they used for cooking. In this way, they practiced literacy, even when they were denied it by formal institutions of learning. (156)

For more on women's culinary writing identities and the importance of publishing alternate histories based on cookbooks and recipes, see Janet Floyd and Laurel Forster's *The Recipe Reader: Narratives, Contexts, Traditions*; editor Anne L. Bower's *Recipes for Reading: Community Cookbooks, Stories, Histories* (U of Massachusetts P, 1997); Susan Leonardi's watershed article "Recipes for Reading: Summer Pasta, Lobster à la Riseholme, and Key Lime Pie"; and Rosalyn Collings Eves's "A Recipe for Remembrance: Memory and Identity in African-American Women's Cookbooks," *Rhetoric Review* 24.3 (2005): 280–97.

/ 45

2. While I believe that the embodied rhetoric of recipes is applicable to those recipes found in typed texts, such as community cookbooks, published cookbooks, and on recipe-swapping sites on the Internet, for the purposes of this essay, I am limiting my discussion to handwritten recipe cards since these add an additional layer of embodiment.

3. In addition to Graham Tomlinson's essay, for careful examinations of the language of recipes, see Cornelia Gerhardt, Maximiliane Frobenius, and Susanne Ley's edited collection *Culinary Linguistics: The Chef's Special* and Colleen Cotter's "Claiming a Piece of the Pie: How the Language of Recipes Defines Community" in Bower, *Recipes for Reading*, 51–71.

4. In Farmer's dedication to her former teacher Mrs. William Sewall, she extolls Sewall's "untiring efforts in promoting the work of *scientific cookery*, which means the elevation of the human race" (n. pag., emphasis mine).

5. See "British Surnames Beginning with 'Anderson,'" British Surnames, *Ancestry*, accessed 22 June 2014; and "Florence," *Think Baby Names*, accessed 22 June 2014.

6. "Oleomargarine," *The Oxford English Dictionary* (Oxford UP, 2014), 24 June 2014. After 1949, the term fell out of regular circulation in the United States, although Cognard said "oleo" (or just "oly") when she meant "margarine" for the rest of her life.

7. See Waverly Root and Richard de Rochemont, *Eating in America: A History* (Ecco P, 1981), 146–49, 156–60, 213–46.

8. The advent of a national food market created by the inventions of the tin can in 1825 and the icebox railway car in 1842 paved the way for an American cuisine that emphasized industrially produced, prepackaged, and ever-consistent food. For a broad summary of the history of food and foodways in nineteenth- and early twentieth-century America, see Jennifer Cognard-Black, "Food and Drink," *American Literature in Historical Context*, ed. Gary Scharnhorst (Gale, 2006), 391–95.

9. Poststructuralist theorists have written widely about how imaginative texts affect and potentially alter a reader's psyche in ways that other kinds of texts do not. See Roland Barthes's *The Pleasure of the Text* (1973), particularly his discussion of the "jouissance" of novelistic reading that occurs when a reader loses himself or herself within the book, as well as M. M. Bakhtin's theory of heteroglossia as a "speaking" discourse within novels in his *Dialogic Imagination: Four Essays* (1975).

10. Situating her work within studies of everyday writing and rhetoric informed by Bakhtin's theory of dialogism, White-Farnham defines "rhetorical heirlooms" as writing practices that are handed down within families and that sustain the commonplace "activity system of a household" (208). To develop her concept, White-Farnham adapted Suzanne Rumsey's notion of "heritage literacy" as realized in Amish communities. See Suzanne Kesler Rumsey, "Heritage Literacy: Adoption, Adaptation, and Alienation of Multimodal Literacy Tools," *College Composition and Communication* 60.3 (February 2009): 573–86.

Works Cited

Bloom, Lynn Z. "Consuming Prose: The Delectable Rhetoric of Food Writing." *College English* 70.4 (March 2008): 346–62.

Bower, Anne. "Cooking Up Stories: Narrative Elements in Community Cookbooks." *Recipes for Reading: Community Cookbooks, Stories, Histories*. Ed. Bower. U of Massachusetts P, 1997. 29–50.

Cognard, Nellie ("Peg") Frances Rogers. "Incidents in My Life." 1999. TS. Collection of Jennifer Cognard-Black, St. Mary's City, Maryland.

Farmer, Fannie Merritt. *The Boston Cooking-School Cook Book*. 1896. Little, Brown, and Company, 1912.

Floyd, Janet, and Laurel Forster. "The Recipe in Its Cultural Contexts." *The Recipe Reader: Narratives, Contexts, Traditions*. Ed. Floyd and Forster. U of Nebraska P, 2003. 1–11.

Gerhardt, Cornelia. "Food and Language—Language and Food." *Culinary Linguistics: The Chef's Special*. Ed. Gerhardt, Maximiliane Frobenius, and Susanne Ley. John Benjamins Publishing Company, 2013. 3–52.

Gerhardt, Cornelia, Maximiliane Frobenius, and Susanne Ley, eds. *Culinary Linguistics: The Chef's Special*. John Benjamins Publishing Company, 2013.

Inness, Sherrie A. *Dinner Roles: American Women and Culinary Culture.* U of Iowa P, 2001.

Leonardi, Susan J. "Recipes for Reading: Summer Pasta, Lobster à la Riseholme, and Key Lime Pie." *PMLA* 104.3 (May 1989): 340–47.

Sceats, Sarah. "Regulation and Creativity: The Use of Recipes in Contemporary Fiction." *The Recipe Reader: Narratives, Contexts, Traditions.* Ed. Janet Floyd and Laurel Forster. U of Nebraska P, 2003. 168–86.

Theophano, Janet. *Eat My Words: Reading Women's Lives through the Cookbooks They Wrote.* Palgrave Macmillan, 2002.

Tomlinson, Graham. "Thought for Food: A Study of Written Instructions." *Symbolic Interaction* 9.2 (September 1986): 201–16.

White-Farnham, Jamie. "'Revising the Menu to Fit the Budget': Grocery Lists and Other Rhetorical Heirlooms." *College English* 76.3 (January 2014): 208–26.

3. UNDERSTANDING THE SIGNIFICANCE OF "KITCHEN THRIFT" IN PRESCRIPTIVE TEXTS ABOUT FOOD

Jennifer E. Courtney

What to make for dinner when the grocery budget is tight? It is a routine but vexing question for many women, one that generations of domestic experts are eager to help home cooks answer. If, for instance, a mother of two school-age children wants economical, family-friendly recipes, she can consult any number of budget-minded cookbooks, from no-frill, spiral-bound collections published by university extension services to the styled boards on Pinterest. A nineteenth-century reader new to homemaking might have referred to Catharine Beecher and Harriet Beecher Stowe's *The American Woman's Home* for instructions on preparing a low-cost piece of meat or making soup (or to learn more from my favorite chapter in the book, "Evils of Hot Bread"). Easily read and digested in small chunks, prescriptive texts about food are ostensibly straightforward and enjoy a long tradition of popularity with American—mostly white, mostly middle-class—women (Ehrenreich and English; Leavitt); they are likely a staple in many home libraries.

A cursory look at such prescriptive literature might yield a relatively straightforward assessment: a stable—even formulaic—informational genre, produced and consumed by mostly women, designed to supplement the domestic instruction of mothers and home economics teachers. This chapter complicates such a limited reading by arguing that the texts, when read through the lens of thrift, are rich contributions to an understudied but ongoing cultural conversation about spending and saving, offering readers not only practical information but powerful alternatives to mainstream discourses of gendered consumption.

This chapter focuses primarily on four popular domestic guides, each clearly part of the prescriptive literature tradition. The first, Lydia Maria Child's *The American Frugal Housewife*, published in 1829, was incredibly popular and remains relevant almost two hundred years later. The comprehensive text is mainly a cookbook, interspersed with advice about cleaning, decorating, and educating girls and women. The second text, *The Complete Tightwad Gazette*, is a compendium of newsletters written by Amy Dacyczyn during the 1990s. Melissa d'Arabian's television show *Ten Dollar Dinners* is the third and most mainstream guide. *The Prudent Homemaker*, the final example, is the website and blog of Brandy Simper, a homeschooling mother of seven. Selected for the strong ethos of the writers and the accessibility of the advice, the collection here—though certainly not exhaustive—showcases representative examples of what I term "kitchen thrift."

Lindal Buchanan and Kathleen Ryan write that, in part, feminist rhetorical practice "entails identifying and examining women rhetors and women's rhetorics, making claims for their importance and contributions to the discipline, and, in doing so, regendering rhetorical histories and traditions" (xiii). Though the domestic writers here do not publically identify as feminist (though Child aligned herself with early feminist causes), they are powerful writers with texts designed to provide women the information and encouragement to make often complex food choices for themselves and their families; they deserve attention as "everyday" rhetors working in a range of discursive spaces. In addition, I call attention to how they participate in the rhetorical tradition of thrift, situating these authors and their texts in the history of prescriptive advice—cookbooks, domestic guides, and self-help manuals.

/ 49

Jack Selzer explains that contextual rhetorical analysis enables readers to understand how specific texts are "parts of larger communicative chains, or conversations," and that "by understanding the larger conversations that surround a specific symbolic performance, an analyst can appreciate better what is going on within that performance" (283). He further argues that contextual analysis shows how ideas are taken up and reformulated in unique ways by individual rhetors (301), depending on time, place, and circumstances. As we will see, Americans have long been interested in talking about thrift; the texts here show how thrift is discussed in a particularly gendered genre.

THRIFT AS A DISCURSIVE TRADITION

Historically, "thrift" has meant, roughly, the act or ways of acting that promote *thriving*. James Hunter and Joshua Yates point readers to the *Oxford English Dictionary*, which defines *thrift* as "the fact or condition of thriving or prospering; prosperity, success, good luck, in early use sometimes fortune, good or bad, etc." (qtd. in Hunter and Yates 11). They argue that thrift, while allowing humans to flourish, also allows us to "sustain and extend a conversation about the inescapably normative dimensions of economic life" (11). In other words, thrift enables us to talk about what resources make possible individuals' well-being.

Thrift also functions as an alternative to America's historically consumerist culture; using the term "simple living" in a way that is akin to thrift, David Shi provides a history of simple-living philosophies and movements in America, explaining the political, economic, and religious foundations of alternate lifestyles that prize intellectual or spiritual pursuits over the acquisition of material goods. Similarly, Terrence Witkowski describes six eras in US history and characterizes the "frugality discourses" that each yielded. He writes that these discourses

> generally have advocated that consumers show more discipline and resourcefulness in their product and service acquisition, use, and reuse . . . This rhetoric has called on Americans not to reject their material culture to the extent of self-inflicted deprivation but to consume more carefully, thoughtfully, and with greater restraint. . . . Frugality discourses have been thus a regular counter-current against the rising tides level of American consumerism. (237)

He further argues that frugality discourses "show both continuity and change over time" but are largely understudied (237). His article offers one of the only treatments of the rhetorical dimensions of frugality, identifying some of the most powerful writers on the topic, including the famously thrifty Benjamin Franklin, Lydia Maria Child (discussed in this chapter), World War II government campaigns, the Adbusters organization, and members of the "voluntary simplicity movement" (249). While Witkowski and Ronald Wilcox—author of *Whatever Happened to Thrift?*—both note the scant overall scholarship on thrift, notably missing from the extant work is the role that domestic advice has played in helping everyday women purchase and prepare food economically and mindfully.

While thrift encourages prudent household spending, it also enables production and interdependence; David Blankenhorn, Barbara Whitehead, and

Sorcha Brophy-Warren argue that it yields "an abundance of good things to savor in life" (xi) and is "big and big-hearted" (x). Ben Franklin, a "thrift advocate," encouraged people to develop self-discipline and individual initiative while cooperating with others in the community (x). Thrift has much in common with other practices and "moral goods" such as self-restraint, conservation, and stewardship and "notions of justice, charity, and the public good" (Hunter and Yates 12). Understood historically, thrift is a mindful and deliberate approach to daily living that considers the welfare of self and others. Hunter and Yates identify thrift trends (rooted in differing ideologies) in American history, including, among others, "Puritan thrift," "consumer thrift," "collective thrift," and "green thrift" (12); to their existing definitions, I add "kitchen thrift." In addition to yielding the food that provides physical sustenance, kitchen thrift gives purpose and pleasure to the daily work of preparing food.

Because *thrift* has the richest definition, I use it here in lieu of *frugality* or related terms. I define "kitchen thrift" as a home-based set of goal-oriented practices that conserves or increases food resources while supporting well-being. Kitchen thrift is community-oriented and production-driven; examples include being involved with food sourcing, such as growing vegetables or shopping outside of grocery stores, such as at farmers' markets. Kitchen thrift requires both food and financial literacy. As constructed by the texts I analyze, individuals practicing kitchen thrift not only prepare food but also create a domestic space in which family members and friends are nourished both physically and emotionally. And, despite the identified dearth of scholarship on thrift—and the contention of some, like Wilcox, that there is a dearth of actual thrift—the texts analyzed here suggest that kitchen thrift and discourses on kitchen thrift are alive and well, running parallel to and sometimes intersecting with mainstream consumer narratives.

/ 51

THE TEXTS

It's important to note that not all advice about budget cooking is thrifty in the sense of promoting thriving. There are myriad websites and books about successful couponing and budgeting. Extension services, community groups, and churches also offer information about shopping and cooking frugally. While valuable, many are fairly one-dimensional in supplying low-cost recipes, sometimes with nutritional information. The US government provides resources for saving money on food while meeting nutritional needs; on its website, the United States Department of Agriculture provides a "thrifty food plan" and recipe finder to citizens working with a modest food budget, particularly those who are Supplemental Nutrition Assistance Program (SNAP) recipients (*Recipes*). During the 1990s, food writer (and *Iron Chef America* judge) Jeffrey Steingarten challenged himself to eat well using the restrictive budget allotted by the department's "thrifty food plan." At the time, the plan was downright dreary: bland dishes and a limited menu rotation, with very little fresh food (it remains little improved). Steingarten gave the plan a "makeover," emphasizing that more nutritious, pleasing dishes could be made with careful shopping and proper preparation (Steingarten 33–49). While his message did not likely reach those it could have best helped, his combination of goals—to eat well and to eat pleasurably while on a budget— are characteristic of kitchen thrift.

A more recent effort to elevate the options easily available to SNAP participants is Leanne Brown's *Good and Cheap*. Originally published as a free pdf of Brown's master's degree in food studies capstone project, the cookbook (still available free online and as a softcover book, with in-kind donations for each purchased) features seasonal foods and cooking methods meant to provide flexibility to readers with a limited budget (about four dollars per day for each SNAP recipient) (Brown vii). Full of color photos and Brown's charming asides, the cookbook shows that—with moderate effort and planning—healthy and delicious food is within the budgets of most readers. Arguably a cookbook that will reach a diverse audience—the free version has been downloaded over eight hundred thousand times (*Leanne Brown*)—*Good and Cheap* speaks to a range of tastes, seasons, and occasions, emphasizing not only budget but the satisfaction of developing kitchen skills and the importance of a generous table.

With the notion of thriving at the forefront, let's turn our attention to four prescriptive texts promoting kitchen thrift. Because kitchen thrift—like thrift—has many ingredients, I will highlight here how each author uses kitchen thrift as a way to frame cooking advice and recipes and, in doing so, evidences the important role of domestic advice in the broader conversation about thrift.

The American Frugal Housewife, written in 1829 by novelist, editor, abolitionist, and cultural critic Lydia Maria Child and reprinted dozens of times (Longone iii), is a comprehensive domestic guide that includes an extensive recipe collection. Despite the title, the book promotes thriving rather than simple frugality; it urges readers to be industrious, disciplined, and of service to others even during difficult times. Child's position is clear: she writes for the poor (6) and criticizes reckless overspending, calling extravagance "the prevailing evil of the present day" (89) and the source of "much domestic unhappiness" (89). Seeking to counteract the stigma about thrift, she writes,

> Economy is generally despised as a low virtue, tending to make people ungenerous and selfish. This is true of avarice; but it is not so of economy. The man who is economical, is laying up for himself the permanent power of being useful and generous. . . . . True economy is a careful treasurer in the service of benevolence; and where they are united respectability, prosperity and peace will follow. (7)

In this passage, we see clear similarities between her notion of "economy" and the notion of thrift-as-thriving described above. For Child, this stance transforms thrift from miserable penny-pinching to purposeful activity that women can use to improve the lives of their families and the community.

Much of her cooking advice would be familiar to today's readers; she tells her readers to make their own bread, noting that the rich can buy bread, "but those who are under the necessity of being economical, should make convenience a secondary object" (9). She urges readers to buy in bulk (15), eat seasonally (33–36), and learn to prepare inexpensive cuts of meat (43). Suggestions like "Look to the greasepot, and see that nothing is there which might have served to nourish your own family, or a poorer one" (8) remind women to remain conscientious about reducing waste and attending to those in need.

/ 53

She also has positions that contemporary readers likely find amusing or difficult to fathom, such as "Beer is a good family drink" (86). In the event that one's husband brings home unexpected company, readers are advised that

> rennet pudding may be made at five minutes' notice; provided you keep a piece of calf's rennet ready prepared soaking in a bottle of wine. One glass of this wine to a quart of milk will make a sort of cold custard. Sweetened with white sugar, and spiced with nutmeg, it is very good. (62)

Though this recipe seems neither appetizing nor frugal, it, nonetheless, underscores her emphasis on preparation and what we might term "food literacy"; the thrifty reader is ready at all times to welcome drop-in guests.

Along with providing recipes and other advice, Child criticizes the societal emphasis on marriage and argues for better domestic education for girls (91–98). Writing that "the greatest and most universal error is, [sic] teaching girls to exaggerate the importance of getting married" (91), she posits that young women should be taught "that usefulness is happiness" (92). Instead of being encouraged to socialize, dress fashionably, and participate in other trends meant to increase their charm and marriageability, Child argues that young women should instead be taught to derive satisfaction from their ability to run efficient, pleasant homes that support the physical, emotional, and financial well-being of their inhabitants. She argues that when women are competent and satisfied household managers, they will not seek useless or destructive consumer distractions (96).

Avoiding useless consumption is the goal of Amy Dacyczyn, founder of *The Tightwad Gazette*, a 1990s newsletter with a devoted following. Dacyczyn and her readers embrace the term "tightwad," joking about achieving "black belt" status in frugality; by assigning the typically disparaging descriptor a high status, she dignifies the money-saving practices she advocates and encourages her readers to see them in a similar light. In addition to sharing her own strategies, she published money-saving tips from readers, such as reusing pickle juice to preserve several batches of cucumbers (313). *The Complete Tightwad Gazette: Promoting Thrift as a Viable Alternative Lifestyle*, a nine-hundred-page compendium of her newsletters, continues to be a popular seller on Amazon, with many readers viewing it as the authoritative source on saving money. Her 2009 appearance on New Hampshire Public Television ("Forever Frugal") has over eighty thousand views on YouTube. Her experiences—raising six children in her dream home in New England on her husband's salary—form the basis of much of her advice.

In many ways, Dacyczyn carries on the thrifty tradition we associate with Child, with more precise recipes and advice and perhaps a bit less didacticism. Her recipes, family-friendly and accessible to most palates, use cost-effective ingredients and are made from scratch. Her ingredient lists include prices, and she counsels readers to keep price books to track the cost of frequently purchased items at different stores. She shows readers how to evaluate the cost-effectiveness of various food preservation techniques, like whether dehydrating food is more economical—from an energy and nutritional standpoint—than freezing or canning (752–54). Her detailed cost breakdowns of many kinds of purchases are highly instructive.

How does Dacyczyn promote thriving through kitchen thrift? She is adamant that "the understanding of the relationship between thrift and the environment has given me the assurance that efforts to reuse and conserve could not be 'too extreme'" (222). In other words, her personal actions—cooking from scratch rather than buying prepackaged foods that generate a lot of waste, for instance—affect the planet. Recognizing the relationship between choices in her own kitchen and landfills and transportation costs aligns her quite tidily with those advocating "green thrift." Her homemade treats (popsicles, jellies, and birthday cakes) are designed to provide enjoyment for her family without the cost and hassle of purchasing new or consuming outside of the home. Finally, she encourages readers to

> develop a very critical attitude toward what seems to be our new, national goal: lying around doing nothing. Being busy, being productive, doing things that improve your family's long-term prospects should not be seen as drudgery to be endured. . . . The happiest people I know have realized a crucial truth: the act of doing things is more fun than doing nothing. If this is not your current attitude, you should work to acquire it. (815)

Her example—not to mention her text—shows that the practice and discourse of kitchen thrift is lively and important.

Melissa d'Arabian, of Food Network fame, shows that kitchen thrift can be easy and fun. Winner of the Food Network Challenge in 2009 ("Melissa d'Arabian Bio"), her Food Network show, *Ten Dollar Dinners*, is a thirty-minute program demonstrating how to cook dinner for a family of four for ten dollars or less. Her popular cookbooks are based on the same ideas—economical, healthy, and accessible cooking. Currently involved in several other projects, like judging Food Network's *Guy's Grocery Games* and running the Picky Eaters Project (*Melissa d'Arabian*), she maintains a high public profile. An active user of social media, particularly Twitter, she blends the personal and professional, advocating for causes that have affected her, like eliminating childhood hunger and promoting suicide awareness. /55

While all the rhetors analyzed here aim for at least some commercial success, d'Arabian has clearly achieved it, attaining celebrity status. Though the set of *Ten Dollar Dinners* looks like an upper-middle-class home and her tableware and cooking tools are new and pristine, she is one of the few voices on Food Network talking about budget-oriented cooking. She frequently uses some version of the saying "the most expensive ingredient is the one you throw away." And though clearly styled for television, she conveys an ethos of expert-peer, empathetic and open. The meals featured on her show are "fun" (like a diner-themed grilled cheese sandwich and soup supper), but she is direct about the necessity of smart shopping and intersperses cooking demonstrations with advice about purchasing and preparing, for instance, economical whole ingredients rather than convenience products. In all, her collection of texts—from her television shows to Twitter feed—creates an aspirational vision of thriving. Cooking fresh, modest, and child-friendly meals—and presenting them thoughtfully—is crucial to contented, middle-class family living.

Different means of thriving are apparent on *The Prudent Homemaker*, a blog and website created by Brandy Simper. Beginning in January 2007, Simper's family lived on no income for eight months, curtailing all shopping for one year. Their income continues to be erratic, and, consequently, they shop infrequently, buying in bulk and growing much of their own produce ("About"). The website and blog, from which Simper makes a small income, provide detailed, creative advice for eating well while struggling with serious financial hardship. Her popular ten-part series, "Eat for 40 Cents a Day," shows readers how to feed a family on very, very little money. The series makes d'Arabian's ten-dollar meals seem downright extravagant. Simper also has a post called "Cutting Expenses When You Think You Have Nothing Left to Cut," which she prefaces with the following:

> I know that many of you are really struggling with your inability to make ends meet right now. This post is for you. I hope it gives you hope—as well as some ideas for how to live well, even when you are living below the poverty line.

This quotation encompasses kitchen thrift when we understand it to mean thriving despite highly restrictive resource constraints.

Simper's beautifully photographed home belies her financial status; a set table, a basket full of fruit, and a flourishing garden convey calm, graciousness, and abundance. Simple meals, like homemade saltine-style crackers and from-scratch salad dressings served on homegrown greens, are nourishing while minimizing meat, dairy, and high-priced seasonings. Her domestic advice—and her gentle, generous presence—has formed the basis of a growing, welcoming web community dedicated to supporting and promoting thrift-as-thriving.

POSITIONING MYSELF AT THE TABLE

My analysis builds on the recent feminist rhetorical work in our field, which, as Jacqueline Jones Royster and Gesa Kirsch show, identifies and values women's texts while "helping to redefine what constitutes rhetoric and recast the ways in which we think about and interrogate the nature and consequences of rhetorical enterprises" (131–32). In situating representative texts promoting kitchen thrift within the tradition of thrift discourses, I show that women rhetors have actively contributed to discussions of how best to thrive despite their near absence in published scholarship. Looking forward, better understanding the impact of kitchen thrift discourses is necessary, as is better "understanding rhetorical agency itself in new, more-dynamic terms with regard to the scope and nature of rhetoric as an embodied social praxis" (132). Both these lines of inquiry could be explored by investigating the daily, nonpublished ways that women promote kitchen thrift and the increasing popularity of alternatives to mainstream consumer discourses. I count myself among the women for whom kitchen thrift is a valuable practice. A few years ago, I returned home following the semester break. After assessing the dreary contents of my post-holiday kitchen and resigning myself to a trip to the grocery store on a cold night, I browsed the two-week-old stack of mail. A relative had mailed my husband thirty-two dollars to repay some small loan. Since my husband was out of town, I decided to claim the thirty-two dollars as my own. Perhaps because of the bills I had also just opened, I decided to limit my grocery spending to only the thirty-two dollars, which I stipulated had to cover all of my healthy meals for the week. And in the spirit of New Year's resolutions, I continued with the shopping challenge well into the spring, eventually dubbing it "The $32 Plan." I thought up creative (and mostly palatable) uses for leftovers, scraps, and seemingly incompatible pantry staples. Planning and shopping for a week's worth of meals, cleaning supplies, and most toiletries was difficult. Throughout the duration of "The $32 Plan"—and subsequently—I sought advice from a variety of texts, and what I learned about recipe planning, food shopping, and cooking led to an academic interest in the understudied notion of thrift. My position of relative socioeconomic privilege—middle-class, food-literate, comfortably housed— afforded me the resources and leisure time to research recipes, cross-reference weekly sales, and assemble meals in a well-appointed kitchen; I grew increasingly—and sometimes uncomfortably—aware of that privilege as a result of my arbitrarily determined (and SNAP-level, as I later determined) budget.

I share this personal experience, mindful of and grateful for Royster and Kirsch's assertion that "stories matter" (3), because it deeply affected how I lived each week and, by extension, the priorities I came to have regarding shopping, food selection, and preparation. The experience informs my analysis of the highly gendered texts here, those that I encounter using "strategic contemplation" (21), Royster and Kirsch's term for a researcher's self-awareness of her material conditions and their relation to research and writing. As I offer my interpretation of their significance, I do so with the recognition that my fondness for and reliance on texts promoting kitchen thrift make me keenly feel a need for their inclusion into our field of study.

There is much to be learned about women's rhetoric by looking to the traditions of prescriptive literature and thrift, particularly when we are conscious of how we position ourselves in relation to the texts, as Royster and Kirsch underscore (135). The ways that we as individuals and scholars interact with and value these texts depend on what our financial circumstances permit and how our dispositions incline. There is also much room for study of how women every day are discursively negotiating their relationship with domestic work and expanding conversations about what it means to thrive.

Works Cited

Beecher, Catharine E., and Harriet Beecher Stowe. *The American Woman's Home.* Ed. Nicole Tonkovich. Harriet Beecher Stowe Center and Rutgers UP, 2002.

Blankenhorn, David, Barbara Dafoe Whitehead, and Sorcha Brophy-Warren. *Franklin's Thrift: The Lost History of an American Virtue.* Templeton P, 2009.

Brown, Leanne. *Good and Cheap: Eat Well on $4/Day.* Workman Publishing. 2015.

Buchanan, Lindal, and Kathleen J. Ryan, eds. *Walking and Talking Feminist Rhetorics: Landmark Essays and Controversies.* Parlor P, 2010.

Child, Lydia Maria. *The American Frugal Housewife.* 1844. Dover Publications, 1999.

Dacyczyn, Amy. *The Complete Tightwad Gazette: Promoting Thrift as a Viable Alternative Lifestyle.* Villard, 1998.

Ehrenreich, Barbara, and Deirdre English. *For Her Own Good: 150 Years of the Experts' Advice to Women.* Anchor Books, 1978.

"Forever Frugal." New Hampshire Public Television. 2009. *YouTube.* Accessed 29 June 2014.

Hunter, James Davison, and Joshua J. Yates. "Introduction: The Question of Thrift." *Thrift and Thriving in America: Capitalism and Moral Order from the Puritans to the Present.* Ed. Yates and Hunter. Oxford UP, 2011. 3–33.

Leanne Brown. 2015. Accessed 11 September 2015.

Leavitt, Sarah A. *From Catharine Beecher to Martha Stewart: A Cultural History of Domestic Advice.* U of North Carolina P, 2002.

Longone, Janice Bluestein. Introduction. *The American Frugal Housewife.* By Lydia Maria Child. 1844. Dover Publications, 1999. iii–viii.

Melissa d'Arabian. 2014. Accessed 30 June 2014.

"Melissa d'Arabian Bio." Television Food Network G.P. 2014. *Food Network.* Accessed 30 June 2014.

Recipes and Tips for Healthy, Thrifty Meals. United States Department of Agriculture. 2000. Accessed 29 June 2014.

Royster, Jacqueline Jones, and Gesa E. Kirsch. *Feminist Rhetorical Practices: New Horizons for Rhetoric, Composition, and Literacy Studies.* Southern Illinois UP, 2012.

Selzer, Jack. "Rhetorical Analysis: Understanding How Texts Persuade Readers." *What Writing Does and How It Does It*. Ed. Charles Bazerman and Paul Prior. Lawrence Erlbaum Associates, 2004. 279–307.

Shi, David E. *The Simple Life: Plain Living and High Thinking in American Culture*. Oxford UP, 1985.

Simper, Brandy. "About the Prudent Homemaker." *The Prudent Homemaker*. Accessed 30 June 2014.

———. "Cutting Expenses When You Think You Have Nothing Left to Cut." 11 February 2014. *The Prudent Homemaker*. Accessed 30 June 2014.

———. "Eat for 40 Cents a Day: Introduction." 31 May 2013. *The Prudent Homemaker*. Accessed 30 June 2014.

———. *The Prudent Homemaker*. Accessed 30 June 2014.

Steingarten, Jeffrey. *The Man Who Ate Everything*. Vintage Books, 1997.

Ten Dollar Dinners. Food Network. Accessed 30 June 2014.

Wilcox, Ronald T. *Whatever Happened to Thrift? Why Americans Don't Save and What to Do about It*. Yale UP, 2008.

Witkowski, Terrence H. "A Brief History of Frugality Discourses in the United States." *Consumption Markets and Culture* 13.3 (2010): 235–58.

4. PROMOTING PEACE, SUBVERTING DOMESTICITY: COOKBOOKS AGAINST WAR, 1968–83

Abby Dubisar

It will be a great day when our schools get all the money they need and the air force has to hold a bake sale to buy a bomber.
> —Velia Dean and Barbara B. J. Zimmerman,
> *The Great Day Cookbook*

If I can't bake, I don't want to be part of your revolution.
> —Rae Abileah and Whitney Hallock, *Peace Never Tasted So Sweet*

In the press release announcing Code Pink's 2010 cookbook, the organization gives its origin story and indicates that its cookbook "tells the story of women 'waging peace' . . . through their personal family recipes as well as sharing their tools and experience as peace activists" (Balicki). This deliberate gesture toward framing the cookbook as a resource that instructs activists and potential activists not only on pie baking but also on organizing follows in a little-known tradition that facilitates understanding peace activists' rhetorical strategies and the available means women locate to be both engaging and subversive.

As the analysis will reveal, feminist peace cookbooks not only serve fund-raising or cooking instruction purposes but also work to persuade individuals to join the peace community and antiwar cause. These cookbooks construct the organizations as accessible, friendly, and strategic. The sources considered in this essay—including the 1968 and 1970 volumes of

Peace de Resistance by members of Los Angeles's Women Strike for Peace (WSP), the 1973 Greenwich Village Peace Center's cookbook *Peacemeal*, and the 1983 *Great Day Cookbook* by Velia Dean and Barbara B. J. Zimmerman of the Women's International League for Peace and Freedom—enact subversive, yet tasty, interventions in women's activist lives; they teach feminist rhetoricians the potential of domestic genres to promote activist causes and frame political identities. Beyond expanding rhetorical horizons, analyzing such texts furthers an understanding of the practices that make up peace activism, which are quite diverse, and broaden concepts of gendered peace actions beyond marches, protests, flyers, political signs, and demonstrations.

These cookbooks, illuminated by the theory of invitational rhetoric (Foss and Griffin) and didactic materials for activists (Del Gandio), demonstrate how historical and contemporary activists ignite engagement, promote community identity for subcultures, and adeptly subvert domestic roles demanded of women. And furthermore, considering these cookbooks as rhetorical texts helps answer questions asked by those concerned about the political and feminist implications of the upswing in fetishizing domestic tasks like pickling and making jam (Matchar) and how gender roles can be rejected while denouncing the tradition that "mainstream American culture   / 61 views the household as a unit of consumption" (Hayes 9).

NOW WE'RE COOKING WITH RHETORIC

In his editor's letter in the 2008 special food issue of *College English*, John Schlib writes, "The field now studies both rhetoric *and* cookery—including the rhetorics accompanying production and delivery of food" (345). What Schlib does not describe in his brief editor's letter is the pathway to arriving at this intersection, the navigation that helped us gather at this place: feminism. The academic study of feminism, the increased interest in women's rhetorics, and the work of women's and gender studies scholars made and continue to make the intersection of rhetoric and food studies not only possible but also now legitimized by major journals like *College English*. For rhetoric specifically, feminist historiographical methodologies and the scholars who revised rhetorical studies to critique its phallocentric focus have, in just the past thirty years, ambitiously and energetically revised the field's notion of what is rhetorical, what rhetorical theory looks like, and who crafts rhetorical thought.

Led by rhetoric and communication scholars like Kate Ronald, Jacqueline Royster, Karlyn Kohrs Campbell, and many others, rhetoricians now engage texts historically ignored by past creators of the rhetorical canon, prying open the field of rhetoric for rhetors who are not included in or enfranchised by the white, masculine, normative tradition. As Kate White writes in her study of pageants performed by women's clubs, "if we continue to use canonical maps that exclude women[,] . . . we lose a rich and complicated history of women's participation in specific, and often local, cultural moments" (515). The same argument could be adapted to studying rhetorical artifacts such as peace activist cookbooks, which illustrate women's political participation and provide a unique and specific perspective on women peace activists' rhetorical strategies.

Rhetoric scholars who have studied conventional, nonactivist cookbooks implicitly highlight the long, pervading shadow of rhetoric's male-dominated, mainstream history by opening their publications with a legitimizing gesture, taking time to prove that cookbooks are worthy of study. Their efforts to validate such study lay the groundwork for studying women's peace activist cookbooks, which no longer requires extended justification.

A brief literature review shows the small yet active body of work established about women's cookbook rhetorics. Marta Hess, for example, studies Junior League cookbooks and how the books revealed community and identity formation. Elizabeth Fleitz shows how online recipes are rhetorical situations, multimodal platforms that enhance the continually revised and communal aspects of recipes. Rosalyn Collings Eves analyzes National Council of Negro Women cookbooks, revealing how they "serve a practical purpose of instructing in the material production of food [and] serve a deeper ideological purpose as a site where a particular group of African-American women combat prevalent cultural stereotypes" (280–81).

By interviewing second-wave white women who belong to the Red Hat Society, Jamie White-Farnham discovers how widely diverse the women's recipes can be when studied rhetorically (39). The women expressed annoyance at times, bothered by the focus on domestic roles instead of professional identities. The women had de-emphasized or simply rejected domestic work and thus revealed the tension of the feminist possibilities of domestic endeavors like cooking. This tension also surfaces textually in peace activist cookbooks; writers deal with being both an activist and a preparer of food. Beyond rhetoric, others explore the significance of cookbooks to construct gender norms (Inness; Neuhaus) and build community (Bower).

Writing about a set of two cookbooks that I also take up in this analysis, *Peace de Resistance*, Isaac West analyzes maternity as a political strategy. West links the WSP cookbooks to Kenneth Burke's characterization of food's rhetoricity, that "in the *meaning* of food[,] there is much rhetoric, the meaning being persuasive enough for the idea of food to be used . . . as a rhetorical device of statesmen" (West 379). West shows how members of the WSP wrote *against* statesmen's motives by positioning their cookbooks against war (379). Beyond West's critique, which focuses on the "affective and embodied dimension of the political practice of everyday life" (360), this analysis positions the WSP cookbooks within a context of other peace cookbooks to show WSP's embedded invitational, radical strategies.

This analysis thus takes up the call issued by West and others to more substantially focus on food, drawing upon a small archive of peace cookbooks spanning fifteen years. The cookbooks' writers, as the next section articulates, see opportunities to subvert expectations for both peace activism and gender, as all members of the broadest possible audiences eat.

INVITATIONAL AND RADICAL RHETORICS

Applying concepts from Sonja K. Foss and Cindy L. Griffin's landmark 1995 essay "Beyond Persuasion: A Proposal for an Invitational Rhetoric" and linking them to Jason Del Gandio's 2008 *Rhetoric for Radicals: A Handbook for Twenty First Century Activists* offers both a historical understanding of the rhetorical work these cookbooks do and how they continue to enact productive strategies for politically engaged citizens.

Foss and Griffin frame their alternative rhetoric, their proposal, as feminist because it focuses on relationships of equality and elimination of dominance and elitism, the value of all human beings, and self-determination (4). The four cookbooks analyzed here reflect these values and, thus, function as invitational rhetoric. The 1970 *Peace de Resistance* cookbook, for example, includes blank pages in the back for readers to put their own recipes, a literal enactment of invitational rhetoric that involves readers in the space of the book.

Foss and Griffin propose an expanded array of communication options, just like the peace activists who develop options for what activism looks like. In 1973's *Peacemeal*, written by a peace organization not defined as a women's group, Sybil Claiborne writes a reflection, "The Politics of Soup" (16). Like other peace cookbooks that feature multiple types of writings and illustrations beyond recipes, Claiborne's piece describes early days of commune living that included pooling resources to eat, outlining the creative cookery of a Venetian "transvestite" who made brilliant soups with few commune resources. Claiborne writes, "But it seemed to me then as it does now that soupmaking was a radical act, for to live cheaply and simply is the dream of every revolutionary" (16). Like Foss and Griffin, Claiborne and others contributing to this cookbook write of collaborative relationships that both built and maintained the Greenwich Village Peace Center and sustained its members with food and ideas.

Ultimately, Foss and Griffin suggest an option for understanding and enacting rhetoric not based on traditional rhetorical goals of persuasion or dominance but, instead, on the value of interaction and connection. In the introduction to the first volume of *Peace de Resistance*, the authors elicit such an invitation. They connect conversations at international peace conferences with cooking conversations, characterizing both as happening simultaneously to describe their practice of strategizing peace building while exchanging recipes. They write,

> Here, then, are some of those recipes, international and domestic, adapted to American kitchens for busy housewives, WSP or otherwise. Some of these recipes are for those harried days when leaflets have to be distributed . . . or urgent telephone calls have to be made. Some of the recipes are for those relaxed days when you want something extra special for your family . . . or for when you're having a party—a cause party or just for fun. All are for you WSPer's and women like you . . . women on the move! (n. pag.)

This introductory note deliberately addresses both members and nonmembers of the organization, inviting all to see the book as relevant to their lives.

Earlier in the introduction, the WSP writers list their many peaceworker actions: "[We've] walked thousands of miles, written plane-loads of letters to our president, our congressmen, and the heads of states. We've vigiled at the Federal Building; we've attended conferences of women like ourselves across the world" (n. pag.). This multiplicity of actions connects Foss and Griffin's invitational strategies with Del Gandio's direct address to activists. The writers here attempt to relate to their audiences of members and nonmembers by showing how they understand the various tasks involved in building connections and activism and cooking.

Del Gandio's *Rhetoric for Radicals* is a guidebook written by a rhetoric scholar for activists. Along with his many suggestions that can help make activists' rhetorical strategies more effective, Del Gandio promotes several ideas that surface in peace activist cookbooks and other practices. Del Gandio builds some of his theories on critiques of present activist strategies: "We have come to believe that our actions, and our actions alone, will change the world.

That is a mistake. . . . Creating networks of world-wide justice must entail *effective rhetorical communication*" (7). Thus, Del Gandio positions rhetoric at the core of productive, sustainable activism. In this same way, the cookbook authors promote their work in a network of other strategies, diverse activities that do not rely on simply one kind of activist practice. Their justifications for the cookbooks support this notion that activists must be prepared to justify their rhetorical strategies and connect them to their mission.

To that end, the introduction to *The Great Day Cookbook*, published in 1983, offers readers a brief history lesson on the Women's International League for Peace and Freedom (WILPF) and describes the myriad issues the organization has addressed. Velia Dean and Barbara Zimmerman detail how WILPF needs money to "make peace and justice a reality" (6), which is why they sell their cookbooks, an extension of their bake sales. Drawing on the adage included as an epigraph at the start of this chapter, they write that the book anticipates the "expectation that one day humankind will learn to live in peace and the military will need our recipes for their bake sales" (6). Right away, then, this book is positioned as a marginal text, a tool of the peace movement without the federal funding of American military enterprises, a counter-narrative against mainstream American policy. / 65

Another one of Del Gandio's rhetorical strategies for activists exemplified by these cookbooks relates to the audiences addressed by such texts. The cookbook writers count on diverse audiences made up of members of their organizations, but they also see themselves as writing to much wider audiences. As Del Gandio implores, "we need to appeal to the widest audience possible while maintaining our revolutionary stance. This double-edged sword is the lifeline of our radicalism" (29). Here the radicalness of a cookbook can be considered. While it is not possible to know how controversial creating a cookbook was for these organizations, all the books work to connect activism and cooking, assuming audiences will not necessarily do so.

Though these cookbooks could potentially find a broad and diverse audience, they come from organizations that were likely populated by white individuals who had the time to participate in political activities and could be engaged against war, not needing to focus their activist energy on gaining civil rights or fighting other layers of oppression. Scholars like Melinda Plastas, for example, study intersectionality and peace activism. Plastas focuses her work on how race and racism contributed to the development of WILPF, for instance, rejecting assumptions that the organization was all-inclusive or that it did not struggle with race as well as addressing peace (4). Organizations themselves strove toward inclusivity in official documentation, but the actual makeup of their groups when these cookbooks were written remains unknown. WSP, for example, described themselves in their 1962 national policy statement by affirming, "we are women of all races, creeds and political persuasions who are dedicated to the achievement of general and complete disarmament under effective international control" (qtd. in Swerdlow 499).

GENDER SUBVERSION AND DOMESTIC REVOLUTION

Peace activists hold unquestioned subversive identities, as antiwar activists place themselves in opposition to mainstream militarization. Likewise, women engaging in peace activism are doubly "othered" since women's experience and authority are often positioned marginally compared to men, long considered the normative citizen and expert. Therefore, women activists must contend with and strategize gender in the peace context.

The cookbooks analyzed here enact strategies for both revealing the performative nature of normative gender roles and revolutionizing domestic spaces and practices. Using discursive strategies that continually remind readers that the cookbook they are reading is different from a nonpeace organization cookbook, the writers combine their activism with the recipes to show how they, as activists, embody multiple roles, including both the radical and the familial. The writers thus implicitly reject assumptions that activists do not perform household tasks or that those who cook are not also very politically active. To exemplify dual roles performed by the cookbooks, a chronological consideration shows multiple strategies enacted in one type of activist material.

The first volume of *Peace de Resistance* is a two-color, spiral-bound, unpaginated book. The cover features a drawing of women carrying protest signs that spell out the title, immediately connecting gender and activism. The title page indicates that the book was created collaboratively, "written, designed, and illustrated voluntarily" by the Los Angeles branch of WSP. Esther Lewin is credited as the writer, Jay Rivkin as the designer and illustrator, and Kay Hardman and Jean Kovner as editors. Twelve additional contributors are also listed, as well as Mary Clarke, who conceived of the book.[1]

Written for other WSP members, this book serves as an artifact of the women's community, and yet it could also find audiences beyond the WSP membership. The opening describes how WSP members have not only "vigiled at the Federal Building," attended conferences around the world, and written "plane-loads of letters to our president, our congressmen, and the heads of our states" but have also fulfilled all their homekeeping duties as well (n. pag.). All the while, WSPers are performing their antiwar actions, as the introduction describes, and they are talking to one another about home and recipes. Thus, in addition to addressing the "proliferation of nuclear weapons and atom free zones," they connect their lives through food and home (n. pag.). The book is, therefore, positioned as a collection of these exchanged recipes, adapted "to American kitchens for busy housewives, WSP or otherwise" (n. pag.). The basic assumption made by the writers is that readers of *Peace de Resistance* have cooking responsibilities, just like the WSP members who wrote the book.

Early in the book, recipes for "Russian Borscht" and, on the following page, "Rushin' Borscht" offer cooks options, depending on how much time they want to (or are able to) spend cooking. The latter recipe opens with the line, "Make in 10 minutes in the morning before rushing off to your WSP meeting," acknowledging the multiple demands faced by WSP women (n. pag.). Throughout the text of the WSP cookbook, writer Esther Lewin and editors Kay Hardman and Jean Kovner position women as equipped to strategically fulfill their domestic roles by saving time and money in the kitchen while also expanding those roles for WSP work. The recipe notes acknowledge the performative nature of gendered roles, enhanced by tips and tricks from experienced WSPers. Additionally, other details note the challenges of WSP's activism, attempting to balance bright optimism with the negative implications of antinuclear, antiwar activism. The recipe for "Italian Veal and Peppers," for example, opens by stating, "Italian exports are known the world over. If only PACEM in TERRIS was as popular as Italian Veal and Peppers. However, until that great day . . ." (n. pag.). *Pacem in terris*, or peace on earth, the goal to which WSP aspires, becomes reiterated in the recipe.

Some of the recipes subvert the expectation of a dedicated cook who commits countless hours to preparing food for her family, encouraging women to employ strategies that will both save time and satisfy family members. One example is "Barbecue Leg of Lamb," which includes the note, "Your family will never guess that while this lamb was cooking in the oven[,] . . . you were cooking up something for WSP on the telephone" (n. pag.). The book does not offer evidence that women should specifically hide their WSP work, but instead, this notion of being strategic surfaces repeatedly, anticipating and refuting the claim that busy people do not have time for activism.

Another feature of *Peace de Resistance* is a focus on international cuisine, connected to peace. "Chicken a la Moscow" includes the detail, "Spread sauce over chicken and serve. Sometimes (maybe due to nuclear testing) the sauce just won't thicken enough to spread" (n. pag.). While this parenthetical note

could be taken as a simple joke, it reminds readers of the environmental consequences of nuclear testing—and that food and its production are political.

A final notable way the first volume of *Peace de Resistance* undermines
traditional gender expectations and radicalizes domesticity is in its positioning of the family as less important than WSP work. The book suggests that,
through cooking, activist women can placate their families easily. WSP work
is not rushed or framed as burdensome or in need of time-saving strategies.
Instead, the construction of the domestic worker/activist throughout the
book privileges her radical role as a peace activist. In the recipe for "Divine
Lime Pie," the introduction asks, "Neglected your family lately? All will be
forgiven with this divine pie" (n. pag.). Even though the more important
mission of peace and disarmament cannot be solved with a pie recipe, the
book proposes that other roles that WSPers likely perform—cook, mother,
wife—can require less time so more can be spent on important activist work.

This theme continues in the second volume. The authors repeat their
first volume's introduction on the cover flap and open the introduction
by writing:

> We tried. We tried every way to bring peace to our land. We protested;
> we marched; we wrote letters; we leafleted; we vigiled; we counseled
> on the Draft. We tried everything but inviting the President to dinner
> and cooking a meal out of the first Peace de Resistance cookbook. We'll
> *have* peace too, we women, with one foot in the kitchen and one foot in
> the world. We're impatient with the hash that has been made of things.
> We're determined, by every means possible . . . to stir things up, to stew
> about what matters, to go on serving Peace.

Again illustrated by Rivkin and written by Lewin, this volume continues
to insist that WSP members and potential members must maintain their
vigilance for peace while also meeting the demands of their roles at home.
Time carries on as a significant theme in recipes like "Beef Bird in Garden
Casserole," which ends with the note, "If you've got a street corner leaflet
distribution scheduled for the next day, make this casserole a day in advance"
(25). Like time, money and the economics of war and peace also surface in
recipe descriptions, including the directions for "Western Chili," which read,
"The defense budget has nothing on the household budget these days. Here's
some welcome relief" (28).

The recipe for "Mary's Mishmash" highlights the urgency of activism
that makes cooking an afterthought, yet a still significant obligation. The
recipe description begins,

Did you rush off to a demonstration with such enthusiasm that you forgot to take something out of the freezer for dinner? Here's the solution to that problem. We wish it were this easy to solve problems like war and Peace. . . . (35)

Again readers see an acknowledgement of the overwhelming work of seeking peace, in comparison to the ease of dinner preparation. Thus the book reinforces its potential domestic revolution by positioning cooking, the focus of any cookbook, as less important than activism. Additionally, by ending with the extended ellipsis, the WSP writers invite readers to continue reflecting on the ongoing, pressing issue of achieving peace.

Decades before Del Gandio insisted that activists employ numerous strategies, this cookbook encouraged that guidance. The description for "Soy and Tomato Round Steak" inspires writing specifically, imploring readers after the recipe details to "get that idea off your chest and into a newspaper—where it counts. While your round steak is cooking, you have plenty of time to write a letter to the editor" (42). These different strategies for actions continually connect to cooking, but the activism is always more important. A recipe note also prompts readers to engage others about the issue of peace in conversation by asking, "A rich relative coming to dinner? Want to set him on his ear and *then* ask for a large contribution to WSP? Serve caviar with aspic with the drinks before dinner" (103).

/ 69

The 1970 volume also features photographs and biographies of Lewin and Rivkin, as well as Mary Clarke, who conceived of the idea of doing a cookbook. These biographies position all the women as career professionals, roles never referred to in the cookbook pages. At the time, Lewin, a University of California, Los Angeles graduate, worked as an advertising copywriter and account executive. Rivkin painted commissioned murals for architects, her artwork featured in many exhibits. Clarke, who started the peace movement in Los Angeles, is described as a businesswoman. With these details, then, the creators become positioned as individuals who take on multiple roles and demands, again complicating the notion of who peace activists are and what their lives are like.

In 1973's *Peacemeal*, the writers frame cooking in the context of their organizing meetings and do not refer to domestic gatherings or family spaces at all, subverting the notion that to cook is to play a role in a heteronormative nuclear family. Instead, cooking is a necessary task to combat hunger and a way to gather people at the Greenwich Village Peace Center. In her introduction, Grace Paley writes,

> I know a lot of these recipes, because in the 45 minutes between work and a Peace Center meeting I have often had to call Mary or Karl and ask, "How the hell did you say I should do that fish?" (n. pag.)

The cookbook then serves to document instructions that are passed around anecdotally among members of the peace center. Continuing, Paley states, "I have also gathered some hot tips at the Resistance dinners which we served once a week at the Peace Center to about a hundred young men who were *not* going to be part of the U.S. plan to torment and murder the Vietnamese people," showing clearly how food gathers people so they can discuss and organize, well nourished and energized (n. pag.). Food is essential to revolution and not just in a home-based environment.

Peacemeal includes contributions from both women and men instead of focusing on a feminine gendered identity being performed by the activists at home and politically. A resounding theme is economics and cooking delicious food for yourself and others while also being poor. Being a peace activist is not a lucrative endeavor. For example, the recipe for "Lentil and Lamb Pottage" includes the variations, "If you're broke . . . if you're really broke . . . if flush" (32). The writers know their readers embody a diverse array of economic circumstances and do not want their recipes to be read as elite or expensive.

Continuing with their positioning of cookery as an endeavor for all genders and challenging the notion that cookbooks are "feminine," *Peacemeal's* recipes also reinforce their vision of cooking as a way to gather activists and engage important political issues. Barbara Dane's recipe "Corned Beef Euphoria," for example, shows how food gatherings facilitate conversation. The opening description reads,

> One way to get through hard times and confusing times is to take a good meal with friends who know how to hear each other. So call up some, even on an impossibly busy day, and tell them to come for a late dinner hour and bring some beer. (39)

The recipe closes with further emphasis on communicating over a shared meal. Dane writes, "Break out the beer and take your time over it all, seeing as far into your friends' gifts of communication as you can. Everything will begin to look better. With luck and organization it can even *get* better!" (39). The continued optimism galvanizes readers to remain engaged with the issues while also trying out the recipes.

The final cookbook under consideration, *The Great Day Cookbook* (1983) by Dean and Zimmerman, uses even different strategies to position domestic tasks and spaces as revolutionary, yet it does so without deliberately addressing or constructing gender. By including only baking recipes, *Great Day* goes beyond the WILPF description covered earlier to pepper its contents with quotations from politicians, activists, and others. The briefest of all the cookbooks considered here, the recipes do not have peace or activism-related descriptions and no short essays about peace appear; the book is focused on baking. The cookbook does, however, feature ten children's drawings randomly positioned throughout its pages, evoking a call for peace to preserve future generations.

Among the quotations that connect food and peace directly are President Dwight D. Eisenhower's statement, "Every gun that is made, every warship that is launched, every rocket fired, signifies in the final sense a theft from those who hunger and are not fed, from those who are cold and are not clothed" (19). This quotation makes a domestic space, like a kitchen, a political battleground due to the fact that issues of hunger and war are concerns about resources and their distribution. Another relevant quotation featured, by songwriter and poet Rod McKuen, makes a disarmament argument by stating, "Guns make lousy plowshares, but oh, they rust so beautifully. Think of how they'd look with snap peas crawling over them" (53). Other antinuclear quotations, sentiments from WILPF founder Jane Addams, and concerns about the waste war causes are found with the recipes. Consistently positioned at the bottom of the page below a recipe, *Great Day* includes eighteen quotations within its ninety-one pages of baking recipes.

Dean and Zimmerman thus place the authority about peace and revolution in the interspersed quotations by known figures instead of positioning the cookbook as a discursive space for their own thoughts and philosophies, beyond the introduction. Unlike the other books that seem to more fully represent the organization's mission, due to its focus on baking, *Great Day* may have been sold alongside baked goods at a fund-raising bake sale, a supplement to other organizational materials.

CONCLUSION

Taken together, these cookbooks exemplify one of Del Gandio's basic communication tenets: balance. He writes,

> To craft a style that both reflects your radicalism and attracts people to it. That's not easy to do. Coming off too radical alienates people. Watering down our radicalism doesn't attract any attention. The trick is to balance these two poles while adapting and adjusting to each and every situation. (165)

In some ways, this philosophy even reads like a recipe, amplifying the balance activists writing cookbooks attempt to achieve.

To close their 2010 cookbook, Code Pink includes on the back cover the line, "If I can't bake, I don't want to be part of your revolution," representing a sentiment of so-called post-third-wave generations who see the performance of cookery and other "domestic" tasks as a key part of their activism. Unlike the cookbooks analyzed here, Code Pink's cookbook revises the trend slightly to assume baking can be a creative, enjoyable activity members can choose to embrace or reject while their commitment to peace remains firm.

Beyond peace organizations, in the contemporary "new domesticity" movement, to be domestic is the revolution itself; individuals who have the means to reject mass-produced consumer capitalism instead reembrace the home and hearth (Matchar 12). When the domestic activity itself is the revolution, however, the actual activist causes and social issues that need attention potentially get lost or ignored. That concern is echoed by Emily Matchar, who writes, "Shopping at the farmer's market and baking bread and curing your own bacon are great, if you love those things, but they're not going to solve the world's problems" (231). While Matchar oversimplifies, the point still very literally drives home what substantial revolution looks like and what relationship it has to current ambivalences about the radical power of food and cooking.

Similarly, the second-wave cookbooks' focus on efficiency potentially liberated women to create a space for activism in their lives but also simultaneously reinforced corporate production of food. The key assumption that women should perform cookery duties thus never gets fully questioned. While third-wave and post-third-wave "makers," like those who submitted recipes to Code Pink's cookbook, resist industrial food production, they also risk highlighting pie over peace. The tension remains concerning the most productive and effective ways to make food progressive and persuasive for revolution. How can activists write cookbooks that resist industrial processing while also resisting gendered power dynamics that construct cooking as women's primary responsibility?

For now, the cookbooks featured here show feminist rhetoricians some ways that activists engaged their audiences and furthered their cause. Each book exemplifies strategies the creators' relied on to make their case and gain entrance into users' homes and lives in ways other peace rhetoric could not accomplish. While some political activities become lost to history, documents like these cookbooks persist and prompt questions about the future of food and peace activism, its gendered implications, and subversive possibilities.

Notes

I am indebted to Jason Palmeri for feedback he provided on this chapter that not only improved it overall but especially helped me articulate this lasting tension.

1. A complete description of the WSP movement cannot fit within the limited space of this chapter. Amy Swerdlow's comprehensive 1993 book *Women Strike for Peace: Traditional Motherhood and Radical Politics in the 1960s* offers a rich history.

Works Cited

Abileah, Rae, and Whitney Hallock, eds. *Peace Never Tasted So Sweet: A Peace Pie Cookbook by Code Pink Women for Peace.* Code Pink: Women for Peace, 2010.

Balicki, Dana. "Peace Never Tasted So Sweet: Code Pink Launches New Cookbook!" 7 May 2010. *Code Pink.* Accessed 18 November 2016.

Bower, Anne L. "Our Sisters' Recipes: Exploring 'Community' in a Community Cookbook." *Journal of Popular Culture* 31.3 (Winter 1997): 137–51.

Claiborne, Sybil, et al., eds. *Peacemeal: A Cookbook from the Greenwich Village Peace Center.* Greenwich Village Peace Center, 1973.

Dean, Velia, and Barbara B. J. Zimmerman. *The Great Day Cookbook.* Quixott P, 1983.

Del Gandio, Jason. *Rhetoric for Radicals: A Handbook for Twenty First Century Activists.* New Society Publishers, 2008.

Eves, Rosalyn Collings. "A Recipe for Remembrance: Memory and Identity in African-American Women's Cookbooks." *Rhetoric Review* 24.3 (2005): 280–97.

Fleitz, Elizabeth. "Cooking Codes: Cookbook Discourses as Women's Rhetorical Practices." *Present Tense* 1 (2010): 1–8.

Foss, Sonja K., and Cindy L. Griffin. "Beyond Persuasion: A Proposal for an Invitational Rhetoric." *Communication Monographs* 62 (March 1995): 2–18.

Hayes, Shannon. *Radical Homemakers: Reclaiming Domesticity from a Consumer Culture.* Left to Write P, 2010.

Hess, Marta. "Projects in the Making: Establishing Community and Identity in Junior League Cookbooks." *Peitho* 14.1 (Spring 2012): 1–6.

Inness, Sherrie A. *Cooking Lessons: The Politics of Gender and Food.* Rowman and Littlefield, 2001.

Lewin, Esther. *Peace de Resistance: A Cook Book.* Women Strike for Peace, 1968.

———. *Peace de Resistance: A Cook Book.* Vol. 2. Ward Ritchie P, 1970.

Matchar, Emily. *Homeward Bound: Why Women Are Embracing the New Domesticity.* Simon and Schuster, 2013.

Neuhaus, Jessamyn. "The Way to a Man's Heart: Gender Roles, Domestic Ideology, and Cookbooks in the 1950s." *Journal of Social History* 32.3 (Spring 1999): 529–55.

Plastas, Melinda. *A Band of Noble Women: Racial Politics in the Women's Peace Movement*. Syracuse UP, 2011.

Schlib, John. "From the Editor." *College English* 70.4 (March 2008): 345.

Swerdlow, Amy. "Ladies' Day at the Capitol: Women Strike for Peace versus HUAC." *Feminist Studies* 8.3 (1982): 493–520.

West, Isaac. "Performing Resistance in/from the Kitchen: The Practice of Maternal Pacifist Politics in La WISP's Cookbooks." *Women's Studies in Communication* 30 (2007): 358–83.

White, Kate. "'The Pageant Is the Thing': The Contradictions of Women's Clubs and Civic Education during the Americanization Era." *College English* 77.6 (2015): 512–29.

White-Farnham, Jamie. "Rhetorical Recipes: Women's Literacies in and out of the Kitchen." *Community Literacy Journal* 6.2 (Spring 2012): 23–41.

PART II

DEFINING FEMINIST
FOOD WRITING

5. THE MEANING OF A MEAL: M. F. K. FISHER AND GASTRONOMICAL KAIROS

Erin Branch

M. F. K. Fisher's place in the history of gastronomical writing is well established. In fact, some even argue that she is largely responsible for the rich
tradition of food writing we now enjoy. In a 1992 obituary for Fisher, *New
York Times* reporter and cookbook author Molly O'Neill credits Fisher with
having "created" the genre of food writing. *Gourmet* magazine ranked Fisher
fifth on its list of "The Fifty Most Important Women in Food," claiming
that Fisher "invented" food writing and noting that aspiring food writers
and bloggers everywhere "want to be her." Her gastronomical books have
remained in print for decades and have been frequently reissued, sometimes
in special anniversary editions, and a popular biography (Anne Zimmerman's *An Extravagant Hunger: The Passionate Years of M. F. K. Fisher*) was
published in 2011. Her influence has been considerable in large part because
she helped us to see eating not simply, as she said, a "thrice-daily necessity" but instead as a practice imbued with deep emotional, spiritual, and
social meanings.

Born in 1908 to Rex and Edith Fisher, Mary Frances Kennedy spent most
of her childhood in Whittier, California. In 1929, she married Al Fisher and
moved with him to Dijon, France, so he could complete his doctorate in
literature. She chronicles that time most fully in *Long Ago in France* (1991),
and the experience made a profound impression on her culinary sensibilities.
She began writing and publishing shortly after they returned to the United

States in 1932. Her first book of gastronomical writing, *Serve It Forth*, was published in 1937, and although it received very positive reviews, it did not sell as briskly as she'd hoped. Nonetheless, the book was the start of her long and impressive career in using language and rhetoric to reshape the way Americans thought about food and eating.

From the beginning of that career, Fisher was something of an iconoclast.[1] Gene Saxton and the other editors at Harper and Brothers (now Harper-Collins), which published *Serve It Forth*, were astonished to discover that Fisher was not the "bookish Oxford don" they had expected but rather an "attractive" and stylish woman (Reardon, *Poet* 92). Indeed, in Fisher's later accounts of the meeting, she reports Saxton assuring her that "no woman could possibly have written *Serve it Forth*" (Fisher, *Dubious Honors* 134). Saxton and the others were no doubt influenced by their contemporary moment, during which unabashed discussions of the pleasures of eating were considered exclusively the purview of male epicures. Women who wrote about food were expected to do so in "correctly female and home economics fashion," as Fisher described it (qtd. in Reardon, *Poet* 92). While Fisher's derisive tone makes clear her feelings about this kind of writing, she is right that most women of her era who wrote about food did not follow the model of writers like Jean-Anthelme Brillat-Savarin (author of *The Physiology of Taste*) or the gourmand Maurice Edmond Sailland, better known by his pen name Curnonsky. Rather, most women wrote more practically about cooking and household management in ways that emphasized economy or nutrition but not pleasure. Few employed Fisher's narrative, anecdotal style; rather, they wrote advice columns, recipes, domestic handbooks. In short, most women who wrote about food or cooking upheld cultural commonplaces about gendered food practices. As Sherrie Inness notes in *Dinner Roles*, popular magazines like the *Woman's Home Companion* encouraged women to prepare dainty and elaborate foods, reflecting cultural ideals about femininity and womanhood (53–54). Even books that promoted the use of time- and labor-saving devices, like Poppy Cannon's series of *Can Opener Cookbooks*, did little to challenge the idea that women were responsible for preparing a family's meals. And very little of this writing focused on whether women ate—let alone enjoyed—the food they prepared.

Fisher, on the other hand, wrote with gusto about enjoying preparing and eating food, whether something as simple as toast or something as elaborate and exotic as escargot or a homemade curry. She is universally praised as a stylist; W. H. Auden wrote in the foreword to the 1963 edition of *How to Cook a Wolf* that he knew of "no one in the United States today who writes better prose," and Raymond Sokolov believed her to be "one of the great writers this country has produced in this century" (qtd. in Reardon, "Art of Eating" xiv; Sokolov 1). In "Feminist Food Studies: A Brief History" (found in Arlene Voski Avakian and Barbara Haber's *From Betty Crocker to Feminist Food Studies*), the authors posit that Fisher's "strong views have had an impact on [her] readers, whose perceptions about food were probably changed forever" (4). Such assessments of Fisher's writing are typical: they are complimentary and certain that Fisher's writing persuaded readers to adopt new attitudes about food and cooking. These assertions may be true, but they do not show us *how* that persuasion has happened. Given the influence so often ascribed to Fisher's writing, the lack of scholarly attention—particularly from rhetoric scholars—paid her work is surprising.

Fisher, I argue, provides a rich case study for feminist rhetorical practice; while she employed strategies we now associate with a feminine style, she frequently wrote about topics—such as pleasure and desire—which were usually associated only with men's writing about food. Though claims abound about Fisher's importance to gastronomical history and American food culture, as well as the novelty of her achievement, these claims have rarely been substantiated with rhetorical analysis. Here, I corroborate such claims by showing how Fisher employs what rhetorical scholars have described as a "feminine style" to argue that the pleasures food can provide are as important as any of its other benefits. I draw from a selection of Fisher's gastronomical essays, each of which illustrates a concept I have termed gastronomical kairos. I define this concept as the "fitness" or "opportuneness" of a given culinary experience. The food itself, as I will show in several examples, need not be particularly impressive or even perfectly recalled for her to find, in Avakian and Haber's words, "deep emotional experience in what others might see as mere ordinary experience" (5). For Fisher, these gastronomically kairotic moments are charged and significant, and her evocation of that significance in language is one reason for her extraordinary success as a writer. /79

In describing Fisher's style, I follow Karlyn Kohrs Campbell, Theresa Enos, and others who have theorized feminine style, a style that frequently involves anecdotes, personal examples, and inductive reasoning. Fisher's style helps make her writing accessible to wide audiences. Further, this style helps her to cultivate a welcoming ethos, that of an ordinary nonexpert whose authority derives from personal experience and experimentation. Readers, I suggest, identify more readily with such a persona than one whose authority derives from more remote sources, such as participation in scientific studies or a professional status. They are, therefore, more likely to adopt the approach to food and cooking that Fisher advocates, since she seems more approachable and unassuming.

I then turn to three examples of gastronomical kairos. In each of these instances, I show how Fisher employs sensory descriptions to invite readers to share, vicariously, in the gastronomic experience, thereby encouraging readers to take pleasure in the sensory, embodied practice of eating and not view it simply as refueling the body. The "evidence" for her argument includes these descriptions of bodily experience, as well as the emotional responses they provoke, rather than the disembodied, decontextualized, rational "evidence" provided in mainstream dietary advice columns or other publications. Ultimately, I suggest that what Fisher offers us, by presenting moments of gastronomical kairos and describing them in deeply personal terms, is a rhetorical alternative to arguments about food that focus on its *quantities*. I respond here to Jessica Mudry's call in her book *Measured Meals* for a *qualitative* rhetoric of food, one that takes pleasure and personal taste fully into account.

FISHER'S FEMININE STYLE

In her study of historical women rhetors, rhetorician Campbell explores how women managed to be persuasive, credible public speakers without neglecting the rhetorical resources available to them, such as prevailing attitudes about women's moral superiority and expertise in domestic matters (Campbell 11–12; Jasinski 253–54). They did so, she argues, by developing a style that "relies heavily on personal experience, anecdotes, and other examples" and that was "structured inductively" (Campbell 13). Furthermore, such speakers endeavored "to create identification with the experiences of the audience" (13). This identification can be "facilitated by common values and shared experience" (13–14). Although Campbell is careful to note that there is "nothing inevitably or necessarily female" about what she describes, she claims that this style "has been congenial to women" partly because it "reflects the learned experience of women" (14). Such a style is at odds with a "masculine style" that tends to value abstraction and whose primary aim is "problem-solving" (Dow and Tonn 288). Furthermore, Dow notes that "feminine style is as much a product of *power* as it is a product of *gender*" ("Feminism" 109). That is, feminine style can be a rhetorical option for those in disadvantaged social positions, regardless of gender, or for those who do not have access to privileged rhetorical forms, such as professional journals or other publications associated with sites of social or institutional power.

Fisher's writing is, in many ways, a textbook example of Campbell's concept. The accretion of personal anecdotes and examples from Fisher's life exemplifies what Campbell and others regard as the "truth emerging out of women's lived experience" (Enos 265). What Fisher shows us, too, is that the "truth" of gastronomic experience can be mutable, changing circumstances and preferences. For example, she writes in *The Gastronomical Me* of not having tasted a jelly roll since she was ten, although they were a favorite childhood treat (365). Early in *Serve It Forth*, Fisher encourages her readers to set about "the pleasant task of educating [their] palate[s]," so they can recognize and respond appropriately to their changing gastronomical needs (11). These recommendations emerge from Fisher's awareness of her own evolving preferences, and they differ from more static, rule-bound popular dietary advice, such as the Recommended Dietary Allowances, first publicly issued in 1941.

Rather than relying on scientific nutritional data or citing repeatedly tested recipes as evidence, Fisher presented her own "lived experience" as the model for readers, often justifying particular choices simply by saying "I like them" (*With Bold Knife* 271). In this way, she encouraged readers to take so-called expert advice with a grain of salt and to recognize that their own experiences were equally, if not more, instructive. In the essay "Borderland," Fisher describes her own secret practice of heating tangerine sections on the radiator in the tiny apartment she shared with her first husband, Al Fisher, in Strasbourg. She then rapidly cooled the fruit in the snow on her windowsill before indulging in the "magical" sections, with the "little shell" that "crackles so tinily," the "rush of cold pulp," and the "perfume" (*Serve It Forth* 28). She admits that she cannot entirely explain or even understand why she enjoys this strange little snack but speculates that "probably everyone" understands the pleasures of a private gastronomical experience (28). Fisher never claims that what she finds pleasurable should please others, but by presenting her own experiences as instructive and meaningful *for her*, she encourages readers to cultivate their own gastronomical preferences. Instead of mindlessly following advice from others, however expert or well intentioned, she states, staunchly, "We must do our own balancing, according to what we have learned and also, for a chance, according to what we have *thought*" (*How to Cook* 192). With this claim, Fisher reminds us that eating is—or should be—a bodily *and* an intellectual experience.

Fisher's style values personal experience and promotes independence and individualization, and these values undergird the other arguments she makes about the kairotic nature of certain gastronomic experiences. In the next section, I analyze three such moments to show how attending to the fitness of certain foods at certain times allows us to recognize the deeper emotional and social bonds forged over shared meals.

MOMENTS OF GASTRONOMICAL KAIROS

Given Fisher's concern with personal tastes and her tendency to "revise" her attitudes and memories,[2] it is little wonder that some of the more poignant moments in her writing appeal to readers' emotions precisely because of their kairotic nature. To describe something as kairotic usually implies a kind of fitness or appropriateness to a particular moment. In kairotic moments, the actual time elapsed is inconsequential; what matters is how that time was filled. As a component of rhetorical theory, kairos is concerned with rhetoric's search for relative, rather than absolute, truth. For rhetoric to be kairotic, it must take multiple perspectives into account in order to produce a "truth relative to circumstances" (Herrick 45). Above all, kairos is concerned with context and with selecting the opportune moment for response to an exigency.

Kairotic moments, of course, are often recognized *in* the moment themselves or, perhaps, even after the moment has passed. Fisher illustrates such a moment in her essay "A Thing Shared," in which she relates a family trip to her great-aunt Maggie's ranch. The purpose of the visit was to help with the summer canning. At the conclusion of the visit, Edith (Fisher's mother) stayed behind to continue helping her relatives, leaving Rex (her father) to drive Fisher and her younger sister Anne back to Whittier. On the way home, the trio stopped to eat at a roadside stand. Fisher claims not to remember much of what they ate, except for a "big round peach pie, still warm from [the] oven, and a jar of fresh cream" (*Gastronomical Me* 358).

Fisher acknowledges that part of the food's appeal is its freshness: the peaches for the pie were "picked that noon" and the cream was "still cold, probably because we all knew the stream it had lain in" (358). Of course, *knowledge* of the stream would not affect the temperature of the cream, but Fisher implies here that knowing the origin of one's food contributes to the pleasure in eating it. But the real significance of the meal lies in Fisher's recognition, for the first time, of "food as something beautiful to be shared with people instead of a thrice-daily necessity" (358). The actual components of the meal matter little in comparison to what the experience showed her about how a shared meal can encourage closeness. "That night," Fisher remembers,

I not only saw my Father for the first time as a person. I saw the golden hills and the live oaks as clearly as I have seen them since, and I saw the dimples in my little sister's fat hands in a way that still moves me because of that first time. (358)

Food, and the sharing of it, functions as a lens through which Fisher can appreciate her surroundings and her relationships with a new clarity because they are so tied to a material reality. By constantly positioning herself as an agent within this narrative (she repeats "I saw") and suggesting an awakening of sorts (it was the "first conscious" meal of her life), Fisher insists on the personal and the particular. She encourages us to position ourselves similarly—as active participants in our gastronomic activities, rather than passive observers or recipients—and to recognize when particular foods contribute to or encourage these kinds of emotionally powerful experiences.

As noted earlier, Fisher spent several years in France with her first husband in the late 1920s and early 1930s, and these years formed the foundation of her gastronomical identity. Not surprisingly, many memories from those years are described in kairotic terms in her later essays. She admits, "Sometimes it is hard to say, even from remembrance, just what magic chord has sounded for you with the right blending of time, space, and the physical sensation of eating" (*Serve It Forth* 87). For her, "there is one time, one souvenir, of eating that I can keep with impunity throughout all seasonal changes" (87). While in France, Fisher belonged to the local chapter of the Alpine Club. She claims to have felt generally "rather lonesome, foreign" while on outings with this club until one day, as she stood shivering on top of a hill, an "old general" in the club unexpectedly offered her some chocolate. He said only, "Here! Try some of this, young lady." Although "he had never done more than bow" to her, she accepted the offering and ate it. At first, the bitter chocolate broke into "separate, disagreeable bits, [and she] began to wonder if [she] could swallow them. Then they grew soft, and melted voluptuously into a warm stream down [her] throat" (88).

The experience alone might be noteworthy: perhaps this was Fisher's first taste of bittersweet chocolate, or perhaps simply the surprise of something initially disagreeable becoming pleasurable was worth recording in such vivid detail. But the chocolate—its taste and eventually sensual texture— tells only part of the story. The more significant event occurs when a "little doctor," presumably another member of the Alpine Club, "came bustling up" and cried, "Never eat chocolate without bread, young lady! Very bad

/ 83

for the interior, very bad!" He goes on to rebuke the old general, telling him
that he was "remiss" for offering chocolate without bread (88). The general
offers to trade, bread for chocolate, and Fisher describes their shared snack:

> We sat gingerly, the three of us, on the frozen hill, looking down into
> the valley where Vercingetorix had fought so splendidly; we peered shyly
> and silently at each other and smiled and chewed at one of the most sat-
> isfying things I have ever eaten. I thought vaguely of the metamorphosis
> of bread and wine. (88)

As she often does, Fisher contextualizes herself, "on the frozen hill," near
Les Laumes-Alésia, the site of the Gallic king Vercingetorix's famous stand
against the Roman army led by Julius Caesar. The most important feature,
though, is the strange "communion" this trio of strangers shares, despite
having so little in common, presumably even language, as Fisher knew little
French when she first went abroad. Fisher suggests that while the bread and
chocolate are tasty and probably complement one another well, the experience is so satisfying because it is shared, perhaps especially so for Fisher
because of the unprompted care and attention she receives.[3] Additionally,
Fisher highlights the value of multiple perspectives by recording dialogue
and allowing these men to speak in their own voices. She presents herself
as a participant in an unlooked-for but welcome experience. As before, the
food acquires significance primarily through the social interaction it inspires.

Like the simple pleasure of the tangerine sections, many of Fisher's fond-
est food memories, and those that seem especially kairotic, involve simple
preparations. For instance, Fisher writes on several occasions of the delight
in eating freshly picked garden peas while living at Vevey in Switzerland with
her second husband, Dillwyn Parrish. Her parents had come to visit from
California, and the family spent much of the day working in the garden,
mostly picking and shelling peas. As Fisher stands in the kitchen, preparing
the peas, she looks toward the table where

> there sat most of the people in the world I loved, in a thin light that was
> pink with Alpen glow, blue with a veil of pine smoke from the hearth.
> Their voices sang with a certain remoteness into the clear air, and suddenly
> from across the curve of the Lower Corniche a cow in Monsieur Rogivue's
> orchard moved her head among the meadow flowers and shook her bell
> in a slow, melodious rhythm, a kind of hymn. My father lifted up his face
> at the sweet sound, and his fists all stained with green-pea juice, said
> passionately, "God, but I feel good!" I felt near to tears. (*Alphabet* 666)

Clearly, the poignancy of this moment—enough to prompt the usually reserved Rex Kennedy to make this proclamation—is not simply the result of eating peas, which are themselves no culinary marvel. The preparation Fisher describes consists only of quickly steaming the peas and then tossing them with some sweet butter—a treatment that suggests a kind of respect, since she gathered them at the peak of ripeness and served them relatively unadorned. With such treatment, the peas enable her and her guests to feel "what really mattered, what piped the high unforgettable tune of perfection," and Fisher writes that the whole experience of sharing "fresh green garden peas, picked and shelled by my friends, to the sound of a cowbell" constitutes her idea of "heaven" (666). The fresh peas are, like the tangerine sections in Strasbourg, the right things at the right moment. The ephemerality of the vegetables, the fading sunlight, and the spontaneous alpine music of cowbells combine in such a way to produce these feelings of well-being and pleasure, thereby contributing to the kairotic nature of this shared meal.

CONCLUSION

For good reason, much of the scholarship on women and food has focused on women's food pathologies (see Silver; Bordo; Thompson; Counihan). One of these pathologies, or at least an undercurrent in the description of other food pathologies, like self-starvation, is an aversion to pleasure. This aversion has long been culturally sanctioned because it fit with powerful cultural commonplaces about the appropriateness of women's self-denial, especially of physical pleasures. In particular, Victorian era doctors argued that women should avoid strong flavors and even meat out of fear that indulging such hungers might stimulate other appetites. While such advice no longer has currency, traces of it remained well into Fisher's life, and even into our own historical moment, which still admires, in some ways, the woman who can resist temptation.

Certainly, Fisher would reject this attitude toward women and food. Critics have long noted her frank discussions of appetite and hunger and her occasional conflation of hungers with other forms of physical desire. As she writes, "there is a communion of more than our bodies when bread is broken and wine drunk" (*Gastronomical Me* 353). Understanding that deeper communion is what led her to write "about hunger, not wars or love"; for Fisher, hunger refers to a complex matrix of desires. "Our three basic needs," she claims, "for food and security and love, are so mixed and mingled and entwined that we cannot straightly think of one without the others" (353). When she writes about food, she also is writing about "love and the hunger for it, and warmth and the love of it and the hunger for it . . . and it is all one" (353). Hunger cannot be divorced from emotions, and so approaching eating *without* attending to our different hungers is thoughtless at best.

Fisher's stylistic prowess makes her worthy of the attention of feminist rhetorical scholars, but more interesting is the way she employs strategies typically regarded as "feminine" to make arguments about food that were often diametrically opposed to other popular arguments made by women in the early and mid-twentieth century. For instance, she rejects the commonplace that meals should be "balanced," calling such a recommendation "one of the stupidest things" (*How to Cook* 189). Further, she often modified genres to suit her rhetorical needs. For example, when she offers recipes, they are often embedded in personal narratives, and she does not present them as unalterable or even finished. Rather, they are suggestions, starting places, for readers to begin their own processes of gastronomical learning. In one recipe for "Edith's Egg Croquettes," she lists both "fine crumbs" and "more crumbs" as ingredients, imprecision that lets the reader determine how much to use (*With Bold Knife* 115). She thus relates her own experience as a possible model but encourages readers to use their own experience and taste as a guide.

86 /   Of course, what Jessica Mudry calls the discourse of quantification remains a potent force in contemporary food culture. A recent article in *The Atlantic* (Hamblin) urged us to stop counting calories in our quest to eat healthfully; the fact that such an urge needs to be made at all reveals that the practice of evaluating food by its numbers is still very much with us. Nonetheless, Fisher's writing compels us to think beyond expert discourses on food—whether from medical, scientific, or culinary professionals—and to undertake our own process of gastronomical learning. Her skillful use of elements of a feminine style allowed her to make what were (at the time) decidedly unfeminine arguments about food. And her evocations of gastronomically kairotic moments offer us a way of thinking about kairos that includes the material and the social. In these ways, Fisher provides us with a compelling rhetorical alternative to discourses of food that privilege its nutritional value at the expense of its social, intellectual, and emotional meanings.

Notes

1. Her unconventional personal life was a factor, too: Fisher was married three times, bore one child out of wedlock, engaged in many affairs with men and women, lived abroad several times, and spent the last twenty years of her life in relative seclusion in a house built for her by her friend David Bouverie on his Glen Ellen, California, estate.

2. Later editions of Fisher's texts, particularly those collected in *The Art of Eating* contain her own bracketed revisions and annotations, which allow us to see her changing attitudes. Additionally, her sister Nora once remarked that Fisher's memories of their childhood were sometimes so altered from reality as to be fictional.

3. While I am reluctant to push the Eucharistic imagery too far, there is a reference, at least in the Episcopal service, to the Eucharist as a "memorial of our Redemption." Interestingly, Fisher's family was Episcopalian—the lone Episcopalians in Whittier, a town primarily populated in Fisher's childhood by Quakers. The scene suggests that these three people, united by nothing except sharing this meal, are somehow commemorating the Gallic army's defeat at the hands of the Romans, just as the Last Supper was Christ's last meal before his crucifixion by the Romans.

Works Cited

Avakian, Arlene Voski, and Barbara Haber, eds. *From Betty Crocker to Feminist Food Studies: Critical Perspectives on Women and Food.* U of Massachusetts P, 2005.

Bordo, Susan. *Unbearable Weight: Feminism, Western Culture, and the Body.* 10th anniv. ed. U of California P, 2004.

Campbell, Karlyn Kohrs. *Man Cannot Speak for Her.* Vol. 1. *A Critical Study of Early Feminist Rhetoric.* Praeger, 1989.

Counihan, Carole M. "An Anthropological View of Western Women's Prodigious Fasting: A Review Essay." *The Anthropology of Food and Body: Gender, Meaning, and Power.* Routledge, 1999. 93–112.

Dow, Bonnie J. "Feminism, Difference(s), and Rhetorical Studies." *Communication Studies* 46.1–2 (1995): 106–17.

Dow, Bonnie J., and Mari Boor Tonn. "'Feminine Style' and Political Judgment in the Rhetoric of Ann Richards." *Quarterly Journal of Speech* 79.3 (1993): 286–302.

Enos, Theresa, ed. *Encyclopedia of Rhetoric and Composition: Communication from Ancient Times to the Information Age.* Garland, 1996.

Fisher, M. F. K. "An Alphabet for Gourmets." *The Art of Eating.* Wiley, 1990. 575–744.

———. *Dubious Honors.* Farrar, Straus, and Giroux, 1988.

———. "The Gastronomical Me." *The Art of Eating.* Wiley, 1990. 353–573.

———. "How to Cook a Wolf." *The Art of Eating.* Wiley, 1990. 187–352.

———. "Serve It Forth." *The Art of Eating.* Wiley, 1990. 5–124.

———. *With Bold Knife and Fork.* Rep. ed. Counterpoint, 2010.

Hamblin, James. "Forget Calories." *The Atlantic* 13 June 2014.

Herrick, James A. *The History and Theory of Rhetoric: An Introduction.* 5th ed. Pearson, 2012.

Inness, Sherrie A. *Dinner Roles: American Women and Culinary Culture*. U of Iowa P, 2001.

Jasinski, James. *Sourcebook on Rhetoric*. SAGE Publications, 2001.

Mudry, Jessica J. *Measured Meals: Nutrition in America*. State U of New York P, 2010.

O'Neill, Molly. "M. F. K. Fisher, Writer on the Art of Food and the Taste of Living, Is Dead at Eighty-Three." *New York Times* 24 June 1992.

Reardon, Joan. "*The Art of Eating*: In Celebration." *The Art of Eating*. 50th anniv. ed. Wiley, 2004. x–xv.

———. *Poet of the Appetites: The Lives and Loves of M. F. K. Fisher*. North Point P, 2004.

Sekules, Kate. "The Fifty Most Important Women in Food." *Gourmet Live* 18 May 2011. Accessed 1 June 2014.

Silver, Anna Krugovoy. *Victorian Literature and the Anorexic Body*. Cambridge UP, 2002.

Sokolov, Raymond. "On Food and Life and Herself." *New York Times* 6 June 1982. *NY Times*. Accessed 1 June 2015.

Thompson, Becky W. *A Hunger So Wide and So Deep: A Multiracial View of Women's Eating Problems*. 2nd ed. U of Minnesota P, 1996.

Zimmerman, Anne. *An Extravagant Hunger: The Passionate Years of M. F. K. Fisher*. Counterpoint, 2011.

6. FEMINIST CULINARY AUTOBIOGRAPHIES: *BATTERIE DE CUISINE* TO PEACEABLE KINGDOM

Lynn Z. Bloom

Our three basic needs, for food and security and love, are so mixed
and mingled and entwined that we cannot straightly think of one
without the others.

—M. F. K. Fisher, *The Gastronomical Me*

Although M. F. K. Fisher inscribed her work with initials to obscure her gender, Mary Frances Kennedy Fisher's food writing, succulent and seductive, evokes not only an ethos of powerful hospitality but of quintessential femininity. As she explains in *The Gastronomical Me*,

> when I write of hunger, I am really writing about love and the hunger
> for it, and warmth and the love of it and the hunger for it. . . . There is
> food in the bowl, and, more often than not[,] . . . there is nourishment
> in the heart, to feed the wilder, more insistent hungers. We must eat. . . .
> There is a communion of more than our bodies when bread is broken
> and wine drunk. (353)

Fisher creates an authorial persona of beauty, grace, generosity, and abundance, becoming the character Botticelli's *Primavera* epitomized as Flora. In Fisher-as-Flora, readers recognize the hostess/chef/wife/mother, mistress too, whose very recipe for milk toast—"4 slices of good bread, preferably homemade," "sweet butter, the seasoning, the cream and the milk"—

provides succor, solace, "sops indeed to the sybarite in even the sickest of us" (*Alphabet* 680–81).

Fisher's writing about food, like Julia Child's *Mastering the Art of French Cooking* (1961), has set the Michelin four-star standard for food writers ever since, women and men alike (consider Adam Gopnik's *The Table Comes First: Family, France, and the Meaning of Food* 2011). Her gracious persona presides over the generous table readers have come to expect from women food autobiographers in such authors of abundance as Frances Mayes (*Under the Tuscan Sun* 1996), Ruth Reichl (*Tender at the Bone* 1998), Amanda Hesser (*Cooking for Mr. Latte* 2003), Madhur Jaffrey (*Climbing the Mango Trees* 2005), and Marcella Hazan (*Amarcord* 2008). If space permitted, I could make the case here that in addition to epitomizing Fisher's feminine virtues, these writers are the very models of feminist executives, in their lives if not necessarily in their rhetoric. Their writings emphasize their literary talents and culinary tastes, yet in accord with the expert (often male) professional model, their autobiographies downplay the hard work behind the scenes that contributed to their highly successful careers. To a woman, they have learned to be well organized, highly disciplined, economically sophisticated decision-makers who delegate the day-to-day business and ancillary activities to others (including supportive husbands). Nevertheless, like Adele Astaire who—as partner to her brother Fred—danced beautifully backwards and in high heels, they make their herculean efforts look easy.

This essay, however, will examine significant ways in which three distinguished feminist autobiographers, Betty Fussell (*My Kitchen Wars*), Gabrielle Hamilton (*Blood, Bones, and Butter*), and Barbara Kingsolver (*Animal, Vegetable, Miracle*), impose their signature stamp on food and food culture. In the process, they subvert (and sometimes expand) the default feminine model of effortless succor and succulence, even while they are preparing and serving (and in Kingsolver's case growing) meals to die for. Although these works are very different from one another, each could be considered a feminist work in its assumptions of equality, energy, and role expectations of men and women (with Fussell's evolving over the years). Yet as this analysis will show, not all feminist autobiographies are created equal, for there is a wide latitude for the label, which to this day remains contentious and contradictory (de Beauvoir; Friedan; Gamble; Meltzer; Thornham).

These authors (white, American, middle-aged, and middle-class) are united in their consuming passion for food as an extension of their egos and personalities, ethos and philosophies. They are united, as well, in their focus, drive, and energy devoted to growing, selecting, preparing, serving, and promoting good food. Their food-oriented autobiographies "bring a conventionally inside space outside" as performances that "make public those intimate, personal, and often private moments historically consigned to oblivion" (Ferris 208). Their temperaments, values, mode and manner of working, and ethical sensibility divide them, not always on gender lines (or willingly), into food amateurs and professionals, insiders and outsiders, at war and at peace.

BATTERIE DE CUISINE, MILITARISTIC MELODRAMA

Fussell's *My Kitchen Wars* (1999) is a bitter reenactment of the sexist, competitive cooking culture of the mid-American 1950s and 1960s, in which, as the wife of distinguished World War scholar Paul Fussell, she was a willing combatant. "Hunger, like lust in action," she explains at the outset, "is savage, extreme, rude, cruel. To satisfy it is to do battle, deploying the full range of artillery—crushers, scrapers, beaters, roasters, gougers, grinders," and it is required in the ever-escalating war among faculty wives (4). These "Serious Competitive Cook[s]"(157), who spent outrageous amounts of money, time, and energy preparing dinner for as many as two hundred guests, were wedded more to Julia Child's *Mastering the Art of French Cooking* and to their unlined copper bowls, wire whisks, and Cuisinarts than to their husbands or their children. Fussell, alone among these authors, relished high-status dishes requiring "multistepped preparation that extended over many days and required much special equipment." To properly prepare *pâté en croûte*, she explains, in a series of self-imposed imperatives, "serious climbers had to first bone a duck, leaving the entire skin intact, then stuff it with truffles and pork and veal, stitch it with thread and a trussing needle, wrap it in pastry dough, and decorate it with little pastry fans . . . to conceal the seam" before baking. For a cold buffet, however, "we then had to chill the *pâté*, remove the top crust, take out the duck, take out its stitches, carve it into slices, and tuck it back into the crust. No sweat" (157–59).[1]

/ 91

In contrast, Child's humane cooking instructions, a roux of compassion and precision (as disclosed in endnote 1), are calculated to provide meals as pleasurable in the cooking as they are savory in the eating. Indeed, these are hallmarks of the bountiful, imaginative repasts that permeate food writing in general, irrespective of the author's gender, or sexual politics. Even Peg Bracken's *I Hate to Cook Book* exudes pleasure on every page, with simple, succulent recipes that make "people think you're a better cook than you are" (89). The only chronic naysayer is Fussell, whose self-staged kitchen wars abound in enough blood, sweat, and tears to override the high quality of the *suprêmes de volaille en chaud-froid*, blanche *neige, mousseline de poisson*, and *gigot de pré-salé farci* (161–62). Eating, and the status drinking that accompanies the food, seldom brings her a soupçon of enjoyment; "spending time, our most precious commodity, was the point" (164). As a combatant, she cooks to show off and to use the resulting viands as aphrodisiacs ("the subtext was always sex" [127]), although dalliances with her husband's colleagues seem devoted more to sumptuous picnics than to passion.

Didn't anyone have fun at the parties? Didn't Fussell ever derive pleasure from preparing or devouring the good food she served? Well, yes. She's exhilarated as the party takes "off on its own," and she enjoys cleaning up afterward: "shards of glass ground into the rug," "ashtrays stinking of stale butts," "a plateful of chicken bones on the piano," "a purgation appropriate to a day of hangover" (164–65). Feminist anger or a feminist urge to rewrite either her personal or social history could allow this fulminating author to examine her scorched-earth style of entertaining without irony or self-mockery, using Betty Friedan's *Feminist Mystique* as a model. Fussell's explanation that she's not a feminist because men (in World War II) "had saved our lives, and in gratitude we protected theirs, often at the expense of our own," loses force over the years as women take empowerment into their own hands, despite her rhetorical claim that she doesn't "want to be liberated forcibly" by "bullying . . . ideologues" (166–67). Indeed, her combative cooking and angry writing style are fully in the strident feminist mode of her 1960s and 1970s peers, including Shulamith Firestone, Germaine Greer, and Kate Millett. Yet of all food autobiographers, Fussell fulminates alone in the kitchen minefield.

THE EDUCATION AND ETHOS OF A CHEF: ONE-WOMAN SHOW

Gabrielle Hamilton's *Blood, Bones, and Butter: The Inadvertent Education of a Reluctant Chef* (2011) presents scenes, sizzling and scintillating, from the author's education. She proffers rapid, incisive snapshots of herself moving from outsider to insider as she learns to become a chef, restaurant owner, and writer. In the background are more casual glimpses of herself as lover—mostly of women, but also of her doctor husband Michele and his magnificent mother—and as the mother of two young boys.

Hamilton constructs herself as a romantic feminist figure. The jacket photo shows a pretty, petite, blonde young woman in a simple black shift, holding with ease a huge wire basket of tomatoes—thirty or forty pounds, about one-third of her weight. She stands on terra-cotta-colored pavement before a green-shuttered stone building, against a sunlit backdrop of trees. Such an Italian-looking setting can't really be her beloved East Village restaurant, Prune (her mother's puckery pet name for her), can it? Hamilton looks delicious, yet vulnerable—bare feet, plunging neckline. But her vulnerability is a rhetorical strategy; she is as tough and sinewy as undercooked brisket and accessible only on her own terms.

Her terms are feminist. Unlike Fussell, perpetually angry in her home kitchen, Hamilton thoroughly enjoys the "fun and urgency" (107) of the process of gaining a professional's complex conceptual understanding, technical skills, balancing economics with aesthetics. She loves doing hard physical work to the point of exhaustion day after stressful day, night after frantic night. Anything men can do she can do better. She masters the brutal art of butchering, going "bare-handed up through an animal's ass [to] dislodge its warm guts," cutting

> two-hundred-twenty-pound sides of beef down to their primal cuts, carv[ing] out the heads of goats, fasten[ing] whole baby lambs . . . onto green ash spits . . . over hot coals, and bon[ing] out the loins and legs of whole rabbits that—even skinned—still look exactly like bunnies. (63)

/ 93

She welcomes "the intense pressure of getting a dinner for two hundred plated quickly"; and she claims that the control and purity that comes from "cleaning out a cluttered walk-in [freezer] and putting impeccable order to it . . . [is] my favorite part of kitchen life" (108). Hamilton, "who thought for sure she knew everything" about cooking when she arrived in Ann Arbor for a two-year MFA program in creative writing, ditches literary theory (while completing the degree) for the real-life satisfactions of kitchen and garden. The only teachers she acknowledges are women: her acerbic, meticulous mother (who could ferret out "the true chanterelles from the poisonous orange look-alikes" and taught her to "eat common clover" [24–25]); her generous Italian mother-in-law; and especially the consummate catering pro, Misty, who can "distinguish between an Indonesian, a Chinese, a Vietnamese, and a Thai ground shrimp paste." Hamilton and her mentor bring "excitement and fresh energy" to cheeses, pickling, bottling, grilling; they bond over "yellow sunbeams and tongues of fire and flageolets—fresh shell beans," described in far more lascivious language than she devotes to either her "big butch Michigander" lover du jour or the man she marries (106–10).

The narrative arc of restaurant tales (will the start-up restaurant succeed and patrons eat happily ever after?) risks being bent out of shape by all the things that can go wrong. Hamilton's love-at-first-sight is a wreck of a restaurant. The thirty-seat space had closed abruptly two years earlier, becoming a toxic stew of putrid food, fetid decomposing meat carcasses, rat shit and urine, mold spores, and "legions of living cockroaches." She shoves to the back burner the knowledge that 80 percent of new businesses fail in the first year and whisks away her inexperience as a chef or sous-chef and her lack of money or knowledge of the significance of "square footage, check average," W-2 forms, FICA taxes, due diligence, or a certificate of occupancy. Come hell or high water, this Indiana Jones of the open range will launch Prune, a decision gutsy, rash, and naive. In her romantic fantasy, she expects to "cook by hand from stove to table" and if necessary "just reach over the pass and deliver the food myself." Prune will be the source of sustenance and solace for people arriving "cold and early and undone" by their day in the city (113–36). The food, incorporating the essence of all the good meals she's ever eaten in her ravenous, wandering youth, will have wholesome integrity:

> There would be no foam and no "conceptual" or "intellectual" food; just the salty, sweet, starchy, brothy, crispy things that one craves when one is actually hungry. . . . [T]he portions would be generous; there would be no emulsions, no crab cocktail served in a martini glass with its claw hanging over the rim. (136)

To bring order out of disaster, Hamilton insists on controlling everything and does most of the work herself. She power washes walls "in a floor-length rubber apron, rain boots, and ventilated goggles," poisons roach nests, traps rats, and enlists her friends in "scraping the walls, scouring every surface, using skewers and razor blades to get into every crevice of every appliance." She makes

> lists that went on for thirty pages and constantly renewed themselves even after I had crossed off the first thousand tasks . . . items I had never encountered in my professional life—
>
> ~~Determine 2nd Means of Egress~~
> ~~Establish Payroll Account~~
> ~~Attend LCB Public Hearing~~
> ~~Estimate Breakage~~. (134–35)

By the time she's through, she "exudes ownership" and authority (145).

Every food autobiography worth its salt has a major kitchen chapter, where the romance of food meets the reality of the chopping block. In Prune's kitchen, "the size of a Lincoln Continental," the field of combat is Sunday brunch, "the Indy 500," in which every forty minutes "hordes of hungry, angry, mag-wheeled, tricked-out customers line up at the door, scrape the chairs back . . . and blow through their steak" and 1,440 eggs, two hundred covers in a "relentless, nonstop five-bout beating." Hamilton, who sees herself as uncompromisingly badass, revels in the "shocking heat of a restaurant's set of burners" and always feels like "a contender in a nicely matched bout" every time she approaches their "immense power" (149). To combat the "forces, events that just conspire to fuck you" in the struggle "to stay psychologically up and committed to the fight," she swears "the dirtiest, most vulgar" words imaginable, for a cathartic power surge. "It can be very Tourette's Syndrome back there when I am working that egg station and the expediter has failed to tell me about a sauce on the side or a well-done poached," she says, but after assuring the staff "that nothing is personal . . . I rip it out, jaw tight, and spewing combinations of the word *fuck* that even David Mamet has not thought to put together." Profane and tough, "I have fired people who can't suffer their setbacks and petty failures," for they threaten "to sink the whole boat." Timing, precision ("five minutes in the life of a cooked egg . . . is the difference between excellence and bullshit"), military drill, attention to minutiae at a flat-out pace underscore the irony of Hamilton's conclusion to combat de brunch: /95

> You want to own your own little place? You want to have a tight relationship with your farmer? Surround yourself with poet-philosopher wine merchants? Make your own ricotta and cure your own lardo? . . . It's not the eighteen-hour days and the hot kitchen that'll get you. It's all that *plus*. (145–52)

Hamilton's macho to-do list, the epitome of her "twenty years of chronic, compulsive list-making," is the one she wrote when thirty-nine weeks pregnant:

> Train CR on a 2-man line
> Call Roodie for fill-in?
> Have baby
> Tell brunch crew vinaigrette too acidic
> Pick up white platters
> Change filters in hoods
> Figure out pomegranate syrup. (200)

About to give birth to her second child, she claims to have ditched her intimidating badass ways and mellowed out:

> I don't want to be that woman who . . . [got] down on all fours and
> scrape[d] the pancake batter off the oven door after having just cooked
> three hundred eggs with a near-constant monologue of *fucking fuck of
> a fuck* issuing from her lips.

But that is the persona who is "throwing the party every night, emptying the
ashtrays, making sure the tonic is cold, the limes fresh, the shifts covered,
the meat perfectly cooked and adequately rested, the customers carefree and
the employees calm and confident. "Someone," she says, "has to stay in the
kitchen and do the bones of the thing, to make sure it stands up" (200–201),
and she is that person: vibrant, strong, hugely pregnant, and proud, Wonder
Woman and Woman Warrior incarnate.[2] The essence of professionalism,
where the buck always stops, also embeds an active definition of a feminist—
one who creates opportunities for growth and change, takes responsibility
for fulfilling these, solves problems, and lives with the consequences, the
profit or the loss.

FEMINIST PASTORAL: SUSTAINABLE FARM, SAVORY TABLE

Barbara Kingsolver's *Animal, Vegetable, Miracle: A Year of Food Life* (2007)
enacts the author's locavore philosophy; she, too, stays in the kitchen and
the garden to "do the bones of the thing, to make sure it stands up." In
league with Henry David Thoreau ("We had come to the farmland to eat
deliberately" [22]), Wendell Berry, and Michael Pollan, Kingsolver interprets
eating as "an agricultural act," and thus also a political act, with profound
ecological, ethical, and economic consequences. Aiming to ensure the future
of the planet, Kingsolver's vision encompasses a pastoral ideal. In accord with
the sustainable agriculture masterplot, she (a novelist) and her husband (an
environmental studies biologist) and two daughters (in elementary school
and college) seek and find an idyllic agricultural kingdom on the edge of
Appalachia. As with many farmers, this is a family enterprise, performed
by Kingsolver and company not in the rigid Pa-and-Ma-American-Gothic
mode but in the interstices of their day jobs and on weekends. The book's
narrative arc recounts the family's journey through a year of growing and
eating food that originated less than one hundred miles from their Virginia
farm, except for coffee, olive oil, and selected spices. Their yearlong abstinence from "industrial food" (the average supermarket product has traveled
fifteen hundred miles from origin to destination) is "a purification ritual
to cultivate health and gratitude," she explains. "It sounds so much better

than wackadoo" (338–39). Although Kingsolver reinforces M. F. K. Fisher's promise that serious food writing offers "food and security and love," her concentration on the principles and practice of ecological farming at times overrides the Barefoot-Contessa-cum-Alice-Waters persona that emerges in this down-to-earth food writing.

Like many agrarian works, the book is structured according to the seasons, beginning "on the new edge of springtime" (41), continuing into June with incessant "hoeing and pulling weeds" (174). July brings "days of plenty," including the dreaded zucchini[3] and fifty pounds of tomatoes; August yields a profusion of green beans, cucumbers, "soft summer fruits," and 302 additional pounds of tomatoes that "take over your life." Kingsolver's communal kitchen scenes emphasize preservation as much as cooking: pickling, "slicing, canning, roasting, and drying tomatoes—often all at the same time." The family digs potatoes, their "homeland security," throughout the summer and fall to accompany the continuous egg supply, the home-reared and slaughtered chickens and Thanksgiving turkey, the pumpkins, "antique apples," "native persimmons" and the summer's bounty, thawed or reconstituted throughout the winter (197–201). That the family rarely works, or eats, alone is reflected in the collaborative authorship of *Animal, Vegetable, Miracle*. Stephen Hopp's environmental, ecological, and technological commentary ("How to Impress Your Wife, Using a Machine") and daughter Camille's recipes ("Four Seasons of Potato Salad," "Pumpkin Soup in Its Own Shell") punctuate Kingsolver's narrative spiced with polemic.

Food is the medium of community and generosity. "We celebrate plenty," says Kingsolver; "We give away our salsas and chutneys, and make special meals for family and friends." Planning "beautiful meals and investing one's heart and time in their preparation is the opposite of self-indulgence," she explains. "Kitchen-based family gatherings are process-oriented, cooperative, and in the best of worlds, nourishing and soulful," in part because "a lot of talk happens first, news exchanged, secrets revealed across generations, paths cleared with a touch on the arm." This heritage endures. Kingsolver expresses the cook's universal understanding: "When I'm cooking I find myself inhabiting the emotional companionship of the person who taught me how to make a particular dish, or with whom I used to cook it" (285–91), just as she acknowledges its romance: "Be warned, the fragrance of your kitchen will cause innocent bystanders to want to marry you" (201).

Animal, Vegetable, Miracle enacts the vigorous definition of contemporary feminism that is woven into the fulfilled, fulfilling lives and work and love of Kingsolver and her family. This definition is analogous to the feminist concepts of Facebook CEO Sheryl Sandberg's *Lean In: Women, Work, and the Will to Lead* (2013), advocating both/and rather than the second-wave feminist choice of either family or career. We women "hold ourselves back," she says, "by lacking self-confidence, by not raising our hands, by pulling back when we should be leaning in." *Lean In*, Sandberg explains, is "sort of a feminist manifesto," but one intended to inspire "men as much as it inspires women." Ideally, women should not compromise their career goals; they should be "ambitious in any pursuit," whether professional or personal, preferably both, and aim "vigorously" for "the top of the field" (8–9). Their work, like their family life, should be meaningful, satisfying, and abetted by men, whether as collaborative colleagues or running the household (172). If that work is in the kitchen, and in the garden (with inevitable Edenic literary overtones), so much the better, Fisher and Kingsolver would agree.

Fisher and Kingsolver share common values and integrity of vision of what constitutes good food and good eating in congenial circumstances. Their well-honed writing, like freshly baked bread, nourishes family, guests, readers with a generous culinary embrace. Yet at the same time, their dedicated professional willingness to "lean in" and work hard without sacrificing other meaningful dimensions of life signifies that they are feminists in Sandberg's contemporary sense. Given fifty years of amorphous and contentious definitions of both second-wave feminism (Thornham) and postfeminism (Gamble), it is tempting to imagine Fisher and Kingsolver, whose works bracket this time span, indifferent to the arguments as they go serenely about their work, which is also their play, and comparing notes over a cup of tea. Were Fussell and Hamilton ever to sit down, they'd be at separate tables.

Notes

1. Julia Child devotes seven good-humored pages to the preparation of this formidable dish, in comic contrast to Fussell's take-no-prisoners stance toward the sacrificial bird. Child begins with,

> You may think that boning a fowl is an impossible feat if you have never seen it done or thought of attempting it. Although the procedure may take 45 minutes the first time because of fright, it can be accomplished in not much more than 20 on your second or third try.

After half the boning is done, "the carcass frame, dangling legs, wings, and skin will appear to be an unrecognizable mass of confusion and you will wonder how in the world any sense can be made of it all" (570).

2. In contrast, Anthony Bourdain's high testosterone *Kitchen Confidential: Adventures in the Culinary Underbelly* (2000) is Animal-House-in-the-Kitchen,

an unreliable chef signaling an unreliable narrator. Like Hamilton, Bourdain writes about how to cook and how to run a New York restaurant. But while the ethos of Hamilton's kitchen is disciplined professionalism designed to produce memorable meals, Bourdain's kitchen is "drenched in drugs and alcohol," including "pot, Quaaludes, cocaine, LSD [and] increasingly, heroin" consumed by the "thuggish assortment of drunks, sneak thieves, sluts, and psychopaths" for whom food seems incidental (122–23). Having created havoc in the kitchen, Bourdain devoted the succeeding decade to exploiting the mayhem for celebrity television status.

3. "Garrison Keillor says July is the only time of year when country people lock our cars in the church parking lot, so people won't put squash on the front seat. I used to think that was a joke" (Kingsolver 188).

Works Cited

Bourdain, Anthony. *Kitchen Confidential: Adventures in the Culinary Underbelly*. 2000. Ecco/HarperCollins, 2007.

Bracken, Peg. *The I Hate to Cook Book*. 1960. Fawcett, 1967.

Child, Julia, Louisette Bertholle, and Simone Beck. *Mastering the Art of French Cooking*. Knopf, 1961.

de Beauvoir, Simone. *The Second Sex*. Trans. H. M. Parshley. Knopf, 1952.

Ferris, Lesley. "Cooking Up the Self: Bobby Baker and Blondell Cummings 'Do' the Kitchen." *Interfaces: Women, Autobiography, Image, Performance*. Ed. Sidonie Smith and Julia Watson. U of Michigan P, 2002. 186–210.

Fisher, M. F. K. *An Alphabet for Gourmets*. 1949. Rpt. in *The Art of Eating*. By Fisher. Macmillan, 1990. 573–744.

———. *The Gastronomical Me*. 1943. Rpt. in *The Art of Eating*. By Fisher. Macmillan, 1990. 351–572.

Friedan, Betty. *The Feminine Mystique*. Norton, 1963.

———. *The Fountain of Age*. Simon and Schuster, 1993.

Fussell, Betty. *My Kitchen Wars: A Memoir*. North Point P, 1999.

Gamble, Sarah. "Postfeminism." *Routledge Companion to Feminism and Postfeminism*. Ed. Gamble. Routledge, 2001. 36–45.

Hamilton, Gabrielle. *Blood, Bones, and Butter: The Inadvertent Education of a Reluctant Chef*. Random House, 2011.

Kingsolver, Barbara. *Animal, Vegetable, Miracle: A Year of Food Life*. Harper, 2007.

Meltzer, Marisa. "Who Is a Feminist Now?" *New York Times* 21 May 2014. *NY Times*. Accessed 15 November 2016.

Sandberg, Sheryl, with Nell Scovell. *Lean In: Women, Work, and the Will to Lead*. Knopf, 2013.

Thornham, Sue. "Second Wave Feminism." *Routledge Companion to Feminism and Postfeminism*. Ed. Sarah Gamble. Routledge, 2001. 25–35.

7. FROM STREET FOOD TO DIGITAL KITCHENS: TOWARD A FEMINIST RHETORIC OF CULINARY TOURISM (OR, HOW NOT TO DEVOUR PARIS AND EAT YOUR WAY THROUGH ASIA)

Kristin Winet

> Since we must eat to live, let's learn to do it intelligently and grace-
> fully, and let's try to understand its relationship to the other hungers
> of the world.
>
> —M. F. K. Fisher, *Conversations with M. F. K. Fisher*

At Rancho Heliconia in the cloud forests of Costa Rica, Roxana pours a cup of coffee for both of us from her homemade *chorreador* and tells me that getting divorced was the best thing that ever happened to her. As we talk about her decision to buy the farm, her devotion to preserving local Costa Rican culture, and her dedication to educating tourists about the many labors of love related to coffee production, I realize that I've learned more about Costa Rica in my few hours over a cup of coffee than I have in a lifetime anywhere else. We began our day touring the farm, examining ripening coffee beans, washing them, laying them out in long rows to dry in a shed, shaking them to find out if they are ready to roast, and carting them down to the kitchen to roast. I learned why dark roasts have the least amount of caffeine, how it takes eighteen minutes to cook a light roast and twenty-two minutes to cook a dark one, and how to lovingly and carefully grind beans to ensure the heartiest flavor.

Roxana does not sell her coffee to corporate buyers, does not export internationally, and does not need to turn a healthy profit on her farm. Her family is one of the founding families of Monteverde, and she secured a sizable sum in her divorce. She has a pet goat, Bella, who wears a pink collar and trots behind her wherever she goes, and she has no problem slaughtering cows and chickens when it is time. She rides Caramel, the chestnut-colored mare, every morning. As she tells me, the American writer who has been brought here to write about Roxana's work, she wants nothing more than for her visitors to realize where the food they eat comes from and how cultivating the products they consume is both joyful and fulfilling, arduous and difficult. I think about the crisp mountain air, the dried coconut husks in our paths, the dried coffee bean hollow like a wooden maraca, the simultaneously sweet and bitter scent of cooked beans wafting from the kitchen, the dark brown residue from ground beans on our hands, and I promise her in my humblest way that I will do my best.

Though I've been on many food journeys—in my own kitchen and abroad—this is culinary tourism at its best. Even though I was sent to cover her work and share her story, I suspect that tasting Costa Rican coffee in context like this offers more insight than simply tunneling through San José sipping every cup of coffee I can find. Roxana does not allow people to fetishize farm life, extol the farmers for simply doing their jobs, or bring tourists down to till her land for free under the guise of "voluntourism." She offers local schoolchildren living wages to come after school and basket ripe berries from the branches, and in her spare time, she teaches Costa Rican dance classes to them for free. She believes in the value of culinary tourism when it is done tastefully and mindfully, when it inhabits the space between putting food and culture into context and sharing stories and lives at the dinner table (or over the *chorreador*).

As both travel journalist and rhetoric and composition scholar, I can appreciate Roxana's position because I straddle a unique place between my deep love for the delightful act of food writing and culinary tourism and my critical stance on the politics and consequences of telling stories about the food and lives of Others. However, as I am ever mindful of my privileged position as a white feminist, and because I believe in the potentially transformative power of traveling and experiencing other cultures through food, I wish to bring this complicated passion to the foreground.

In this chapter, I think about my own work as a travel journalist and consider that work in light of the rhetorical strategies that some food writers and bloggers have come to rely on to tell their stories. Though each of the examples I cite below is far more complicated than the space of this chapter allows me to analyze, I wish to draw attention to the ways in which writing about culinary tourism can stray from joyful and tantalizing and veer toward colonizing and sometimes even patriarchal. Lucy Long defines culinary tourism as "the experiencing of food in a mode that is out of the ordinary, that steps outside the normal routine to notice difference and the power of food to represent and negotiate that difference" (20). For those of us who wish to respect the work of people like Roxana and feel a deeper sense of connection to the communities and cultures in which we are taking part, we must consider our lives and food stories as feminist scholars do, as "messy, changing, non-essential, heterogeneous, embodied, [and] diasporic," and not as a Western subject, as bell hooks reminds us, who goes out to eat an exotic Other (Cook 824). In this chapter, I consider four rhetorical strategies in food writing—cosmopolitanism, decontextualization, devouring, and escapism— that can have unintended negative effects, and I then consider possibilities for a more feminist perspective on food in culinary travel writing.

COSMOPOLITANISM

Under the wider umbrella of consuming foods while traveling, cosmopolitanism—a stance widely recognized across a number of scholarly disciplines—is perhaps the most well-known technique among foodies and food writers because it is often driven by an acceptance of all cultures, a willingness to engage with the Other, and a genuine openness to different ways of living and being in the world. As David Bell and Gill Valentine write in their coedited text *Consuming Geographies*, the cosmopolitan often enacts the personae of a Diogenes-like "citizen of the world" while traveling, claiming a high degree of literacy across multiple cultures, a deep and loving knowledge of food around the globe, and a willingness to try any cuisine once—however mundane or exotic. As a rhetorical construction, these travelers have a ready list of interesting and unusual food stories to rattle off (often to delight and demonstrate a cultural prowess to interested listeners) and make sure that their audience knows they recognize "[their] rambutans from [their] kiwanos" (187). This traveler, quite often, is someone like me.

As sociologist Jennie Germann Molz has noted, the practice of cosmopolitanism is not theoretically considered negative, as it is most often associated with "a stance toward diversity itself" through a demonstration that willingly wishes to engage with the Other in curious, appreciative ways—an orientation that is not, at its heart, necessarily colonizing by design (80). Cultural anthropologist Ulf Hannerz agrees, suggesting that as it pertains to travelers, it often takes the form of "an intellectual and aesthetic stance of openness toward divergent cultural experiences, a search for contrasts rather than uniformity" (239). In terms of culinary tourism, then, the concept transfers easily: for cosmopolitan travelers who love to eat, difference is constantly constructed, recognized, celebrated, and even shared though the act of eating the Other.

In this way, taking a cosmopolitan stance toward eating often has its consequences, particularly in terms of making exotic someone else's home cuisine or meal preparation methods (even when the traveler comes with the best and most curious of intentions). According to Molz, some travelers *rely* on the notion of cosmopolitanism to uncompromisingly veil their colonizing attitudes in curiosity or to simply perform a sense of adventure and adaptability to themselves and their audiences at the expense of exoticizing another (79). In a sense, the entire rhetorical circuit depends on a relationship to a person, place, or food that is *different from* or alien to the eater, a construction that upholds—rather than downplays—the tenuous binary between visitor and host and eliminates the contingent and discursive nature of identity/identities and history/histories we consider crucial to our feminist food work. Cosmopolitans are often Euro-American, Christian, white, middle-class, well educated people who "long to 'spice up' their diets (literally) with the flavours of exotic cuisines" and are often well intentioned / 103 but naive (Heldke xxi). They enact a performance of "dilettantes as well as connoisseurs," presenting themselves as self-proclaimed foodies whose sense of competence amid cultural diversity includes a readiness and ability to make their way into another's home or kitchen and who believe they can maneuver "more or less expertly within a particular system of meaning and meaningful forms" (Hannerz 239). In this way, scholars are torn on the concept, wondering if it simply enacts Karl Marx's theory of commodity fetishism, namely the idea that social relationships between people are perceived as economic relations among objects. For some, it resembles what bell hooks calls "consumer cannibalism," a kind of "Other-eating" that thrives on foreignness and a lack of critical engagement with the people involved in food production and dissemination and can lead to the constant production of cultural difference as a consumable commodity (31).

Within travel discourse, these nuances matter. Take the example of Valen Dawson, an American expatriate whose food blog, *Eating the Globe*, aims to inspire people to literally "consume" the world as a culinary cosmopolitanist—by trying all the world's culinary delights. As Ian Cook and Philip Crang suggest in their work, the idea of "eating the globe" is reminiscent of the cosmopolitan's desire to have "the world on a plate," so at first glance, Dawson's work seems similarly aligned, a blog full of celebratory eating experiences (132). However, in a post entitled "Date a Girl Who Eats," which she wrote in response to Aleah Taboclaon's "Date a Girl Who Travels," a blog post that went viral in late 2014, Dawson argues that women who eat their way around the world are more suitable dates. As she writes, instead of having closets full of shoes, a girl who eats is

> the one with the cabinet full of saffron spices she brought from Morocco, dark honeys that she smuggled from Spain, dried chilies that an old woman handed over from a smoky fire in Mexico, and lavender that she picked from the fields of France.

Complementing this list of culinary pursuits are a number of photos in which Dawson eats a number of foods, including such "foreign" delicacies as fish bones, mango slices, legs and thighs from unidentified animals, cupcakes, sugared pastries, and ice cream cones. Her tongue, which is present in over half of the photos, is a cosmopolitan representation of having her world on a plate—and eating it, too.

Despite the fact that there is plenty to analyze here, it is Dawson's performance of culinary cosmopolitanism that is clearest across her blog. Unlike Taboclaon's post, in which she encourages her readers to remember humility, Dawson, instead, offers posts like "Pig's Blood, Brains, Tongues, and Frogs: I Tasted It All to Follow the Anthony Bourdain Chiang Mai Food Trail," in which she takes up the task of following Bourdain's episode on Chiang Mai from his television show *Parts Unknown* by stopping at all the street-food vendors and restaurants he visited. Unlike in Taboclaon's post, humility is nowhere to be found in Dawson's; instead, there are a number of cosmopolitan moments in which she pits her bravery against dishes like pig's tails, bloody soup, and bile. Like many food cosmopolitanists, her desire to engage with difference is physical, a negotiation of corporeal risk that allows her to further demarcate the boundaries between herself and her innocent body and the locals who prepare and serve food many Westerners would not dare to touch. As Molz and others have argued, the cosmopolitan often depends on this demarcating of the physical body, a way that the traveler can perform an identity that is "less about experiencing the local culture than it is about exploring the boundaries of these travelers' own bodies and cultural identities" (86). As Dawson states before trying *loo*, a raw blood soup, "now, this is where I took my life in my hands. People have died from parasites from eating this stuff, but I still had to try it" ("Date"). She then posts an extreme close-up photograph of the soup and another with her arm around the unnamed, anonymous female chef who has ostensibly prepared the food for her. Through such processes of commodification, Dawson has crossed into colonizing cosmopolitanism, eradicating the history and necessity of *loo* without acknowledging the complex histories, power relationships, mobilities, geographies, and even migrant laborers who made this "dangerous" food available in the first place by privileging, instead, her bravery in trying it. Her cosmopolitan stance—and the stress she places on the parasitic dangers involved in its consumption—foregrounds Dawson as a daring eater who will try anything in the name of travel rather than as someone who is interested in genuine engagement with local communities and foodways. By emphasizing the fact that she "had to try it" in order to continue her narrative of daring foodie, Dawson does exactly what Roxana hopes her global visitors will never do when they visit her farm: consume simply to consume.

DECONTEXTUALIZATION

While cosmopolitanism is the most well-known stance in telling food stories, the act of decontextualization is perhaps the most common—although it is sometimes not obvious. Those who decontextualize food present it as fixed, static, and often without the influence of human hands. As Cook writes, /105 this strategy relies on promoting an essentialist and "pure past" model that presupposes that cuisines emerge, fully formed, for the traveler to consume (822). Though Cook's examples concentrate on the ways that Mexican food advertisements and Vietnamese restaurants decontextualize the complicated histories that brought those foods to American consumers in the first place, his theory remains critical in any discussion of tourism, whether within one's own city or halfway across the globe. In a way, the belief that food is easily categorized because it is fixed and stable is a millennia-old belief, a belief going back to Aristotle's fascination with classification and transitioning well into European exploration of the New World with the belief that places, plants, and animals can be identified, tagged, and put into organizational categories. These beliefs, which are shaped by what Cook calls a long-standing "romantic fantasy of the 'primitive,'" translate almost too perfectly to contemporary culinary food tourism in ways that bell hooks has documented: as she writes, by decontextualizing food, we engage in a kind of eating that "not only displaces the Other, but denies the significance of that Others' history" and allows for a kind of multicultural rhetoric without migrants by projecting regional practices into the global realm (31).

Though food decontextualization occurs across texts as diverse as cooking blogs to travel guides to food photography to opinion sites like TripAdvisor and Yelp, decontextualization happens in any space where the contexts in which the food is made possible are implicitly—and even accidentally—erased. As a unique example, take Ashley and Jason Bartner's live cooking demonstrations, shot on their Tuscan farm in Italy. American expatriates from New York, the Bartners provide their digital audience the opportunity to cook "authentic" food from their own kitchens in the United States by paying five dollars and watching a live cooking demonstration from their organic farm in Tuscany. Though they also invite interested gardeners, farmers, and those interested in Slow Food movements to come and visit their residence, they have recently begun to promote their online podcasts and live cooking classes as excellent ways to experience Italy's peasant foods "without leaving the comfort of your kitchen." This is, in some ways, the kind of Internet-based decontextualization that celebrates global food practices without really understanding them. As food photographer Penny De Los Santos says in her interview with Lynne Rossetto Kasper, it boils down to relatability: foreign food is simply more digestible when it's made apolitical. "If you photograph this amazing meal that you had somewhere in Italy and you post it on your Facebook page," De Los Santos says, "more people can relate to that because it's food rather than politics." Food, then, becomes little more than an amalgamation of ingredients that creates the garden-friendly, backyard-inspired cuisine (a.k.a., the *cucina povera*, or "food of the poor") that the Bartners market on their site and that has become such a widely popular motif in Tuscan tourism marketing.

Though the history of *cucina povera* practices are rooted in socioeconomic realities of farm labor and poor working conditions, Italian cooks have resurrected the term to be synonymous with "fresh and local," a kind of cooking that, inspired by less wealthy Italian chefs, makes the most of gardens, forests, seas, and backyard produce in their quest to create abundant and affordable dishes (Bartner). The Bartners have embraced this sister to Slow Food and promote it as the kind of cooking they embrace on the farm. On their "Hosts" page, they claim that because "food is the most accessible, and one of the most unique and enjoyable, ways to get to know a new destination" and because culinary experiences allow "immediate immersion into the local culture," participants can get to know rural Italy without ever stepping foot on an airplane. By promising to divulge the time-tested secrets of peasantry and eliminating the need to travel, the Bartners have incidentally brushed aside the circumstances that have, as Lisa Heldke writes, "conspired to bring these cuisines into the world in the first place" (xv). Though their infectious love for organic farming and teaching sustainable cooking practices is real and admirable, I worry that armchair experiences like this eviscerate regionalism and commodify the lives and histories of Italian peasants. If nothing else, the conditions are decontextualized because there is no meat to salt, no pasteurization process to consider, no need to think of ways to refrigerate certain items to keep them cool and antimicrobial—all realities that Italian peasants have faced for generations.

While the theoretical concerns and opportunities of armchair travel are perhaps too much to include in this chapter, it is worth noting that the Bartners, along with a host of other armchair travel companies, are using digital media in ways that can incidentally create a lack of context that, like Cook and others have argued, eliminates the need to cross borders, grapple with gender and labor issues, and address the hybrid geographies of food and how they work in "everyday practice" (824). Even "live" audience members and participants do not have to muddy their feet, try out a few words of Italian, wind up on a street they never imagined they'd find, or even push the limits of their knowledge and understanding in any real profound way. Though the Bartners are enacting their dreams of teaching others to love gardening and cooking, sometimes learning the context and history of different food traditions is a first step, as the epigraph I included by Fisher suggests, toward contextualizing food culture(s) as we travel.

/ 107

DEVOURING

Etymologically, the word *devour* has a number of meanings, all of which echo distinctly John Urry's theory of the "tourist gaze" as being a one-way, top-down, disembodied stance toward Otherness that continually upholds the unequal and often asymmetric power relations between the conqueror— one who devours—and the conquered. As a rhetorical strategy in travel discourse, it is actually quite common, stemming back to travel accounts in which white, male European explorers detailed their accounts of everything they ate, sexually violated, and took home as souvenirs. However, what the devourist does with food is actually quite complex because the conquest of food almost always leads to the essentialist idea that posits place—and the people within that place—as a consumable product that can be swallowed whole. In "Consuming Nations," Shannon Peckham argues that food works as a powerful metonym for culture writ large, citing, for instance, the ways in which tacos have become a metonym for Mexico and Coca-Cola has become one for the United States. These associations are strong, often grounded in racist, essentialist ideas that espouse culture as uniform and fixed, reducing the complexity of culture to a single equation. Turning her discussion to travel guides, Peckham also demonstrates how food is often discoursed about as both a promotional object representative of an entire nation or region and a list of items to be sampled and avoided. This kind of metonymic representation of food assumes both food linearity and universality, regardless of race, gender, class, and other important socioeconomic markers. Like the process of decontextualization, it erases critical context and eliminates the need to engage with imperialism, forced coercion, slavery, immigration, and displacement—anything that might unravel the ease of simply eating to eat. In taking a photograph of a fish market in China, a plate of *pot thai* in Thailand, or a sausage in Germany and presenting that photograph as emblematic of the entire country, there is no more critical reflection than perhaps the composition of the photograph.

Consider a modern example of this: Andrew Dobson's blog, *Dobbernationloves*, is well read and award-winning; not only is he often plugged to be a speaker at travel blogging conferences and social-media networking events, he also belongs to a number of professional food and travel writer associations. In a post titled "Eating My Way through Penang, Malaysia," he details his exploits of a short trip to Penang in which he plans to eat everything he can. The post is chronological and problematic from the start, beginning with his assessment of Georgetown, a place where he "was not expecting to see such a large number of massive high rise condominiums on an island [that he] thought was going to be, shall [he] say, quaint." During his two days there and in Penang, he claims that he devoured an exorbitant amount of food, ranging from pork shoulders in a tangy sauce to a cold pastry stuffed with bean sprouts to vegetable samosas and battered onions in sweet chutney. In rendering his extensive list, Dobson eliminates any kind of critical reflection regarding the gendered and classed realities of the people who are serving these dishes to him. In his post, he writes about the "flock of incredibly eager ancient Chinese women who hobbled across the floor" to shower him with hot pots of green tea and about a "maniacal little Chinaman," who he claims bombarded him and insisted he try a plate of fried noodles free of charge. He shares his exploits of running into a lady at a food cart who motioned for him "to look down at a slippery gruel which she insisted was 'good good'" but that he was entirely too repulsed to try (this is the only example of something he did not devour). At the end of his post, having taken food from nearly all of the hands who put food in front of him, he writes that he waddled back to his hotel room, collapsed onto his bed, and decided, dreamy from his food coma, that "Penang tastes delicious!"

The case of Dobson's conquering of Penang is not rare within travel circles. For one, his characterization of the city as a composite collection of servers and cooks wishing to please him by offering him their goods and products is a primary example of the colonizer entering a space of Otherness with the belief that everyone is there to serve him. He is, in many ways, enacting the personae of what communication scholar Jean Duruz likens to a kind of culinary plunderer, someone who is "greedy to devour the commodified products of other people's home-building practices" by placing himself as the Anglo subject "reembodying h[im]self in a new location" (65). Though Dobson clearly enjoys his food-conquering activities and ultimately decides that Penang equals delicious, reducing the city to a tasty adjective, his rhetoric is nevertheless imperialist, connoting the white, male patriarch entering, penetrating, devouring, and leaving the submissive Other behind. In this way, he exhibits—no doubt without realizing it—the overwhelmingly masculinist tourist gaze, a stance unobstructed by gender, racial, class, or socioeconomic realities, and one in which a city of millions is reduced to a sheer number of dishes he consumed, one after the other. While the experiences of new dishes, spices, flavors, and methods of preparation are no doubt an inspiration and a source of joy for Dobson, there are other ways of enjoying and writing about food—ways that promote thinking more deeply about interactions with others and building more productive and critical relationships with ourselves, others, and the food that binds us across borders, cultures, landscapes, and languages.

ESCAPISM

The concept of cultural anhedonia—or, as Kelly Donati defines it in her work on Slow Food movements, the idea of self-loathing or a lack of interest in one's everyday activities and experiences—finds itself at the heart of escapism because it allows travelers to engage in "cultural raiding" by finding ways to "spice up" their otherwise boring palates and find deeper and more fulfilling connections abroad (Donati 228; Duruz 428). The lack of appreciation that escapists have for their own home cultures and traditions is both disheartening and predictable because it reinforces the idea that Othered cuisines are inherently more interesting than those at home. It perpetuates the convenient idea that consuming spicier, more vibrant food can enlighten, delight, and entertain because it is inherently more interesting. As Heldke writes, escapism either promotes nostalgic renderings of a past the writer did not experience in an attempt to create distance from his or her white (in other words, blank, empty) roots and find deeper solace in another culture, or shows the history of the writer's "plain, white plate" as perfect for "setting off features of a cuisine without imparting any flavors of its own" in order to emphasize difference (2).

Above all else, escapism suggests monotony in one's home culture, that a person's own history with food is hardly satisfying and deprived of the magnificent flavors of the world's foods. Difference is presented as better: simply because it is different. When written about from the subject position of a Western traveling subject, the dish will often feature yellow saffron, kaffir leaves, or Thai *longons*; it might be eaten raw, boiled, or baked. As long as it is different from the meat-and-potato dishes the writer might have grown up with, it is worth documenting. Escapism promotes an overidentification with difference, a glorification of another's food or culture in an attempt to prop that difference up as better, superior, or just zestier.

Consider the example of *Legal Nomads: Telling Stories through Food*, a blog started by former Montreal lawyer Jodi Ettenberg in 2008 to chronicle the year that she and a friend spent traveling the world after abandoning their law practices. Though her friend eventually returned to law, Ettenberg—a

white, middle-class Canadian who suffers from celiac disease—turned her blog into a thriving business, taking sponsored trips, giving social-media presentations at national and international tourism and blogging conferences, writing food reviews, leading local food tours around the cities she visits, crafting photo-essays (what she calls "visual adventures") and writing e-books on ways to properly eat street food. On her blog, she posts philosophical musings about travel, ruminates on her favorite noodle dishes, and writes about her travel experiences as a woman.

Ettenberg demonstrates both cosmopolitanism and escapism in her writing. As she writes in the introduction to her e-book, *The Food Traveler's Handbook*, "from a childhood with no spices and very little international food, my travels catapulted me into a world of people and places connected through history and an intersection of flavors" (n. pag.). By quitting her law practice, selling her material items, and living a life of nearly constant mobility, she was able to embrace the world's cuisines and flavors full force. On the surface, Ettenberg's celebration of international cuisine is inspiring and sensuous, but it also suggests that "white" food is worthless, spiceless, and altogether uninteresting. However, this dismissal of Euro-American foods suggests a deeper need to grapple with the underlying reality that Krista Ratcliffe calls the accountability logic—that learning to listen rhetorically "does not mean beating oneself up for one's history, culture, or Freudian slips" but instead signifies recognizing that "our standpoints are not autonomous points of static states but rather complex webs of dynamically intermingled cultural structures and subjective agency" (31, 34). From a food perspective, proceeding from an accountability logic should remove the distaste, shame, or guilt associated with eating a particular way throughout childhood and instead invite writers to consciously locate themselves in places of commonalities *and* differences. However, escapism often obscures this important part of cultural literacy, instead focusing on how far the writer has come from her home roots.

Ettenberg's blogs, photo-essays, and pages often promote escapism. In one post, "An Ode to Spices," she shares the story of how she discovered spices when she met a Moroccan man at a street market in France while studying abroad. In a more recent post, "Travel to Northern India: The Good, the Great, and the Ugly," she chronicles her food and cultural journeys in Jaipur. In these posts, Ettenberg often refers back to her uninteresting past in order to celebrate the beauty and color of the world's foods. As she re-members her first encounter with Moroccan spices, she writes that "with a British mother and a Polish father, spices never figured prominently in my childhood cuisine and the pungent smells were fascinating to me." However, once she began giving English lessons in exchange for spice and cooking lessons, she realized that spices could be her gateway to eating more richly and more fully than she ever had, and that everything she was learning was "a far cry from [her] usual, casual salt and pepper dusting. This was a whole new world." She includes a collection of extreme close-ups of spices ranging from mustard-yellow turmeric and black and red Jordanian peppercorns to close-ups of dishes topped with sumac and *za'atar* to long shots of markets and women and men preparing and serving dishes. Ettenberg understands that instead of eating to feel at home, she eats to feel displaced, to find herself among others whose cooking practices more closely align with her love for color, flavor, and, perhaps above all, Otherness.

/ 111

EXPLORING THE POSSIBILITIES OF A FEMINIST FOOD TRAVELER

In recent years, plenty of feminist food writers and scholars have opened up conversations about more ethical ways to engage with food, leading to a renaissance in food writing circles. I wish to use my own experience and the words of Fisher to consider how travelers and eaters can avoid falling into traps of colonizing discourse when they share their food stories. I realize that transformative work is not easy because for all its messiness and inconsistency, colonialism is pervasive, resilient, and malleable—it leaks into well-intentioned exchanges, inhabits our travels, and benefits the privileged in ways that the privileged are not often even aware of. However, while I recognize that imagining travel stories differently does not inherently change the power dynamics innate in these exchanges, I worry that by not examining new ways of seeing the relationship of Western travelers to their Other-eating, we run the risk of perpetuating a hopelessly superficial, nonreflective, inadvertently ignorant perspective. I believe that food stories can become intentional—that travelers can learn to refuse the us/them framework and upset the packaged idea that the world's foods are there for them to consume as they desire.

In the twentieth century, Fisher became a highly respected advocate for healthier and more passionate interactions with food, writing more than twenty books and a number of essays on food that both transcended genre and experimented with the boundaries of literature, food writing, and memoir. Her work consistently grapples with the nature of hunger as both an emotional and physical part of being human, and I believe that her insightful work can lead toward a more feminist perspective on culinary tourism. In *The Art of Eating*, which Fisher published about sixty years ago, she writes

about the need for intentional exchange in food writing, for a passionate, civil engagement with food that is opposed to the uninformed, automatic behavior created and maintained through dominant power systems. As she writes,

> gastronomical writing at its best is almost as much touched with the spirit as the bread and meat and wine with which it deals. There are no gross foods, only gross feeders; and by the same token even the homeliest prose about food, provided it be honest, can penetrate to the heart as do all words that deal with real things. A lordly dish of terrapin—or good bread and cheese—can be as uplifting as any landscape, and more so than many works of art at which we are to bid to "Oh!" and "Ah!" (xiv)

Fisher's passion for eating and love for sharing food stories is, at best, infectious. While I realize, of course, that not all relationships to food are positive and that many food stories are fraught with the residue of colonization, rape, political turmoil, and imperialism, I believe that Fisher's perspective can lead us toward a more self-reflective, careful, and compassionate relationship to food both at home in our own kitchens or abroad in someone else's.

In working against the tourist's gaze as it is traditionally understood, food writers must first recognize the way that food and stories about food make meaning and then must acknowledge that food discourse rhetorically transmits attitudes that are often deeply tied to ideologies about gender, race, class, and other identity markers. Because of this, a feminist food perspective must actively oppose the uninformed, automatic behavior created and maintained through beliefs that reinforce dominant powers and promote a lack of intentionality. With Fisher's reminder that there "are no gross foods, only gross feeders," food writers might reconsider their writing about exploits eating bugs, clambering through cities to devour noodles, and complaining about their boring home palates. They may also come to recognize that by putting food into context and being inquisitive and mindful about the choices they make, travel—and eating—become all the more joyful. By actively contextualizing food, remedying cultural amnesia, and assembling our culinary stories with an eye toward the entangled histories that comprise many foods, we will not only be able to encounter alternative stories but immerse ourselves more fully in our own lives and the lives of others.

In her work on geopolitics and feminist rhetorics, Wendy Hesford argues for a shift from consumptive feminist cosmopolitanism to a critical transnational feminism, asking travelers and rhetoricians alike to focus on the local with an awareness of overlapping localities and interarticulations of both the local and the global. What this means, in the context of culinary tourism, is that by shifting uncritical cosmopolitan practices—what she and Caren Kaplan call a "foundational Western idea"—and dismantling the idea that "travel produces the self, makes the subject through spectatorship and comparison with otherness," we can move from nationalism to transnationalism, acknowledging shifting relations between community members and foreigners (Kaplan qtd. in Hesford 68). Therefore, if we rethink culinary tourism as less of a performative, consumptive act and more as an opportunity to examine the asymmetry of tourism by placing it, as Heldke posits, "in the center of the dining table," traveling and eating can become less of a shameful act and more of a place for possibility (182). By engaging in rhetorical positioning that values listening and critical cultural knowledge, as Ratcliffe suggests, culinary tourism—and by connection, travel discourse—can begin to change. It is possible that by embracing the messiness, we can begin to see that our lives—Western or otherwise—are always already imbued with entanglements of food colonialism and anticolonialism, and that we are all products of globalization and conquest.

The difficulty with reimagining food and travel is that the rhetorical strategies and categories presented in this chapter are not always imbued with negativity. I end this chapter, then, by revisiting a later portion of Ettenberg's *The Food Traveler's Handbook*, in which she begins investigating the intersections between food, history, and the people(s) who harvest, cook, prepare, and sell the products with which she has fallen in love. As she recounts the story of her journey, she writes that many of her impromptu street meals turned into friendships, invitations to learn about spice blends, dinners at local homes, and opportunities to learn about the communities and people she was visiting. Precisely because Ettenberg works to contextualize her food adventuring, highlighting the people she meets and learning about the histories and politics behind the foods she eats, her approach—while privileged—does hold possibilities. In addition to being acutely aware of her positionality as a white, Western woman, she highlights the relationships she has developed with those who have been kind enough to teach her their culinary expertise; she features the women behind the pots, pans, and stoves in ways that are removed from a patriarchal, one-way gaze. Instead of embracing a kind of blanket multiculturalism, Ettenberg recognizes and writes about both the solidarity and acknowledged differences she identifies in these women and herself. In some ways, she puts into practice Audre Lorde's belief that we should not be reluctant to recognize difference in our desire to build communities but instead build on those differences. As Lorde writes, "it is not our differences which separate women, but our reluctance

to recognize those differences and to deal effectively with the distortions which have resulted from the ignoring and misnaming of those differences" (122). Instead of perceiving humans and their food practices as dominant/subordinate, good/bad, superior/inferior, travelers should bring with them "a mind open to connecting and learning with and from others, and, of course, a good appetite" (Ettenberg, *Food* n. pag.). With a bit of practice, those "good appetites" can, I believe, turn into great ones—ones that thrive on recognizing and understanding difference and that feast upon beautiful foods with finesse, love, and care.

Works Cited

Bartner, Ashley, and Jason Bartner. *La Tavola Marche*. 2014. Accessed 20 July 2014.

Bell, David, and Gill Valentine, eds. *Consuming Geographies: We Are Where We Eat*. Routledge, 1997.

Cook, Ian. "Geographies of Food: Mixing." *Progress in Human Geography* 32.6 (2008): 821–33.

Cook, Ian, and Philip Crang. "The World on a Plate: Culinary Culture, Displacement, and Geographical Knowledges." *Journal of Material Culture* 1.2 (July 1996): 131–53.

Dawson, Valen. "About." *Eating the Globe*. Accessed 21 July 2014.

———. "Date a Girl Who Eats." *Eating the Globe*. 17 June 2014. Accessed 28 June 2014.

Dobson, Andrew. "Eating My Way through Penang, Malaysia." *Dobbernation-loves*. 25 January 2010. Accessed June 2014.

Donati, Kelly. "The Pleasures of Diversity in Slow Food's Ethics of Taste." *Food, Culture, and Society* 8.2 (2005): 227–42.

Duruz, Jean. "Eating at the Borders: Culinary Journeys." *Environment and Planning D: Society and Space* 23 (2005): 51–69.

Ettenberg, Jodi. *The Food Traveler's Handbook*. 1st ed. Full Flight P, 2012.

———. *Legal Nomads: Telling Stories through Food*. 2014. Accessed 21 July 2014.

Fisher, M. F. K. *The Art of Eating: Five Gastronomical Works*. Vintage Books, 1976.

Hannerz, Ulf. "Cosmopolitans and Locals in World Culture." *Theory, Culture, and Society* 7.2–3 (1990): 237–51.

Heldke, Lisa. *Exotic Appetites: Ruminations of a Food Adventurer*. Routledge, 2003.

Hesford, Wendy S. "Cosmopolitanism and the Geopolitics of Feminist Rhetoric." *Rhetorica in Motion: Feminist Rhetorical Methods and Methodologies*. Ed. Eileen S. Schell and K. J. Rawson. U of Pittsburgh P, 2010. 53–69.

hooks, bell. "Eating the Other: Desire and Resistance." *Poetry Genius*. Rpt. of *Black Looks: Race and Representation*. South End P, 1992. Accessed 29 April 2014.

Kasper, Lynne Rossetto. "The Language of Food Photography Is Universal: Interview with Food Photographer Penny De Los Santos." *The Splendid Table*. Accessed 25 March 2014.

Lazar, David, ed. *Conversations with M. F. K. Fisher*. U of Mississippi P, 1992. Literary Conversations Series.

Long, Lucy, ed. *Culinary Tourism: Food, Eating, and Otherness*. UP of Kentucky, 2004.

Lorde, Audre. "Age, Race, Class, and Sex: Women Redefining Difference." *Sister Outsider: Essays and Speeches*. Crossing P, 1984.

Marx, Karl. *Capital: Critique of Political Economy*. Vintage Books, 1977.

Molz, Jennie Germann. "Eating Difference: The Cosmopolitan Mobilities of Culinary Tourism." *Space and Culture* 10.1 (2007): 77–93.

Peckham, Shannon. "Consuming Nations." *Consuming Passions: Food in the Age of Anxiety*. Ed. Sian Griffiths and Jennifer Wallace. Mandolin, 1998.

"Rancho Heliconia." *Costa Rica*. 2014. Accessed 31 July 2014.

Ratcliffe, Krista. *Rhetorical Listening: Identification, Gender, Whiteness*. Southern Illinois UP, 2005.

Taboclaon, Aleah. "Date a Girl Who Travels." *Solitary Wanderer*. 24 February 2012. Accessed 20 July 2014.

Urry, John. *The Tourist Gaze*. 2nd ed. Routledge, 1995.

PART III

RHETORICAL REPRESENTATIONS OF FOOD-RELATED PRACTICES

8. NOT YOUR FATHER'S FAMILY FARM: TOWARD TRANSFORMATIVE RHETORICS OF FOOD AND AGRICULTURE

Abby Wilkerson

The June morning sun is already hot as Riet Schumack leads visitors through the Farmway in Brightmoor.[1] She and other community members took action when their Detroit neighborhood faced 40 percent poverty and vacancy rates and many related challenges, such as no supermarkets, hence no access to fresh produce. In addition, many residents didn't own cars and were, therefore, unable to purchase groceries from neighboring towns (Wey). In 2006, Schumack and other women in the community began to create gardens and turn abandoned houses into art spaces. Schumack's was the first, on four contiguous lots, complete with vegetables, flowers, goats, rabbits, and hens. Now, the twenty-two-block area boasts at least thirty-five community gardens within its boundaries. Vacant houses throughout the neighborhood are now boarded up and sport neatly mowed lawns; murals painted by children and adults make the Farmway a bright and vibrant space. Many residents have no Internet access, so when the neighbors designed murals for a vacant house on a centrally located corner lot, they incorporated a blackboard-wall community bulletin board that now displays colorful notices for meetings and events.

Schumack walks her visitors through the Youth Development Garden, where young people may come for the profit sharing but find other reasons to stay involved. Smiling, Schumack reminds a teenager engrossed in her work that the morning shift ended forty-five minutes ago. The youth learn about cultivation and conservation at the same time; a clever water catchment system keeps down the water bill as it conveys sustainability lessons. Just as important, Schumack points out, are the larger life lessons that are absorbed, the ones that motivated her and her neighbors to start this work: "For me, it's the kids. A childhood is only so long, and I don't want them growing up thinking that a boarded-up house is the norm." She is the first to point out the serious political and economic challenges facing the community but insists, "there's something you can do to make your environment better." You can't always "take houses down, but for $100 you can board them up and make some art on them." And work together to see that everyone has fresh vegetables on the table.

Hundreds of miles east lies Grafton County, New Hampshire, "a low-income rural community" (McEntee 240) where many residents participate in local traditions of fruit and vegetable gardening, raising poultry in their yards, hunting, and fishing. Although the Grafton County foragers' and gardeners' rural landscape is quite different from that of Brightmoor, both communities depart from the stereotypical, politically correct sustainable food consumer with disposable income, and their motivations and practices likewise depart from assumed norms of sustainable food consumption. Food systems researcher Jesse McEntee's interviews with forty Grafton County low-income "community respondents" reveal a "traditional localism" characterized by desires for "obtain[ing] fresh and affordable food, reciprocal exchanges, tradition"—in marked contrast to a "contemporary localism" motivated by an "explicit desire to support local farmers, promote environmental sustainability, etc." (250). He writes, "Many respondents who found locally produced products too expensive to purchase happily shared garden produce (from blueberries to squash) with neighbors, relatives, and even strangers through reciprocal exchange" (251). Hunting and foraging are also part of these traditions. When a local food pantry received five hundred pounds of moose meat from a hunter, one of its employees recalled that "it flew out of here. I mean, people were calling us and asking us for some" (251).

Family rhetoric serves a significant role in the sustainable food movement in the United States, in terms of both production—the family farm—and consumption, which a host of cultural references prescriptively situate within the kitchens of nuclear families. The respective settings and food exchanges of Brightmoor Farmway and Grafton County may contrast in a variety of ways, but they share patterns of sustainable local food production and distribution that cannot be fully understood through either a conventional nuclear family lens or typical assumptions regarding sustainable food consumers. In this chapter, I will consider the potential of family rhetoric in movements for food justice and sustainability to reinforce existing social hierarchies and inequalities, concentrating particularly on family farm rhetoric but also on the role of family in the consumption side of sustainable food rhetoric. I will also consider sustainable food practices and settings (such as those just mentioned) that are not conveyed by a family farm mythos and their implications for more equitable rhetorics of food justice and sustainability.

SCHELL'S "ALTERNATIVE AGRARIAN RHETORIC"

In the 2007 collection *Rural Literacies*, Eileen Schell calls for an "alternative agrarian rhetoric" in pursuit of sustainable, equitable food systems. More specifically, Schell advocates—following Kenneth Burke—a rhetoric of persuasion. She notes the frequent depiction of small farmers losing their land as tragic. Such depictions construct farmers as passive victims—a "sympathetic" form of identification that denies them agency while it obscures the political economy that gives rise to the phenomenon (95). Instead of appeals to sympathy, Schell calls for persuasion based on "mutual identification," "emphasizing the common interests of farmers and consumers," and grounded in "an ethic of sustainability" (98).

Since Schell's chapter appeared, connections between the needs of eaters /121 and farmers have materialized everywhere from the *New York Times* to a raft of documentary films and even Walmart commercials. Yet Schell specifies that sustainable food rhetoric must also be constructed in ways that provide tools for exploring systemic forces structuring the food system, including neoliberalism (not something Walmart commercials are prone to highlight), and for taking action—using consumer power and advocacy to create change (118–19). Ultimately, Schell insists that just and sustainable rhetorics of food attend to the interactions of economic and cultural forces in shaping food systems and our experiences of them. Part of the task, then, is to construct an alternative agrarian literacy; thus Schell herself both draws on and engages in critical literacy studies, as her analysis incorporates a condensed political economy of "the farm crisis" (83–92).

In this chapter, I contribute to the larger project that Schell's work typifies by exploring inegalitarian consequences of family rhetorics in sustainable food movements within the dominant neoliberal economic context. While Schell focuses on an alternative agrarian rhetoric that conveys the shared interests of eaters and small family farms, I address small-scale agricultural operations that include but also go beyond the rural settings typically associated with agrarianism. I take up explicit and implicit rhetorics of futurity, kinship, property, and nation circulating in US-based food justice and sustainability movements.

The rhetoric of "the family farm" is linked to a number of values and assumptions with troubling ramifications, including a reinvigorated gender conservatism and a white, economically stable, heterosexual nuclear family norm—an image that tends to obscure any notion of food as an issue of racial justice and socioeconomic inequality. Drawing on queer theory and disability studies, I offer the concept of rehabilitative consumption,[2] which I use to analyze family farm rhetoric in sustainable food projects, consumption norms underlying these efforts, and their impact on how we imagine food justice and sustainability. Applying these critical insights on rehabilitation to family rhetoric in food reform facilitates an assessment of unexamined ideologies of family that can inadvertently undermine the very social justice imperative underlying much-needed calls to transform the food system.

REHABILITATING FARM AND FAMILY

The US family farm has long served as the keystone of the American pastoral idyll, symbol of heartland, image of productivity and abundance—both an egalitarian world of yeoman farmers and a family setting at its most pure and wholesome. Today, the family farm takes on great urgency as a site of cultural investment, embattled by a range of forces from toxic chemical inputs to real estate development and E. coli outbreaks. Indeed, in ways extending far beyond its direct role in food production, it has become invested with the task of preserving, or perhaps rescuing, a fabled American way of life.

The family farm now appears to have become an instrument for rehabilitating both the nuclear family cultural norm and the spectacle of US consumption for which "families"—especially women, mothers above all—so often take the blame. This idealized farm does double duty (or more) by providing sustenance innocent of factory taint, even as it reenshrines endangered foundational myths. The family farm is a potent symbol and target of rehabilitative consumption, a voluntaristic sensibility that tells us if we just "eat this, not that," we'll be saved. This attitude both reflects and reinforces a neoliberal context that maximizes transnational corporate profits and minimizes spending on social safety nets. This economic program, in turn, imposes a physical or fiscal health imperative to reduce consumption—in one case, of fatty snacks and sugary sodas, and in the other, public education, health care, and utilities—austerity and belt-tightening all round.

As for the United States in particular, we hear daily that the nation is experiencing a crisis in food and eating, as supposedly evidenced by the dreaded scourge of obesity, which critics of all stripes seem to agree is a crime and have rounded up quite a lineup of accused parties. But while these critics disagree on which party is guiltiest, they frequently agree on the remedy: people should just "eat right." Yet as conversations on the negative environmental and social justice impact of the US agro-industrial food system have greatly intensified, obesity often stands in for a somewhat more complex array of food-related health problems, broader social inequities, and even environmental concerns.

No wonder, then, that prominent voices are calling for the nation to go into rehab for a toxic addiction to both the substances in our groceries and those in our agricultural production. Rehabilitation has received a great deal of scrutiny at the intersections of queer theory and disability studies, fields whose very existence owes a debt to the cultural studies insight that cultural understandings of human bodies are shaped by ideologies of the body politic and citizenship. Thus, bodily difference becomes bodily defect, and bodies considered defective are associated with defective personhood. From this vantage point, mainstream notions of rehabilitation are configured to preserve gendered hierarchies of family and sexuality, in ways that support capitalist ideologies of production and determine which bodies are absorbed into the economy and which are not (Stiker 164).

Robert McRuer introduces the notion of "compulsory able-bodiedness" in which social inclusion is predicated on societal standards of normalcy. Those who don't meet those often arbitrary standards are not accorded full membership in society, particularly if they do not attempt rehabilitation, or worse, are read as rejecting those standards. Drawing on Adrienne Rich's notion of "compulsory heterosexuality," McRuer identifies family formation as an element of compulsory able-bodiedness: membership in a conventionally structured family has been a significant component of cultural normalcy (88). We can look at dietary standards—intended as they are to produce a certain kind of body (fit, healthy, able)—as a key instance of compulsory able-bodiedness and consider how they are linked to assumptions about gender, family structure, and household practices.

"THAT STEREOTYPICAL FARM THAT YOU SEE ON THE TELEVISION"

The farmers' market is one site that reflects the significance of family rhetoric in sustainable and healthy food efforts. (I'll return shortly to the dietary aspects of compulsory able-bodiedness.) An ethnography conducted by Ryanne Pilgeram demonstrates the power of heteronormative family constructions at a northwestern US farmers' market, where consumers associate family concepts with farmers' markets and sustainability. Producer-vendors' "heterosexual coupling" is visible "at the majority of stands," and their marketing materials rely on family imagery as a central theme (n. pag.).

When Pilgeram asked consumers at the market "what makes sustainable agriculture different from conventional agriculture," a number invoked a "romanticize[d] . . . idea of the family on the land." One "woman envisioned the farmers as 'family members, [a] closer group of people, family run most [of] the time. It is colorful . . . vibrant . . . a sense of lost traditional values in terms of community . . . more like family type farms.'" A twenty-eight-year-old woman felt that conventional grocery stores don't measure up to farmers' markets, which are "really small and family oriented . . . kinda like, you know, that stereotypical farm that you see on the television" (n. pag.).

Pilgeram contends that "the dominance of male/female dyads working the stands at the market suggests the symbolic importance of heterosexuality to the construction of sustainable food." One lesbian vendor reported that "everyone always assumed that her business partner was her mother. . . . [I]t bothered her" that the market community failed to "realiz[e] that there could be any number of reasons that two women were working together." Pilgeram suggests that the market itself "makes it easy to make that mistake" by symbolically "fram[ing] heterosexuality as 'normal'" (n. pag.).

Many of the market's farmers "specifically use images of 'the family,' meaning a white, heterosexual family, to sell their farms to consumers." In these images, farming men are positioned as rugged individuals while farming women are typically situated in relation to men and children, as in a market photomontage including "four images of single men, [while] all the women were accompanied by a man, and in most cases also children."[3] Pilgeram "found that even though on most of the farms [she] interviewed[,] there were no children present," images of children were marketing staples, for example, on the market directory of participating farms, on farms' own websites, and posted at an event promoting seasonal Community-Supported Agriculture shares (n. pag.).

One farmer who displays photos of her children working with animals on the farm acknowledged that such images are "'huge, it really is a selling point for people. I don't mean to diminish it, like it's like I'm using my kids that way, but it's really helpful.'" Pilgeram sees "Images of children . . . as representing multiple ideologies that are present at the market: . . . the ways that sustainable farming preserves the environment for future generations as well as the ways sustainable food helps young, growing bodies thrive"—while "also . . . linking the wholesomeness of sustainable food to the perceived wholesomeness of this hegemonic family form" (n. pag.).

I want to extend Pilgeram's claim here in the ways I suggested earlier: in the current crisis of American identity, linked to perceived excess consumption in so many ways, the sustainable farming family takes on the highly seductive recuperated image of a wholesome, righteous, productive American identity—a most pleasing appeal to pathos. Yet not all families, or family farms, or sustainable farms conform to these familial configurations. It's a vision that fails to reflect reality, even as it limits our cultural and agricultural imagination. While the image effectively conveys a sense of connection to farmers, its appeal to mutual identification may give consumers a stake in the fates of farmers, as Schell advocates, but it also reinscribes an implicitly hierarchical vision of gender relations (one that she also traces in some instances of alternative agrarian rhetorics). At best, it fails to challenge heteronormative patriarchal patterns and, at worst, romanticizes them.

FAMILY RHETORIC AND "INDIRECT FORMS OF EXCLUSION"

There are more ways in which the image of the traditional family farm fails to reflect the diversity and contingency of actual US (and other) farming families and hence of US (and other) farms. A recent survey finds that certain "progressive" agricultural regulations intended to ensure safe working conditions on farms (Minkoff-Zern et al. 66) function as "indirect forms of exclusion" of Hmong immigrant farmers in California (67). Regulations designed for corporate farms impose burdens that small Hmong farms cannot bear.

> Most of the Southeast Asian–owned farms are significantly smaller and less capitalized than the average owner-operated small farm, particularly in California. . . . [T]he cultural institution of labor reciprocity, in which families share labor or in kind services with extended family members, is central to the economic viability of their farms. (75–76)

State inspectors have cited Hmong farmers for violations of regulations that do not recognize the extended nature of family and the related practices that are fundamental to the existence of their farms. Minkoff-Zern et al. report,

> These citations have required poor famers to pay onerous fines for having minors (often nieces and nephews) working in their fields, not buying workers' compensation insurance for extended family members, . . . not having an illness and injury prevention plan, not training employees about heat-related illness, and not providing single-use cups for their

workers' use. (77)

State law specifies that farmers must purchase workers' compensation coverage "for each and every person who is not named on the title of the farm. This applies to both nuclear and extended family members, to those who work for pay or exchange labor, and to permanent and temporary laborers" (78). For the Hmong farmers, many of whom already face a language barrier making the regulations hard to understand, these labor regulations pose further cultural and economic obstacles: a notion of "family" as a land-owning nuclear unit with a clear distinction between "owner" and "worker" that is foreign to Hmong culture, even as it problematizes the extended family interdependence so necessary to the very existence of many small immigrant farms (78–79).

Here, the law setting out the conditions for "rehabilitation" into the norm presents a classic catch-22 for the Hmong farmers: nuclear family ideology and practice define the norm to which all family farms are expected to conform, yet doing so would render their very existence tenuous or impossible. These California policies may well have sprung from advocates' sense of mutual identification with farmworkers but fail to consider the multiplicity of "family" on small farms. Thus, in order to counteract the effect of hegemonic conventional family rhetoric, we must also employ the second element of Schell's alternative agricultural rhetoric, critical literacies—which we must expand from assessing the impact of neoliberalism on family farms and the interconnections of global political realities (including the impact of US policies abroad), to considering cultural variations in family formations and their implications for agricultural practice and policy.

FAMILY VALUES IN THE KITCHEN

Cultural representations of food consumption within the household indicate rehabilitation's linkage to gender ideology. The Left's advantage in matters of gender and sexual egalitarianism becomes murkier in certain ways when we look at food. The Right and the Left's differences regarding gender and sexuality sometimes stop at the farmhouse—or the kitchen—door; much as it wants to, the Left just doesn't know how to quit its romance with naturalistic conceptions of gender.

Both the Right *and* Left demand with equal force the kind of national and nationalistic food rehabilitation that I have described. Conservatives castigate women for failing to ensure proper eating habits for their households, while the sustainable food movement, at best, fails to intervene in this discourse and, at worst, participates in it. Prominent advocate Michael Pollan is also a leading proponent of what I call rehabilitative consumption, which he explicitly links to the family meal, revealing the role of family formation in compulsory able-bodiedness through the demand for nutritional discipline. In a famous 2008 *New York Times* open letter to President-Elect Barack Obama, Pollan outlines a program to rehabilitate the "nation's food system," not only for environmental reasons, but to "confron[t] the public-health catastrophe that is the modern American diet" ("Farmer"). He seeks to "rebuil[d] America's food *culture*," calling for an extensive public food education campaign and urging the president to serve as national role model by informing the public that he sits down with his family "every night that [he is] in town." "What is a higher 'family value,' after all," Pollan asks rhetorically, "than making time to sit down every night to a shared meal?"

In another piece, Pollan blames the family meal's legendary "decline" on "several causes: women working outside the home; food companies persuading Americans to let them do the cooking; and advances in technology that made it easier for them to do so" ("Out"). Just when Pollan seems on the verge of empathizing a little with women whose long hours at their jobs make it difficult to cook, he states: "Women with jobs have more money to pay corporations to do their cooking, yet all American women now allow corporations to cook for them when they can." Pollan does not seem to consider whether men in any of these households may have some role in this apparently universal domestic capitulation to corporations. Somehow he doesn't quite make the leap to considering the role of fathers in cooking for children or—with the exception of President Obama and presumably himself—in educating them about eating well. /*127*

Pollan typifies both the cultural insistence on rehabilitative consumption and the failure to meaningfully intervene in the demand that women—wives, mothers, girlfriends—observe and reinforce this norm in the home as part of our life's work. However, the impetus to rehabilitate in the domain of food must also be explored in the context of food production, and for that, I turn to the queer theory concept of heteronormative temporality. Judith "Jack" Halberstam recites the plotline "of adolescence—early adulthood—marriage—reproduction—child-rearing—retirement—death," a sequence whose "narrative coherence" reflects cultural ideologies of its inevitability and rightness (Dinshaw et al. 180). This familiar—and normative—story arc, Roderick Ferguson frames as "the rational time of capital, nation, and family" (Dinshaw et al. 182), a characterization of great use in thinking about the family farm as cultural symbol—and the contribution of family rhetoric to racial differentials in the success of small farms, as the experiences of the California Hmong farmers and other groups indicate (Alkon and Agyeman).

In the normative heterosexual nuclear family narrative, one generation acquires property in order to sustain the next generation and—speaking metaphorically—plant seeds to provide for subsequent ones. The "stereotypical family farm on television" appears to render this idyllic metaphor literal, as Pilgeram's farmers' market research illustrates so clearly. Heteronormativity is thus made to seem inevitable, righteous, and the generative foundation of society, casting the accumulation of private property as a selfless gift to future generations rather than self-interested profit seeking. In particular, the capitalist goal of accumulating and passing down wealth becomes a veritable public service when it is land devoted to sustainable farming that is passed down—epitomizing future life-preserving benevolence while presenting the private ownership of property as a pastoral idyll.

One reason why family farm rhetoric may have such power in the sustainable food movement is its ability to evoke a nostalgic sense of smallholder farms as an American norm, obscuring the current reality of giant industrial farms dominating food production. Yet, despite the appeal of this cultural imagery, family farm rhetoric limits our agricultural imagination by suggesting that in order for people to be well fed and to foster the health of the planet, our food must be grown by a family on land they own and that will remain under their control—a white, heterosexual, economically stable family with children, and headed by a man, at that.

These comments, to be clear, are most emphatically not a critique of actual family-owned small farms, given the heroic work being done there, nor of the particular ways their households are constituted. My concern rather is with the hegemonic power of family farm *rhetoric*, which is striking, given the difficulty in present political-economic circumstances of any lone household making it a reality. As farmland across the nation is sold, real estate developments spring up, often trading on the pastoral associations of former farmland. Agro-industrial corporations have managed to convert many of the remaining smallholding US farmers, the proud symbol of productivity, from producers into consumers, dependent on the purchased inputs required for industrial agriculture. Yet this process is not a done deal, as the many alternative farms and farmers indicate.

For the Brightmoor Farmway community, working the land to generate food, income, and vibrant public space is a strategy to make life better in the here and now, while resisting ongoing political and economic forces, including corporate development efforts that would eradicate their community. Riet

Schumack was compelled to work with others to create the Farmway in large part because "a childhood is only so long." This is not the sense of reproductive futurity as a channel for the transmission of wealth that is integral to heteronormative temporality. Insisting on a livable present, Schumack's rhetoric has a compelling immediacy, providing an alternative to notions of wholesomeness and sustainability predicated on an increasingly tenuous private property model of farming.

In the same city, the Detroit Black Community Food Security Network works to "'creat[e] a model of community cooperation and self-determination'" through food, "the lens we use to present this model for Black people in Detroit," says the group's executive director, Malik Yakini (qtd. in Wey). They are forging an alternative to the capitalist-controlled food system and its patriarchal dynamics of "gross gender inequalities," with "women doing the vast majority of the work" (Yakini qtd. in Wey). Like Brightmoor Farmway, the network's projects also provide concrete alternatives to the commodification of land and food often taken for granted in family farm rhetoric—as do the reciprocal exchanges of the Grafton County, New Hampshire, gardeners and foragers, even if they don't frame their practices overtly in these terms. Yakini identifies the "'root cause of food insecurity'" as "'dispossessing people of their land'" (qtd. in Ginsburg). Much of his efforts and those of the network involve the critical literacy work that Schell contends is necessary for the creation of alternative farm and food rhetorics.

The family farm, offering up a uniquely powerful image of both American families and American identity writ large, has emerged as an ideal site of and for rehabilitation: first, rehabilitation of the land itself to restore it to its originary harmony with nature, then rehabbed farming practices to maintain that harmony, which then enable rehabilitated consumption by dispensing what we should consume. This process symbolically renders the American family as a site of wholesome production—the family farm—and simultaneously a site of wholesome, virtuous consumption—the consuming household that the family farm enables—thereby rehabilitating our national image. Yet this symbolic operation occurs at great cost to women, people of color, and poor people, even as it renders other models of food and social justice invisible at best.

Meanwhile, projects such as the Brightmoor Farmway generate spaces of conviviality and reciprocity not only intergenerationally but across a range of cultural divides. More than working for food access, they create oppositional spaces where food becomes a channel for community building and generating resistance to entrenched power. These projects are not constrained by rehabilitative consumption, a vision of food that revolves around minimizing the public cost of some people's alleged poor "choices." Instead, these projects are predicated on a vision not just of food access but a world in which everyone has the chance to live well, a vision that understands the interconnectedness of all the social goods necessary for a community to live well together and individually. To promote real change in the food system, from agricultural labor regulations to farmers' market promotions and youth gardens, sustainability and food justice rhetorics must challenge the commodification of land and food—and the presumed whiteness of "family values." These rhetorics must embrace a diverse array of possibilities across urban, rural, and suburban contexts. This shift will also require transformations in domestic life, which in turn require policies that support the diverse configurations of human connection that generate conviviality. And these domestic and convivial transformations require serious support for domestic labor, which in turn requires a reorganization of workplaces, and much more. Ultimately, if we are going to eat well, we need a broader vision, a more pluralistic and diversified rhetoric, than the family meal or the family farm. The tools of critical literacy and intersectional rhetorical analysis have a vital role to play in expanding the bonds of mutual identification in these ways.

Notes

I am grateful to Melissa Goldthwaite, Katie King, Pat McGann, Pam Presser, Carol Reeves, and Karen Sosnoski for their invaluable responses to earlier drafts of this paper; to Kim Hall and Lisa Heldke for the inspiration they provided through our panel at the Association for the Study of Food and Society; and to audiences there and at the University of Maryland Queer Studies Symposium and the Conference on College Composition and Communication for useful comments and questions.

1. These observations are based on a tour of Brightmoor that I attended in June 2013, led by Riet Schumack as part of the Association for the Study of Food and Society conference.

2. See Wilkerson, "'Obesity'" and *Thin Contract*.

3. Rachel Rybaczuk's analysis of farm websites and newsletters also found a preponderance of text and images associating farming women with child care and farming men with farm machinery, farm labor, fields, and supervision of crews.

Works Cited

Alkon, Alison Hope, and Julian Agyeman, eds. *Cultivating Food Justice: Race, Class, and Sustainability*. MIT P, 2011.

Dinshaw, Carolyn, et al. "Theorizing Queer Temporalities: A Roundtable Discussion." *GLQ* 13.2–3 (2007): 177–95.

Ginsburg, Eric. "Conference Explores Dimensions of Food Justice." *Yes! Weekly* 27 February 2013. Accessed 18 July 2014.

McEntee, Jesse C. "Realizing Rural Food Justice: Divergent Locals in the Northeastern United States." *Cultivating Food Justice: Race, Class, and Sustainability.* Ed. Alison Hope Alkon and Julian Agyeman. MIT P, 2011. 239–59.

McRuer, Robert. *Crip Theory: Cultural Signs of Queerness and Disability.* New York UP, 2006.

Minkoff-Zern, Laura-Anne, et al. "Race and Regulation: Asian Immigrants in California Agriculture." *Cultivating Food Justice: Race, Class, and Sustainability.* Ed. Alison Hope Alkon and Julian Agyeman. MIT P, 2011. 65–85.

Pilgeram, Ryanne. "Social Sustainability and the White, Nuclear Family: Constructions of Gender, Race, and Class at a Northwest Farmers' Market." *Race, Gender, and Class* 19.1–2 (2012): n. pag.

Pollan, Michael. "Farmer in Chief." *New York Times Magazine* 12 October 2008. Accessed 7 July 2013.

———. "Out of the Kitchen, onto the Couch." *New York Times Magazine* 29 July 2009. Accessed 7 July 2013.

Rybaczuk, Rachel. "Selling the Pastoral Ideal: The Commodification of Heteronormativity in Contemporary Agriculture." Joint Conference of the Agriculture, Food, and Human Values Society and the Association for the Study of Food and Society, University of Vermont. June 2014. Conference presentation.

Schell, Eileen E. "The Rhetorics of the Farm Crisis: Toward Alternative Agrarian Literacies in a Globalized World." *Rural Literacies.* Ed. Kim Donehower, Charlotte Hogg, and Schell. Southern Illinois UP, 2007. 77–119.

Stiker, Henri-Jacques. *A History of Disability.* U of Michigan P, 2000.

Wey, Tunde. "D-Town Farm." *Urban Innovation Exchange* 30 August 2012. Accessed 7 July 2014.

Wilkerson, Abby. "'Obesity,' the Transnational Plate, and the Thin Contract." *Radical Philosophy Review* 13.1 (2010): 43–67.

———. *The Thin Contract: Social Justice and the Political Rhetoric of Obesity.* Open Court P, forthcoming.

Yakini, Malik. "Tensions and Contradictions of Addressing Racial Justice in Detroit's Food System: The Experience of the Detroit Black Community Food Security Network." Association for the Study of Food and Society, Michigan State University. June 2013. Conference presentation.

Yeoman, Barry. "The Death and Life of Detroit." *The American Prospect* 30 April 2012. Accessed 19 March 2014.

9. BAKLAVA AS HOME: EXILE AND ARAB COOKING IN DIANA ABU-JABER'S NOVEL *CRESCENT*

Arlene Voski Avakian

Diana Abu-Jaber has published short stories, two novels (*Arabian Jazz* and *Crescent*), *The Language of Baklava* (what she calls a food memoir), and *Origin* (a mystery). She teaches creative writing, film studies, and contemporary literature, and she is a food writer. The main character of her second novel, *Crescent*, is Sirine, the daughter of an Iraqi immigrant and a white American mother who is the chef in a café that serves "real Arab food." Food, a ubiquitous ingredient in the book, is symbolic of identities, nationalities, artistry, connection and disconnection, humanity, generosity, community, and love. Always specific to Arab cuisine, the descriptions of dishes in this book are so richly described that an experienced cook could cook from them, and for those who are less skilled, Abu-Jaber ends the book with three actual recipes from food featured in the narrative. Abu-Jaber's deployment of food in *Crescent* creates a cultural space for the characters to explore national, ethnic, and gender identities both in diaspora and exile. Additionally, her use of food and cooking in the novel helps counter Arab American stereotypes.

Abu-Jaber is a central figure in Arab American literature. Few Arab American writers have produced novels so the publication of *Arabian Jazz* was met with great interest. While lauded by non-Arabs, though the publisher tried to get her to take "Arabian" out of the title, many Arab Americans criticized her for what they saw as stereotyped depictions. Like writers from other marginalized groups, Arab Americans are faced with representational dilemmas—

trying to tell a story true to their vision while not feeding into the mainstream cultures' assumptions about whom Arabs and Arab Americans are.

Racialization or marginalization of Arab Americans is based primarily on politics rather than phenotype. The legally based discrimination like that directed against African Americans, Asian Americans, Latinos, and Native Americans has not existed for Arab Americans since 1914 when a US Supreme Court decision ruled that George Dow, a Syrian, was white and eligible for citizenship. While Arabs continued to experience prejudice and sometimes even violence, the legal protections of citizenship were available to them after the Dow decision. Arab Americans became more and more visible and reviled after the six-day war in 1967, the oil embargo of 1973, the Iranian hostage crisis of 1979, and the Gulf War of George H. W. Bush and Bill Clinton. Of course, Arab Americans have been particularly vulnerable after 9/11. Nurtured in the fertile ground of orientalism, representations of Arab Americans by the dominant culture have focused on men as terrorists and women as super-oppressed by a backward and barbaric patriarchal culture. These assumptions also make no distinction at all among the many and varied Arab cultures. All Arabs are the same.

Arab American memoirs have followed the common pattern of immigrant literature of looking nostalgically back to the homeland represented as having a simpler and more fulfilling family and communal life or, conversely, coming from poverty in the homeland to finding economic comfort and a home in the new world. Neither of these narratives seriously critique the dominant culture and uphold some of its assumptions even while possibly presenting a more humanized depiction of Arabs and Arab Americans in loving families and able to adapt to Western culture—perhaps even welcoming it. Contemporary Arab American literature is more critical of both dominant representations and issues within Arab American life.

/ 133

Arab American feminist writers face particular dilemmas. Harkening back to a glorified past, for example, is specifically dangerous for them since in much of the Arab world, the past is patriarchal—or may be represented as patriarchal by dominant forces in their home countries. Like other people in diaspora, holding on to the reality or myth of a patriarchal past may be seen as essential to protect threatened cultures. On the other hand, Arab American feminist writers who explore the patriarchy of their cultures, at home or in diaspora, can play into Western assumptions of Arab cultures as backward. Even Laura Bush represented herself as a woman who wanted to protect poor, helpless Afghani women in order to justify the war on that country. Arab American feminists face the added problem of feminism being identified with Western imperialism and, therefore, an anathema.

Confronting many of these issues in *Crescent*, Abu-Jaber relies heavily on food imagery. Salah D. Hassan and Marcy Jane Knopf-Newman, editors of the 2006 issue on Arab American literature of the journal *MELUS*, suggest that the use of food imagery might be a type of accommodation, making Arab culture more accessible to hostile Western readers. Food imagery is, indeed, very common. Over the past twenty-five years, three of the four anthologies of Arab American literature that have been published use food imagery in their titles: *Grape Leaves: A Century of Arab-American Poetry* and *Food for Our Grandmothers: Writings by Arab-American and Arab-Canadian Feminists*, for example. *Food for Our Grandmothers* uses food for the titles of the volume's six parts, including a recipe for each. For example, part 1 is "Olives, Our Roots Go Deep: Where We Come From" and includes a recipe for tomato salad made—of course—with olive oil. Many of the pieces in this volume also feature food imagery. Abu-Jaber's 2005 memoir *The Language of Baklava* is full of food imagery as well as many recipes. On the other hand, this focus on food may merely be a reflection of cultures in which cooking and eating carefully prepared and well-seasoned food is highly prized.

Another major issue for Arab and Arab Americans, like other broad categories of diverse people, is what composes the group. Who is in and who is out? There is neither consistency nor clarity about which countries are Arab and which are not. Leila Ahmed argues that Arabs are primarily a political grouping with little basis in a shared history and culture constructed by Gamal Abdel Nasser in response to the Palestinian situation. In the US context Arab Americans are either invisible as a group or highly visible as terrorists and oppressors of "their" women with little awareness of either these complexities or the diversity within the group. This problem has made both political organizing and literary representation very difficult.

Abu-Jaber addresses many of these issues in *Crescent*, and food imagery is central to her literary and rhetorical strategies, allowing her to emphasize both cultural connections and differences. The main character in the novel is Sirine, the chef of Nadia's Café, where much of the action takes place. The café is positioned as a home away from home and a kind community center for Arab students and faculty from the nearby University of California, Los Angeles (UCLA) department of Middle Eastern studies. Abu-Jaber writes,

> Nadia's Café is like other places—crowded at meals and quiet in between —but somehow there is also usually a lingering conversation, currents of Arabic that ebb around Sirine, fill her head with mellifluous voices. Always there are the same groups of students from the big university up the street, always so lonely, the sadness like blue hollows in their throats,

blue motes for their wives and children back home, or for the American women they haven't met. . . . The few women who do manage to come to America are good students—they study at the library and cook for themselves, and only the men spend their time arguing and being lonely, drinking tea and trying to talk to Um-Nadia, Mireille, and Sirine. . . . They love her food—the flavors that remind them of their homes. (19–20)

Um-Nadia, a Lebanese immigrant, bought the café from an Egyptian who sold it after the two CIA agents began to regularly come to it, scaring his customers away and terrifying him by asking if he knew about any terrorist plots. After Um-Nadia buys the café, the CIA comes back, but being Lebanese, she says, she knows how to deal with them, chasing them off neither afraid of them nor allowing them to sit in her café. At the very beginning of the novel then, Abu-Jaber signals that Arabs are under surveillance and feel threatened, that not all Arabs are the same, and that Arab women can be stronger than men.

In addition to serving the "food of home," the café provides Arabic television, "news from Qatar, variety shows and a shopping channel from Kuwait, endless Egyptian movies, Bedouin soap operas in Arabic, and American soap operas with Arabic subtitles" (22–23). Patrons come in the morning with their newspapers before classes begin, waiting outside of the café until Um-Nadia opens the doors. Knowing all of them, she lets them in one by one, making the younger ones wait outside until the older ones have had their first cup of coffee. They argue about Middle East politics and poetry, but the food is central to making the café their home.

/ 135

This "home," however, is contested. Who is Arab? Um-Nadia is Lebanese, and there is confusion about whether she is an Arab. Sirine's uncle, who teaches in the Middle Eastern department at UCLA, responds with "God only knows" and asks her why she put her café in the middle of Tehrangeles, an Iranian neighborhood. Iranians are not Arabs, and Um-Nadia complains bitterly that Americans have no idea about the major differences between them and relations between Iranians and Iraqis are hostile as a result of the Iran/Iraq war. She responds, "God only knows. Where else am I going to put it?" (28). And while the Iranians do not come into the café because of Sirine, who is half Iraqi, the neighborhood does have easy access to ingredients needed for Arab cuisine: the Turkish butcher saves the best lamb for Sirine, and the Persian grocer Khoorsh gives Sirine special foods. He came into the café on opening day and announced "that he was ready to forgive the Iraqis on behalf of all Iranians" and asked if Sirine knew how to make *khoresht fessanjan*, his favorite walnut and pomegranate stew. When she promised to learn, he came back later that day with a pomegranate tree for her. The *khoresht* and the tree are food offerings, a way to connect across differences, and to underscore this positive exchange, the tree bears fruit at the end of the novel.

But even among those who are identified as Arabs, there are major political disagreements and endless, heated political discussions about who is Arab, how to be Arab, gender relations in Arab countries, who is the best poet in Arabic. Identities, as Stuart Hall argues, are never fixed either for individuals or groups but are in flux in response to both outer material conditions and inner responses to them. The customers at the café, for example, may never have watched news from Qatar when they were in their own countries, but in the context of being in the United States, Qatar may feel like home, and they may develop a stronger sense of being Arabs rather than connecting more nationalistically.

What there is no argument about is the food. Sirine always makes baklava because it "cheers the students up." Abu-Jaber writes, "They close their eyes when they bite into its crackling layers, all lightness and scent of orange blossoms" (66). While neither Sirine nor Um-Nadia are practicing Muslims, they honor the importance of religious ceremony to the patrons of the café by preparing special foods to break the fast in the mornings and evenings for the whole month of Ramadan.

How and why does food play such a crucial role in creating a home away from home? We know that food is linked to identity. Deborah Lupton argues that food is centrally implicated in whom we become—beginning in infancy with early bodily experiences. She suggests that food discourse and the power relations within it and which it produces construct who we are.

Focusing on the sensory as well as the social aspect of food, David Sutton argues that "eating the foods of home becomes a particularly marked cultural site for the reimagining of 'worlds' displaced in space and/or time" (102). Food memory, a shared *sensory* experience of taste and smell, held in the body through both ceremonial and everyday performative ritual, can reconstruct a cultural whole, an essential factor in creating social bonds and divisions.

Who we are both as individuals and socially is linked, then, to our psychic/bodily experiences of and discourses about food. Food memories can evoke both powerful emotions and a sense of a whole—reconstructed—cultural context. The most famous literary example of course is Marcel Proust's madeleine. But we also have Mimi Sheraton's bialy: "A bread," she says, "that in my psyche, summons up even today the mystical dreamworld of Marc Chagall and Isaac Bashevis Singer" (239). Cornish pasty, a mainstay of immigrant miners from Cornwall in Michigan's Upper Peninsula, is a meal of meat, vegetables, and even dessert wrapped in pastry, baked at home, and then put on a shovel and heated with the miner's lamp. Leslie Cory

Shoemaker argues that although the pasties were eaten in the depths of the earth by miners away from their families, they "are deeply embedded . . . in the very core of people's life stories" and have come to "speak of home, of grandmothers and mothers in the comfort of their warm kitchens" (248). Even in the extreme situation of the Terezín concentration camp, inmates managed to write a cookbook attempting not just to record recipes but to recreate the specific culture in which the dishes were embedded, at least in their imaginations, the act of recording defying the final solution (de Silva).

Through serving Arab foods, Um-Nadia's café functions to reconstruct a home. Many patrons are students who will go back when they finish their studies, others are immigrants, but some are exiles. Han, a brilliant and charismatic linguist, translator, expert on contemporary American literature, and faculty member at UCLA, is an exile from Iraq. He explains,

> The fact of exile is bigger than everything else in my life. Leaving my country was like . . . part of my body was torn away. I have phantom pains from the loss of that part—I'm haunted by myself. . . . It's a dim, grey room, full of sounds and shadows, but there is nothing real or actual inside of it. You're constantly thinking that you see old friends on the street—or old enemies that make you shout out in your dreams. You go up to people, certain that they're members of your family, and when you get close their faces melt away into total strangers'. . . . You forget everything you thought you knew. . . . You have to . . . or you'll just go crazy. (182)

/ 137

Involved in politics just as Saddam Hussein was coming to power, Han escaped when it became clear that he would either be conscripted into the army to fight with Iran or be arrested for his resistance to the regime. We learn that he can't go home early in the novel, just as he and Sirine begin their love affair. She becomes his home. He says,

> You are the place I want to be—you're the opposite of exile. When I look at you—when I touch you—I feel at ease. I feel joy. It's like you know some sort of secret, Hayati, a key to being alive—to living. (158)

The relationship between Sirine and Han is expressed initially and throughout the novel with food imagery. Sirine tells Han she learned about love when she made baklava with her parents. She not only felt their love for her but for each other. Abu-Jaber writes,

> Her mother said that a baklava maker has to have sensitive, supple hands, so she was in charge of opening and unpeeling the paper-thin dough and

placing them in a stack in the tray. Her father was in charge of pastry-brushing each layer of dough with a coat of drawn butter. It was systematic yet graceful; her mother carefully unpeeling each layer and placing them in the tray where Sirine's father painted them. It was important to move quickly so that the unbuttered layers didn't dry out and start to fall apart. This was one of the ways that Sirine learned how her parents loved each other—their concerted movements like a dance; they swam together through the round arcs of her mother's arms and her father's tender strokes. (66)

Sirine and Han make baklava together in a sensual scene much like the one she described with her parents. We expect that Sirine, the chef in a café that is a home away from home for people like Han, will feed Han special foods, but early in their relationship Han also cooks for Sirine. His gift of food, an American dinner of meat loaf and mashed potatoes, both acknowledges and accepts their differences. Later, when their relationship is in trouble, Han engages Um-Nadia to cook another meal for Sirine; this time it is Lebanese dishes, and he feeds her with his hands. Sometimes the food signifies love. Sirine realizes her attraction to Han when she wants to feed him pastry *knaffea* with her hands. Other times, sensuality and love are powerfully expressed by the couple feeding each other, even if it is a piece of meat loaf that Han picks up like an olive and offers to Sirine.

In creating this representation of Han as a giver of food, a feeder, a nurturer, of a man who tells Sirine he loved being in the kitchen with his mother, aunts, and sisters and would often join them there after he had worked in the orchards with the men and listen to their stories, Abu-Jaber is quite clearly countering the stereotype of Arab men oppressing their women. She underlines this representation when Han is able to follow Sirine's lead as she guides him into the bedroom when they do make love and is not put off when she asks him to wear a condom.

But Sirine is wary of Han as well. When he gives her a scarf that belonged to his sister as a token of his love, she is moved but is suspicious of his gift, asking him if he wants her to wear a veil. The reality that Arab culture is patriarchal and that many Arab men oppress women is voiced in the novel by Um-Nadia's daughter Mireille who rejects both Arab food and Arab men. Referring to a group of men in the café, including Han, Mireille says,

> Look at them . . . probably all waited on since the day they were born.
> . . . All these guys really want is to get us back into veils, making babies,
> and I don't know what, nursing goats or something. You watch out, I
> am telling you. (42–43)

In another scene, a large group argues over the different gender relations in the Arab world, some of which are very oppressive while others are not so, again countering the stereotype, even held by many feminists, that all Arabs are alike and that all Arab women have been oppressed for all time.

Yet the character of Sirine counters representations of Arab American women as having no life outside of the family. While she is cooking and serving others, Sirine is a chef, a professional who was reviewed as brilliant by the *Los Angeles Times*—though that was before she was cooking Arab food at Um-Nadia's café. Cooking is both her passion and her art and, perhaps, also has a spiritual dimension. When Rana, a very strong woman character who wears a hijab, asks her what her religion is, "Sirine looks down at her hands and notices a fine crease of flour between her fingers and under her nails. She stuffs them into her pockets. 'I suppose I don't actually have one'" (192). But she does have cooking and food—the implication is that they might be as important to her as religion is to Rana.

In addition to having a profession, Sirine is thirty-nine, sexually active, often having two or three boyfriends at a time, and not at all interested in getting married. She is clearly in charge in her relationships and often quickly tires of them, especially when the café is busy. Before falling in love with Han, she felt that

> food was better than love: surer, truer, most satisfying and enriching. As long as she could lose herself in the rhythms of peeling an onion, she was complete and whole. And as long as she could cook, she would be loved. (217–18)

When she does fall in love with Han, she doesn't lose herself, and her cooking becomes even more interesting as she mixes ingredients with opposite qualities together, such as chocolate and pepper.

While Sirine's gender identity is generally uncomplicated, her ethnic identity is unclear to her and working it out is a major theme in the novel. Food and cooking are central to that process. Her uncle, who raised Sirine after her parents were killed when she was nine, is deeply immersed in the Arab community, yet tells her very little about the Iraq he and her father left when they were young men. Perhaps because of her American mother, Sirine did not learn Arabic, and Abu-Jaber makes clear that she knows very little about the region, perhaps even less than well-informed non-Iraqis. She does not know, for example, that Iraq is a dangerous place even though it is headed by a dictator and the United States is bombing it, or that US citizens cannot travel there.

Sirine also does not read poetry, which figures prominently in the novel and is perhaps the major literary form in Arab writing, but her relationship to this form is also mediated by her cooking. At a poetry reading that her uncle insisted she attend, Sirine is made breathless by Han's eloquent introduction of Aziz, a Syrian poet: "She has never heard anyone speak so eloquently and longingly of Arabic before. Suddenly she misses her father" (30). As the poet begins to recite his work, she tries to listen, but is uncomfortable perhaps because she does not understand poetry or because she is already powerfully attracted to Han. She looks down at her hands and "smells traces of butter left over from cooking lunch" (30). The sentence ends with a poetic metaphor to describe the fragrance, "an incense of oil and grass" (30). Just as the novel implies that cooking may be a religious experience for Sirine, there is the sense that cooking may also be her poetry—and poetry is an Arabic form. Later in the text in a discussion about cultural politics and cultural theory, Aziz says that the "difference between first person and third person in poetry . . . is like the difference between looking at a person and looking through their eyes" (220). When Sirine responds that "tasting a piece of bread that someone bought is like looking *at* that person, but tasting a piece of bread that they baked is like looking out of their eyes" (221), Aziz tells her that she has the "soul of a poet" and that "cooking and tasting is a metaphor for seeing" (221).

Clearly, Sirine's entry into the culture is through food. When she becomes the chef at Nadia's Café, she goes back to her parents' recipes. She recalls that her father said that her mother thought about food like an Arab—and when cooking her recipes, she "felt as if she were returning to her parents' tiny kitchen and her earliest memories" (22). She also is in an Arab context for most of the day, hearing the Arabic she does not understand from the patrons and the television, and for much of the time when she is not there, she is thinking about creating new dishes, always Arabic food.

But Sirine is only half Iraqi, and we are frequently reminded of that by references to her blonde hair and white skin. Her biculturality is expressed most graphically in the Thanksgiving dinner she and Nadia prepare. Aware that American holidays are particularly lonely times for the café regulars who don't have families, they invite them as well as the workers in the café to a Thanksgiving dinner. The night before the feast, the two women pour over the handwritten recipes Nadia brought with her from Lebanon but has not prepared for thirty-five years. After Nadia falls asleep, Sirine stays up all night researching Iraqi recipes for food that Han mentioned from his childhood. Honoring her American side, Sirine still has turkey as the centerpiece, but it is stuffed with rice, onions, cinnamon, and ground lamb. Lentils and onions accompany maple-glazed sweet potatoes, green bean casserole, and pumpkin soufflé. Sirine's identity is a combination of her white mother and her Arab father; she and the meal are bicultural.

Never essentializing her characters, Abu-Jaber complicates both their ethnic and racial identities as well as gender formations. The questions of who is an Arab and what being an Arab means are never answered definitively but consistently questioned while the racialization and marginalization of Arabs are always in the forefront. Most of the characters' cultural identities are inflected by their particular histories as Lebanese, Jordanian, Iraqi, or, in the case of Sirine, her biculturality. Gender is similarly complicated. Sirine as well as other female characters challenge the stereotypes of passive Arab women; the character of Han questions essentialist notions of Arab masculinity; and the central characters argue about women's "proper" place. All of the social positionalities are not only complicated but are mutually constitutive. This novel also encapsulates what is centrally important about food for individuals, groups, and nations. It is 394 pages of delicious feasts—both literary and gustatory.

Works Cited

Abu-Jaber, Diana. *Crescent*. W. W. Norton, 2003.

———. *The Language of Baklava*. W. W. Norton, 2006.

Ahmed, Leila. *A Border Passage: From Cairo to America—a Woman's Journey*. Penguin, 2012.

de Silva, Cara, ed. *In Memory's Kitchen: A Legacy from the Women of Terezín*. Jason Aronson, 1996.

Hassan, Salah D., and Marcy Jane Knopf-Newman, eds. *Special Issue on Arab American Literature*. Spec. issue of *MELUS* 31.4 (Winter 2006).

Kadi, Joanna, ed. *Food for Our Grandmothers: Writings by Arab-American and Arab-Canadian Feminists*. South End P, 1994.

Lupton, Deborah. *Food, the Body, and the Self*. SAGE, 1996.

Orfalea, Gregory, and Sharif Elmusa, eds. *Grape Leaves: A Century of Arab-American Poetry*. U of Utah P, 1988.

Sheraton, Mimi. "The Bialy Eaters: The Story of a Bread and a Lost World." *Food and the Memory: Proceedings of the Oxford Symposium on Food and Cookery 2000*. Ed. Harlan Walker. Prospect Books, 2001. 238–44.

Shoemaker, Leslie Cory, "Passionate for the Pasty: The Cornish Pasty in Michigan's Upper Peninsula." *Food and the Memory: Proceedings of the Oxford Symposium on Food and Cookery 2000*. Ed. Harlan Walker. Prospect Books, 2001. 245–53.

Sutton, David E. *Remembrance of Repasts: An Anthropology of Food and Memory*. Oxford, 2001.

10. FEELING GOOD AND EATING WELL: RACE, GENDER, AND AFFECT IN RUTH OZEKI'S *MY YEAR OF MEATS*

Winona Landis

Ruth Ozeki's first novel, *My Year of Meats*, follows two Asian/Asian American women, whose lives intersect due to their involvement with a "documentary" television show premised on marketing beef. Jane Takagi-Little, the biracial Japanese American director of *My American Wife!*, initially takes on this production in earnest, but she soon realizes the insidiousness of the beef industry and seeks to expose its flaws to her viewers. Akiko Ueno is the wife of a Japanese beef executive and an avid viewer of *My American Wife!*, who becomes so inspired by Jane's work that she travels to the United States in order to meet the woman responsible for her own personal transformation.

With its focus on gendered reproduction and global feminism, *My Year of Meats* is a primary text often taught in introductory women's and gender studies courses. It demonstrates to students the ways in which the concepts they are learning about can be applied in a fictional setting and in the lives of individuals more broadly. Through *My Year of Meats*, students are often able to visualize and understand the intersections of gender, race, and global capitalism and consumption. What is most noteworthy in teaching this text is the reactions that students often have to the characters, scenes, and content. When discussing the novel in my introductory women's studies class, students expressed a wide range of specifically emotional responses. Some remarked that they felt that moments in the text were "over-the-top" or "hard to believe." Others expressed a great deal of shock and revulsion in response to the details Ozeki included regarding the production and consumption of meat products. And still others felt a degree of pleasure or comfort in Ozeki's inclusion of unconventional, multicultural characters and families—especially those students who came from similar backgrounds and thus found themselves identifying with the characters in question.

Despite the variety of reactions, the common thread for all my students in reading *My Year of Meats* is the emphasis on *feeling*, the author's appeal to pathos, and it is this emotional and affective response that I will further explore in this chapter. More specifically, I aim to demonstrate the ways in which Ozeki's novel utilizes affective identification as a rhetorical strategy to promote her political vision. That is, Ozeki's text relies on the production of "good feeling" amongst her characters, emphasizing transnational connection and the importance of kinship. In order to persuade her readers of the dangers of meat consumption, Ozeki connects more conscious consumerism to positive affective feelings, such as love and inclusion. She foregrounds traditionally feminine desires, such as procreation, and shows how unsustainable food practices impede such desires. Therefore, her readers, as my students show, are made to *feel* the negative implications of unmanageable and unhealthy foodways, while simultaneously feeling a positive affective identification with the multicultural and diverse characters and families.

/ 143

By relying on emotions and affect as a lens through which to read Ozeki's text, I am situating *My Year of Meats* squarely in the context of the neoliberal, multicultural project of the 1990s, during which the novel is set and in which it was first published. At this time, the United States was simultaneously anxious about and encouraging of new economic and personal global relationships, particularly with its Asian friends and rivals like Japan. Therefore, it stands to reason that in a politically conscious novel such as *My Year of Meats*, Ozeki would include textual details, such as a main character of mixed-race and another from Japan, a family comprised of transnational Asian adoptees, and a family with same-sex parents. Not only do these details resonate as personally and politically relevant to many readers, but they also enable affective identification between reader and character. *My Year of Meats* exemplifies the neoliberal project of identification across difference; that is, it relies on the production of positive feelings and simplification of difference in order to promote inclusive political change.

I take my claim from those of other theorists of food and rhetoric, such as Allison Carruth, who argues that "[Ozeki's] fiction analogizes cultural diversity and biodiversity as a rhetorical tactic for rejecting 'global economic exchange networks'" (118–19). I expand on this idea by also considering Ozeki's emphasis on emotional reactions and identification. This identification reads as explicitly gendered, especially when considering the ways she tethers food production and consumption to familial (re)production and motherhood. Therefore, I argue that Ozeki's use of gendered rhetoric and a logic of identification can be seen as problematic and seemingly at odds with her more radical political message. That being said, my goal is also to demonstrate the ways in which, particularly through the use of the documentary medium, Ozeki's text may also demonstrate a level of self-awareness in regard to these problematic rhetorical moves. *My Years of Meats* thus pushes readers to make the affective connections necessary to understand Ozeki's message regarding unsustainable food production while perhaps also prompting them to productively question and critique the gendered, politically saturated tactics and content used to convey this message.

Although composed of several intersecting stories, the main narrative of *My Year of Meats* involves filmmaker Jane Takagi-Little. Jane, as her hyphenated name suggests, is the offspring of an American father and a Japanese mother, and as a mixed-race individual, she is chosen as the perfect candidate for producing *My American Wife!*, the target audience of which is Japanese housewives. The goal of the show is to depict "happy" American families and their meat-filled dinner recipes in order to market meat (specifically beef) to Japanese families. Jane, by inhabiting both a female and a kind of hybrid racialized body, is therefore seen by the Japanese meat marketers as someone who can most successfully communicate that "meat is the message" to Japanese female viewers.

Much critical work has already taken up the notion that Jane's mixed Asian and American identity allows her to most appropriately relay the narrative to Ozeki's readers. While Jane's racial and ethnic identity is certainly noteworthy in the context of the story, Ozeki's choice of a mixed-race character as one of the central storytellers is an important rhetorical move, considering the novel's temporal context. As Emily Cheng notes, Jane emerges as a protagonist at a time when there was already a great deal of discussion surrounding "racial mixing," as is evident from the 1993 *Time* cover, "The New Face of America"; the iconic cover depicts a computer-generated woman of ambiguous racial background, but who is most notably *not* white. Thus, Jane as a narrator would register with readers as an important component of what Cheng calls their "temporal narrative" (195). More importantly, emphasizing Jane as a character allows Ozeki to tap into affective responses of her readers to the rhetoric of neoliberal multiculturalism; Jane registers as an uncomfortable individual for some and a reminder of "happy" multicultural

US society for others, but she, nonetheless, plays into readers' feelings surrounding the ever-changing racial makeup of the nation.

In the television series *My American Wife!*, Ozeki has also created a prime example of this promotion of "good feeling," one that readers are initially meant to view critically. Jane conveys her own skepticism of the show's intent while filming a scene at a Walmart, in which she realizes:

> *This* was the heart and soul of *My American Wife!*: recreating for Japanese housewives this spectacle of raw American abundance. So we put Suzuki in a shopping cart, Betacam on his shoulder, and wheeled him up and down the endless aisles of superstores, filming *goods* to induce in our Japanese wives a state of *want* (as in both senses, "lack" and "desire"), because *want* is *good*. (35)

In this instance, Jane recognizes the difficult and uneven economic aspects of representation on *My American Wife!*, as well as the fact that it is pure "spectacle." That is, it is specifically and rhetorically constructed to persuade Japanese viewers to purchase meat products, no matter the price or consequences. The use of the "spectacular" here is evocative of Wendy Hesford's arguments regarding contemporary human rights discourse. As she writes, feelings and affective reactions, such as compassion, are frequently induced through visual representation, and thus the "spectator is configured as the holder of rights and their distributor to those who are unable to claim them independently" (4). Although the United States and other Western nations are not the audience for *My American Wife!*, the television program in the text, nonetheless, relies on the notion of spectatorship to garner a particular emotional response; in this case, happiness and the desire for happiness, which—according to the show—can be attained only through the consumption of meat.

/ 145

Jane, as a documentary artist, comes to learn not only of the disastrous effects of this unhealthy consumption but also, as is evident in the passage earlier, the ways in which the constructed and inherently inauthentic nature of the show creates and maintains unequal transnational relationships between east and west, the United States and Japan. Jane, therefore, begins to subtly subvert the "Meat Message" by foregrounding diverse kinds of families as well as alternatives to the unsustainable beef products. The question becomes, however, whether this narrative's turn toward inclusion of unconventional individuals, groups, and meals in Ozeki's novel is, in fact, a subversion, or if it is, instead, still playing into the dominant rhetoric of cooperation and happiness on which the neoliberal cultural project is so reliant.

One of the most frequently discussed families that Jane focuses on in *My American Wife!* is the Beaudroux family of Louisiana, composed almost entirely of internationally adopted children. The recipe they share with Jane is for Cajun-style baby back ribs, which her boss, John Ueno, emphatically refers to as a "second-class meat." And notably, Vern Beaudroux, the patriarch, prepares this meal, rather than his wife, Grace. When the reader is presented with the large southern and yet racially mixed family, most come to understand that this is a more ideal version of the modern American family and that their consumer practices are, therefore, to be admired and emulated. And yet, such a response to the Beaudroux family is only possible because of the way in which they are continually framed (in both the television show and the text itself) as a family that emphasizes love, compassion, and belonging across racial boundaries. The choice to adopt, in addition to having two biological children, is not only a means of addressing the earth's overburdened population but also to provide loving homes to "children in need." Children like, as Grace puts it, "all the little Oriental babies from Korea and Vietnam who don't have anyone to care for them or buy them toys or educations" (69). And so, the act of adopting ten children from around the globe (but primarily Korea) becomes an act of care coupled with political engagement. The term "Oriental," of course, also evokes a sense of discomfort, as it is easily recognizable to most readers as no longer politically correct. Therefore, by having Grace justify her affective and familial choices with this contentious term, Ozeki provides a moment in which readers may be prompted to question or unsettle the (re)productive and affective logic at hand. However, keeping in mind the affective logic that Hesford identifies, the Beaudroux family is, nonetheless, configured as doing the "good" and "right" thing for these children based on their position as privileged visual consumers. They even choose their adopted children based on pictures in a catalogue that visually capture their neediness as well as their potential to be loved.

Through both literal and figurative framings, the Beaudroux family emerges as not simply an important multicultural plot point but also as a fictional family that is doing crucial affective work. David Eng specifically discusses the affective component of adoptive kinship, arguing that "transnational adoptees today, in turn, provide a new type of affective labor, one helping to consolidate the social and psychic boundaries of white middle-class nuclear families in the global north by shoring up Oedipal ideals of family and kinship" (20). In other words, although the Beaudroux family seems to subvert the conventions of the normative Western family, through its transnational children and the fact that the husband rather than the wife is primary food preparer, they, in effect, solidify certain notions of the conventional family by emphasizing reproduction and familial love and kinship. Moreover, especially when considering the autobiographical/documentary angle of *My American Wife!*, the family becomes an important axis of identification for fictional viewers and actual readers. For example, John Ueno, the Japanese coordinator for *My American Wife!*, is infuriated by Jane's representation of the multiracial Beaudroux family, exclaiming, "She [Jane] has been instructed to make programs about beef, but no. . . . She goes and chooses pork, clearly a second-class meat. I mean, really! A pig-roasting festival! Not to mention all those Korean children" (78). By contrast, John's wife, Akiko, responds quite positively to the Beaudroux episode. While preparing dinner for John,

> the small apartment was filled with the sweet, fragrant steam of the stewing meat and the happy, humid music of the bayou. . . . All that was missing was the children. . . . Maybe she and "John" could adopt, if this problem of hers didn't work itself out. (78)

The problem to which Akiko refers is her seeming infertility. The framing of the Beaudroux family as explicitly "happy" and full allows Akiko to see them as a model to solve her problem, just as she finds herself drawn to and replicating Vern's baby back ribs.

Readers of *My Year of Meats*, in turn, are also invited to identify with the supposedly model Beaudroux family and their various modes of sustainable living and eating. Indeed, Eng notes that through such literature as *My Year of Meats*, transnationally adopted students felt able to "come out" and reveal this aspect of their identity to him in class (1), and so, too, did my own students describe the ways in which the Beaudroux family reminded them of their own families or at least other blended, multiracial families they knew. Including this family in the text of the novel itself, in this regard, feels both unique and familiar and allows readers to understand the political and social issues highlighted by Ozeki without appearing overtly radical. Framed both visually and textually through the positive affects of inclusion and familial love, the Beaudroux family reify certain norms while simultaneously pointing out the flaws with our society's economic and bodily consumption—and it is this affective rhetorical framework that then allows the reader to so easily consume Ozeki's message.

Even more seemingly subversive than Vern, Grace, and their dozen children are Dyann and Lara, the "biracial vegetarian lesbian couple" that Jane decides to include in the television show, knowing full well that their lifestyle will be unpalatable to Ueno and the beef industry sponsors for several reasons (177). Jane, however, feels compelled to film them, again as part of her goal to create an ideally modern and diverse *My American Wife!*. It is through her depiction of Lara and Dyann that Jane learns the most about the dangers of meat consumption and is, therefore, able to communicate these issues to her viewers, just as Ozeki does to her readers. As Dyann prepares her pasta primavera, she explains to Jane and the camera that

> you know, we're vegetarians by default. I mean, we like meat, like the taste of it, but we would just never eat it the way it's produced here in America. It's unhealthy. Not to mention corrupt, inhumane, and out of control, you know? (177)

Here, both audiences understand the political implications of a meat-free lifestyle, especially as it is couched in terms related to a kind of universal humanity and excess. Their understanding is predicated on Dyann's characterization as, above all, an earnest and thoughtful mother—a trusting caregiver who strives to provide the best and make all the "good" and "right" choices for her family. Dyann makes it clear that meat consumption in the United States is logically unsound as well as emotionally fraught and destructive. It is this pronouncement that makes Jane decidedly uncomfortable but also pushes her to construct what she sees as a politically important episode of *My American Wife!*. She notes that "the program was a good one, really solid, *moving*, the best I'd made. *It could even effect social change*" (179, emphasis mine). Here, the reader sees that Jane's decisions as director and documentarian are explicitly connected to the evocation of the "good" and right feelings in her viewers. In order to potentially "effect social change" with regard to unhealthy, unsustainable consumption, viewers must be affectively moved by Dyann, Lara, and their children. They are a queer but also decidedly homonormative couple in that they are framed by their procreative futurity and investment in family. In this way, Dyann and Lara are read as novel and progressive and yet also familiar and comfortable, allowing the reader to more readily draw these emotional and political conclusions (and perhaps also begin to question them).

In this way, by including a lesbian couple within the novel as the tipping point for Jane's political motivations, readers are also made to recognize that it is this queer kinship structure that holds a degree of social and rhetorical power. This power, however, is located in their visibility as good, modern neoliberal subjects. More to the point, while Lara and Dyann are queer by definition, their lifestyle still channels heteronormativity and procreative

futurity in a very conventional manner. Lee Edelman, in his text *No Future*, directly critiques the fact that the queer community and its activism is often caught up in normative narratives of success, especially as this drive connects to the creation of nuclear families, proposing instead that we not be so caught up in the notion of "reproductive futurity" or futurity at all. Judith Halberstam further takes up this critique in *The Queer Art of Failure*, articulating the notion that to "fail" might be more queer and politically radical than to succeed. That is, Halberstam is interested in probing the "darker territories of failure associated with futility, sterility, emptiness, loss, negative affect in general, and modes of unbecoming" (23). Dyann and Lara, with their concern for fertility, fullness, and positive affects, such as care for the bodily health and diet of their children, are prime examples of what Edelman and Halberstam want to avoid in the realm of queer life and theory. They are, in spite of their queer coupling, legible to most readers because of their adherence to conventional modes of success and the way in which Jane frames them through a lens of positivity and love: as "uplifting, a powerful affirmation of difference, of race and gender and the many faces of motherhood" (Ozeki 177). Constructing Dyann, Lara, and their emphatically vegetarian food practices in such a way encourages readers /149
to identify with their ethical, bodily and emotionally sustainable way of life. Similarly, Akiko feels so intimately connected to these women that she begins to question her own marriage and sexuality—though notably never her desire for a child of her own.

Akiko, the second protagonist of Ozeki's novel, therefore also emerges as an important rhetorical figure through her framing as a non-Western other who desperately craves the life that Jane presents to her via *My American Wife!*. In addition, the manner in which she unquestionably consumes and identifies with the families and women on Jane's program—as well as the wide variety of food they prepare—sets her up as a model for the reader's own affective, identificatory responses to these diverse characters. In a noteworthy example, Akiko writes in a fax to Jane:

> But I am most wanting to say that I listen to the black lady say she never want man in her life, and all of a sudden I agree! I am so surprising that I cry! (I do not know if I am Lesbian since I cannot imagine this condition, but I know I never want marriage and with my deep heart I am not "John's" wife.) I feel such sadness for my lying life. So I now wish to ask you where can I go to live my happy life like her? Please tell me this. (214)

Akiko has such a strong emotional or *affective* reaction to the program with Dyann and Lara that she is moved to tears. And through Jane's framing of their lives as happy and (literally and emotionally) healthy, Akiko is persuaded to seek out this happiness in her own life, even as it requires her to physically migrate to a new location in order for her to construct a life of safe, healthy consumption and "good feeling" for her and her child. Although her pregnancy results from the violent circumstances of an assault by her husband, Akiko nevertheless strives to produce a "positive" outcome by deciding to carry and love her future offspring in what she deems to be a better environment.

In the end, after the graphically intense scene in which she is raped by her husband,[1] Akiko is, nonetheless, so inspired by the wives like Grace Beaudroux and Lara and Dyann, that she decides to leave her husband and travel to the United States to give birth to her own child. The violent—almost sensationally violent—rape scene is obviously meant to evoke outrage and pity in the reader, just as Jane feels equally moved to compassion for these women she has never met. At the same time, any negative feelings are quickly pushed aside in favor of emphasizing the love for her unborn child that motivates Akiko's decision to leave Japan for the "happy" location of America. This

location becomes especially important to Akiko when she learns that she is going to have a daughter. She explains to the nurse who befriends her while recuperating after the rape that "that's why I'm going to America. . . . It doesn't matter so much for a son, but since she's a girl, I want her to be an American citizen. So she can grow up to be an American Wife" (318). Discourses of citizenship, access, and rights are shown here to be intimately tied up with gender—and the West is the location that provides the greatest safety and access for women. In this way, *My Year of Meats* taps into the discourse of global feminism and the more problematic rhetoric of transnationality.

Akiko, through Japan's economic and mediated relationship with the United States, has come to understand what it means to be an American citizen but primarily via consumer culture and marketing. Inderpal Grewal explains that, particularly during the time of the novel, "America functioned as a discourse of neoliberalism making possible struggles for rights through consumerist practices and imaginaries that came to be used both inside and outside the territorial boundaries of the United States" (2). In other words, America comes to represent both a desired location and an idealized model of the "good" (in other words, healthy, safe, sustainable, and nourishing) life. And by propelling Akiko to the United States in what reads at times like a trite self-help narrative, *My Year of Meats* seems to corroborate this troubling use of politicized affect that produces and maintains unequal relationships between the United States and its seemingly less modern foreign counterparts.

The "feel good" narrative arc of Akiko's journey, and of *My Year of Meats* as a whole, is most apparent in a concluding scene of the novel, wherein Akiko is leaving Louisiana on a passenger train after visiting the Beaudroux family. In a moment rich with affect and sentimentality, the hyperracialized black conductor, Maurice, welcomes Akiko, an obviously foreign body, to the "Chicken Bone Special." And after introducing herself, Maurice encourages the other passengers (who are all families of color) to share their food with her. Filled with intense feelings of joy, "Akiko clapped her hands in time and looked around her at the long coach filled with singing people. This would never happen on the train in Hokkaido! For the second time since she left Japan, she shivered with excitement" (339). Akiko, in this instance, has been fully embraced and nourished by a collective body of friendly, loving, and accepting Americans, who are notably racialized, though in a way different from her. The passengers on the train—and thus America writ large—are, in fact, configured as a literal body into which Akiko is "absorbed" and then starts to "infuse her small heart with the superabundance of feeling" (339). This superabundance of feeling is directly connected to the excess of good feeling that Sara Ahmed identifies as crucial to assimilation into a multicultural body politic. As Ahmed writes, "the shift from unhappy to happy multiculturalism involves the demand for interaction. Happiness is projected into the future: when we have 'cracked the problem' through interaction, we can be happy with diversity" (122).

The scene of cooperative and multiracial interaction on the Chicken Bone Special exemplifies this kind of happy multiculturalism—a multiculturalism that also relies on gendered and racialized stereotypes. America is represented in this isolated moment as a racialized and feminized body that promises to nurture those who need it, to provide sustenance in particular to immigrants from far-flung and unsustainable locations. At the same time, it problematically renders African American men and women as little more than kindhearted caricatures, as symbolic providers of American generosity, rather than individuals who have been victimized by neoliberal capitalism. Naturally, to have Akiko's emotionally trying story end in such a way simplifies experiences of difference for racialized citizens and immigrants alike but also effectively (and affectively) foregrounds food and nourishment as a promise of the American experience for those who seek it out. The trope of the "happy ending" in this moment may ring false to some readers but also meets the generic expectations of many others, who read on hoping to see the positive results of social and political change that Ozeki and her narrator Jane continually emphasize.

My Year of Meats utilizes a rhetoric of good feeling and embodied love and care to varying degrees of political effect, oftentimes in problematic or contrived ways. I would, however, like to end with a gesture toward a generous reading of Ozeki's text, in which perhaps the very frustrations and tensions that emerge in the novel are, in fact, moments of necessary and intentional critique. Monica Chiu suggests a similar reading when she states that "Jane's propensity to showcase a troubling form of immigrant nostalgia eventually guides her actions. . . . This seeming textual schizophrenia is Ozeki's criticism of both Joichi's [John's] whitewashed views of America and Jane's presentations of happy multiculturalism" (144). Read in this manner, Ozeki's novel utilizes this troubling affective-laden neoliberal discourse as a means to also demonstrate its flaws. I think such a reading is possible when taking the ending of Jane's own story into consideration. While she was able to persuade a fair number of viewers with her exposé of the meat industry, she still feels unsatisfied with the results. She explains that she is "haunted by all the things—big things and little things, Splendid Things and Squalid Things—that threaten to slip through the cracks, untold, out of history" (360). Jane is troubled by the fact that, as a documentarian, she is ultimately unable to tell the complete story, the whole truth.

The difficulties with truthful and (auto)biographical representation appear in Ozeki's other work, especially her own film work, which Eve Oishi refers to as "fake documentary" for its explicitly fictionalized and inauthentic framing of "true" stories. Ozeki's "documentaries" push the limits of truth and memory (Oishi 204), and it is this framework that may allow us to consider the documentaries of *My Year of Meats* in the same fashion. That is, by having Jane express her own doubts about the effects of her work, it can be said that Ozeki herself is aware of the limits of the rhetoric, the appeal to pathos, she relies on to convey her political message.

It is certainly the case that, while my students often felt a degree of attachment to characters and events in *My Year of Meats*, they were also at times quite skeptical of the sensational, the sentimental, and the overly positive aspects of the text. They admire the Beaudroux family's ethical inclinations toward adoption and the way gender roles are reversed in their kitchen, but they also find the sentimentality of their full and loving family overwrought and are hesitant to embrace their "spectacular" motivations. They are glad to see Akiko escape her abusive husband, but sometimes even find themselves scoffing at her idealized adventure on the passenger train.

Given these affective reactions, it is worth considering that Ozeki's novel is meant to provoke readers to "question whether the emphasis on cultural diversity [is] really meant to understand people from different cultural and racial backgrounds, or whether it merely serves as an advertisement of 'America'" (Chae 119), an advertisement whose truth both Ozeki and Jane seem to display skepticism towards. With this nuanced reading of Ozeki's affective rhetorical strategy in mind, it seems to me that *My Year of Meats* offers a great deal of pedagogical possibility. By identifying and analyzing the moments in the text that produce and reinforce good feeling and critiquing the limits of these moments, readers may be able to understand the political importance of sustainable food production and consumption, while also being cognizant of the troubling racialized and gendered "superabundance of feeling" that is so often embedded in the framing of food practices. Such framing is most troubling, as can be seen in *My Year of Meats*, because of the way it reinforces binary notions of transnational economic and food systems that place the United States at the center, even as it points out the bodily hazards and unsustainable results of US modes of consumption. Although Ozeki does not necessarily offer an unproblematized alternative, her novel and its rhetorical strategies can push readers to theorize how alternative consumption, lifestyles, and meals might look.   / 153

Note

1. The inclusion of this rape scene, as well as a scene in which John sexually assaults Jane, is another problematic aspect of Ozeki's novel, in terms of both feminist praxis and affective response. However, due the scope of my argument, I do not have time to thoroughly unpack this aspect of the text.

Works Cited

Ahmed, Sara. *The Promise of Happiness*. Duke UP, 2010.

Carruth, Allison. "Postindustrial Pastoral: Ruth Ozeki and the New Muckrakers." *Global Appetites: American Power and the Literature of Food*. Cambridge UP, 2013. 117–53.

Chae, Youngsuk. "Counteracting the Hegemonic Discourse of 'America': Ruth Ozeki's *My Year of Meats*." *Politicizing Asian American Literature: Towards a Critical Multiculturalism*. Routledge, 2008. 107–25.

Cheng, Emily. "Meat and the Millennium: Transnational Politics of Race and Gender in Ruth Ozeki's *My Year of Meats*." *Journal of Asian American Studies* 12.2 (2009): 191–220.

Chiu, Monica. "Inside the Meat Machine: Food, Filth, and (In)fertility in Ruth Ozeki's *My Year of Meats*." *Filthy Fictions: Asian American Literature by Women*. AltaMira P, 2004. 133–66.

Edelman, Lee. *No Future: Queer Theory and the Death Drive.* Duke UP, 2004.

Eng, David L. *The Feeling of Kinship: Queer Liberalism and the Racialization of Intimacy.* Duke UP, 2010.

Grewal, Inderpal. *Transnational America: Feminisms, Diasporas, Neoliberalisms.* Duke UP, 2005.

Halberstam, Judith. *The Queer Art of Failure.* Duke UP, 2011.

Hesford, Wendy S. *Spectacular Rhetorics: Human Rights Visions, Recognitions, Feminisms.* Duke UP, 2011.

Oishi, Eve. "Screen Memories: Fakeness in Asian American Media Practice." *F Is for Phony: Fake Documentary and Truth's Undoing.* Ed. Alexandra Juhasz and Jesse Lerner. U of Minnesota P, 2006. 196–219.

Ozeki, Ruth L. *My Year of Meats.* Penguin Books, 1998.

11. SUGAR AND SPICE: COOKING WITH THE GIRL POISONER

Sylvia A. Pamboukian

From the Queen in "Snow White" to the White Witch in *The Lion, the Witch,* / 155 *and the Wardrobe* (1950) to Yubaba in Hayao Miyazaki's *Spirited Away* (2001), women poisoners in children's literature and films pervert the traditionally feminine roles of food-preparer and caregiver. In place of wholesome food and pleasing treats, these women, pejoratively labeled witches, offer tainted food and drink, whether impregnated with toxins, as Snow White's apple, or with magic, as the White Witch's Turkish delights and Yubaba's buffet. One might expect girls who offer noxious food and drink to play a similarly villainous role; however, the girl poisoner is more likely to be a high-spirited and likable figure who offers tainted food and drink to her family and friends with amusing results. In stories from *Anne of Green Gables* (1908) to *Brave* (2012), the girl poisoner's activities are treated as lighthearted misadventures rather than sinister signs of perverse femininity. Or are they? Do girl poisoners ultimately reinforce traditional femininity? Or, is the girl poisoner a subversive figure who undermines the "angel in the house" ideology so common in children's literature?

As Wendy Katz contends, children's literature is "filled with food-related images, notions, and values" (192).[1] Many heroines of classic children's literature are strongly associated with food sharing, as with Sara in *A Little Princess* (1905), Rebecca in *Rebecca of Sunnybrook Farm* (1903), Beth in *Little Women* (1868), and Helen Burns in *Jane Eyre* (1847). The heroism of food sharing is readily apparent in Helen Burns, who shares her meager ration of bread with Jane Eyre while literally starving herself.[2] By the end of *The Secret Garden* (1911), even contrary Mary Lennox arranges picnics for her sickly cousin Colin as a sign of her amelioration. In these texts, food sharing highlights the qualities that make a girl good: selflessness and caregiving. This configuration of girlhood is similar to that of Victorian womanhood, famously described by John Ruskin in *Sesame and Lilies* (1865):

> [The Victorian woman] must be enduringly, incorruptibly good; instinctively, infallibly wise—wise, not for self-development, but for self-renunciation: wise, not that she may set herself above her husband, but that she may never fail from his side: wise, not with the narrowness of insolent and loveless pride, but with the passionate gentleness of an infinitely variable, because infinitely applicable, modesty of service—the true changefulness of woman. ("Lecture Two")

Ruskin suggests two methods by which girls become such women. First, Ruskin advises reading about womanly qualities in "a good library of old and classical books" ("Lecture Two"). Second, his "Preface to the Later Editions" recommends that girls study cooking and practice food sharing:

> Learn first thoroughly the economy of the kitchen; the good and bad qualities of every common article of food, and the simplest and best modes of their preparation: when you have time, go and help in the cooking of poorer families, and show them how to make as much of everything as possible, and how to make little, nice; coaxing and tempting them into tidy and pretty ways, and pleading for well-folded table-cloths, however coarse, and for a flower or two out of the garden to strew on them.

Although he prefers the classics, Ruskin shares the values of the literary good-girl heroines who possess his quintessentially feminine qualities of selflessness and caregiving and who, through food sharing, model appropriate behavior for real-life readers. But what of literary heroines who poison instead of nourish?

The girl poisoner engages in a perverse form of food sharing and so might expect to be viewed as an unfeminine, unsympathetic figure, akin to the witchy woman poisoner. But that is not the case. A quick example clarifies the girl poisoner's transgressive yet likable nature. Frances Hodgson Burnett's Mary Lennox appears in many critical works about children's literature and food, but one significant meal is often overlooked. In the opening chapter of

The Secret Garden, young Mary, described "as tyrannical and selfish a little pig as ever lived," finds herself abandoned in the nursery (2). She eventually emerges to eat the remnants of her parents' deserted dinner. This meal is peculiarly significant because it establishes not merely the contrariness of Mary's character but her sympathetic, even heroic, status. Mary defies a boundary when she emerges from the nursery, the part of the house to which children are relegated in the proper Victorian/Edwardian home. She transgresses another restriction when she chooses adult foods, such as wine, biscuits, and fruit, rather than foods thought appropriate for children at the time. All of her choices are described as "sweet" and thus are, quite literally, forbidden fruit. In eating and drinking from other people's half-finished plates and cups, Mary crosses another social boundary, since scraps are not proper food for a well-brought-up girl. In feeding herself, Mary rejects the self-lessness of the good girl, who does not give in to appetite. Most significantly, Mary unwittingly dares a most horrible form of food poisoning. Readers, if not Mary herself, understand that the house is in the grip of a cholera epidemic. Often fatal, cholera is transmitted by tainted food or drink (including food handled by the improperly washed hands of victims). No adult would eat from the plate of a cholera victim. But Mary's transgressions, especially her almost-self-poisoning, do not function in the negative fashion of the woman poisoner's. In eating this forbidden, possibly poisoned, meal herself, Mary displays the mixture of stubbornness, resilience, and ignorance of the adult world that turns the unpleasant little girl into a heroine. Mary's offences transform her contrariness, a trait with negative connotations of selfishness, disobedience, and willfulness, into independence and resilience, positive traits not usually applied to Edwardian girls.[3] In presenting the specter of a most terrible type of food poisoning, Burnett at a stroke makes readers warm to this unattractive child because of Mary's neglected and unfed condition and because of her plucky, if dangerous, self-assertion at the table.

/ 157

In the case of Mary, food poisoning (or potential food poisoning) involves the transgression of many cultural norms. Similarly, critics of sensation fiction and of real-life Victorian poisoning cases assert that the horror of the woman poisoner lies in her transgression of gender norms, in addition to breaking legal statutes.[4] For example, Judith Knelman's study of Victorian women murderers, including noted poisoners Mary Ann Cotton and Florence Maybrick, finds such women represented in the press as "inhuman" (82) and "monster[s]" (53), because they seemed to break natural laws dictating that women be domestic caregivers, whether wife, mother, or servant (228). Words such as *monster* highlight the dissonance between Ruskin's domestic ethos and the woman poisoner's deliberate introduction of external toxins, such as arsenic in Cotton's case, into food for the purpose of escaping domestic responsibility. Even when noxious food is accidentally introduced into the home, as with the cholera-tainted food and drink in *The Secret Garden*, there is the potential to destabilize gender norms. Rebecca Stern claims that commercially adulterated food undermines the notion of separate spheres because it may "invade and infect that home life [and] emphasizes the proximity of economic and domestic concerns" (91). Tainted food destroys the notion that homemade food (and the home in general) is somehow privileged, exempt from public concerns, such as sanitation and public health. Mary Lennox's mother stays in her bungalow and hosts a dinner party, but her prettiness, fine manners, and food sharing are no barrier to the cholera. Both Mary's cholera and Cotton's arsenic are life-threatening; however, nonfatal gastrointestinal distress due to mistakes in food handling, whether the accidental introduction of bacteria and toxins or the failure to recognize food's natural spoilage, is more commonly what we mean when we use the term *food poisoning* in everyday speech. Whether serious or minor, criminal or accidental, food poisoning potentially transgresses gender norms, but women poisoners are not viewed sympathetically. For sympathetic poisoners, one must turn to children's literature.

Unlike the woman poisoner, the girl poisoner is applauded by readers. Holly Blackford argues that literary scenes of food and of food preparation are ambivalent, reinforcing or challenging cultural norms. She writes,

> Cooking is a form of self-control and a way to prepare the female character for repressing inner needs, packaging the self and female body for the pleasure of others. However, cooking is also an aesthetic expression of the female self, a subtle expression of female desire that can take on a life of its own . . . and contradict the intended lesson in self-denial. ("Recipe" 42)[5]

Like Mary, girl poisoners display traits not usually associated with good-girl heroines: independence, resilience, and naiveté, and readers warm to them expressly because of these qualities.[6] The naiveté of the girl poisoner is important. Sarah Bilston identifies age as vital in controlling sympathy because some writers "were prepared to represent *girls* yearning for self-actualization and self-determination when they were unwilling to depict *women* exhibiting these desires" (7). Similarly, U. C. Knoepflmacher argues that children's literature is able to represent female aggression because of the heroine's age: "Women writers began to portray little girls who were allowed to express hostility without the curbs on female rebelliousness that had been placed earlier, in children's literature as well as adult fiction" (14). Bilston and Knoepflmacher agree that literary girls and women may serve different rhetorical purposes. In poisoning stories, the woman poisoner is depicted with malicious and selfish purpose and often using a serious or horrified tone. Depicted in a comic register, the girl poisoner is credited with innocent purposes, merely making mistakes or displaying her imperfect stage of education. Following Bilston, one might argue that the girl poisoner is a naive child who toys with but ultimately maintains hegemonic femininity. Conversely, one might expand on Knoepflmacher and view the adolescent girl poisoner as subversive, both in the text and in the real world. In the latter case, the authors' purpose is to mount a serious critique of gender using the comic figure of the naive girl poisoner. Because she is likeable and fun, the girl poisoner potentially offers readers, both children and adults, a model of positive femininity (kind, generous, affectionate) without the self-negation and restraint of the Victorian/Edwardian ideal.

Louisa May Alcott's *Little Women* has been called ambivalent because Jo March is often viewed as a rebel, while the novel as a whole explicitly promotes the ideal in which girls are domestic, self-sacrificing, and obedient.[7] A chapter called "Experiments" depicts this tension between bolstering the dominant hegemony and subverting it. In this chapter, the girls shirk their usual tasks, so Marmee, determined to make them regret it, leaves them the cooking. Meg and Jo serve Marmee an inedible breakfast of bitter tea, burned omelet, and unmixed biscuits, and Marmee "laughs heartily" over the mess, disposes of it and eats a secret meal in her room (345). In charge of dinner, Jo does the shopping, but her "good bargains" consist of a "young lobster, some very old asparagus, and two boxes of acid strawberries" (346). In preparing dinner for herself, her sisters, Laurie, and a visitor, Miss Crocker, Jo overboils the asparagus, burns the bread, ruins the salad dressing, mangles the lobster, salts the fruit, and sours the cream (347). After this inedible meal, Jo serves another dinner of "bread and butter, olives and fun" (347). At the conclusion of the chapter, Marmee lectures the girls on the evils of selfishness and shirking and suggests Jo study cooking. On one hand, Marmee's lecture and the girls' promises of future obedience explicitly encourage a model of traditional femininity based on domesticity, self-sacrifice, and submission to authority. On the other hand, the symbolism surrounding the noxious food in this chapter subverts the lesson.

As with Mary, there is an association here between noxious food and transgression. In serving Marmee upstairs, Jo and Meg transgress between spaces usually segregated in the middle-class home. They cross the limits of

/ 159

childhood by choosing which foods to eat and how to prepare them. Their breakfast challenges the boundary of proper food: the omelet and tea are too cooked, the biscuits not cooked enough. If not as dangerous as cholera, undercooked food is unappetizing at best, a source of gastrointestinal distress (in common parlance *food poisoning*) at worst, and this is true also of Jo's dinner, which includes spoiled dairy and questionable seafood. As Stern asserts, Jo's purchases undermine the boundary between public and domestic by revealing the external roots of home-cooking. Jo's dinner is noxious because her purchases are noxious: too young, too old, too acidic. On one hand, Meg and Jo's desire to prepare and share food reinforces food sharing as a symbol of femininity. On the other hand, the harmful food symbolizes qualities not usually associated with good-girl heroines: independence, resilience, creativity, and naiveté. The little women share noxious food because of their desire to make independent choices and to assert individual preferences. They want a vacation from obedience and selflessness, and, although toxic food may be viewed as a punishment for these desires, the reader's enjoyment of their adventures and of the comedic tone seems to celebrate such desires.

Bilston argues that girl heroines may be allowed latitude not permitted to women, and the girl poisoner's naiveté seems to support this contention: we sympathize with Mary, Jo, and Meg because we see, as they do not, the pitfalls surrounding them. If adding to their likability, naiveté does not wholly undermine the girl poisoner's subversiveness because readers admire the girls for bravely plunging ahead anyway and for coping with unexpected results, conduct that might otherwise be labeled selfish, disobedient, or, in Mary's case, contrary. The girl poisoner is also subversive because of her influence on women: by transgressing food norms, she encourages women to change their symbolic relationship to food and thus to femininity. For example, Marmee's decision to leave the cooking to the girls is explicitly framed as a lesson, but it makes Marmee admit, "I never enjoyed housekeeping, and I'm going to take a vacation today, and read, write, go visiting, and amuse myself" (345).[8] This can be read simply as part of the lesson; however, Marmee's admission echoes the girls' language and her secret eating in her bedroom echoes Jo's snacking on apples in the attic. Both Jo and Marmee evidently enjoy eating purloined food in improper places at unusual times, temporarily defying propriety. Although an adult, Marmee is applauded by readers for escaping domesticity because Alcott depicts her purposes as innocent, enjoyment for herself and education for the girls. Moreover, Alcott represents Marmee with a comic tone, just as she depicts the wayward girls. When Marmee laughs about Jo and Meg's breakfast, she abandons her usual grave and wise demeanor (345). There are few chapters in which we see the emotions she usually represses. Similarly, Jo's terrible dinner frees censorious old spinster Miss Crocker from her narrow female interests of visiting and gossip. Where the girls called Miss Crocker "Croaker" because of her usually sour disposition, Jo's dinner turns her into a laughing girl again. She is part of the childish meal of bread, butter, olives, and fun, rather than enforcing the strict standards of domesticity symbolized by complex dishes. In this chapter, the cheerful tone with which noxious food is treated undermines Marmee's dreary lesson and the novel's conventional plot, both for the little women and for the grown women, including, of course, the novel's child and adult readers.

Like Jo and Meg, Anne Shirley in Lucy Maud Montgomery's *Anne of Green Gables* is associated with food poisoning and transgression. Anne is an unattractive, red-haired orphan who is adopted by siblings Matthew and Marilla Cuthbert of Prince Edward Island, Canada. At first, gossipy Mrs. Lynde objects because an orphan girl, she asserts, might put "strychnine in the well" (7). In one sense, Mrs. Lynde's association between orphans, transgression, and poison proves accurate, for Anne has a strong association with food poisoning, if not with malice. Where Jo and Meg merely mishandle food, Anne, like a woman poisoner, often introduces external toxins, but not the strychnine that so worries Mrs. Lynde. First, Anne invites her friend Diana Barry for tea and serves currant wine instead of raspberry cordial. After three glassfuls, Diana drunkenly staggers home and is forbidden from associating with Anne, whom Mrs. Barry believes gave Diana alcohol maliciously. Julie E. Fromer examines tea rituals in English literature and finds that adulterated tea and disrupted tea services represent major disruptions of the social order (166).[9] Second, as Diana is drinking her wine/cordial, Anne tells of another incident in which she was to cover the sauce for the plum pudding. Imagining herself a nun, Anne left the pitcher open overnight and then discovered a drowned mouse in the sauce. Imagining herself a frost fairy, Anne forgets to tell Marilla about the mouse before company arrives, and Marilla serves the pudding and sauce. Anne shrieks a warning before anybody eats, but Anne and Marilla are embarrassed at almost serving guests mouse-tainted sauce (125). The third incident involves Anne imagining herself as a nurse in a smallpox hospital and results in Anne forgetting to put flour in a cake, ruining the recipe. Finally, Anne prepares a layer cake for the minister's wife, Mrs. Allan, which the lady gamely tries to eat. However, Marilla tastes it and discovers it is flavored with liniment instead of vanilla (175). On one hand, these incidents highlight Anne's desire to share food and her humiliation at being a bad cook, implying that this is an area in which girls should excel. On the other hand, these incidents undermine the notion of women as naturally domestic. Like Jo, Anne is not a natural cook. The scenes also emphasize Anne's imaginative fascination with roles outside the domestic sphere, whether nun, nurse, fairy, or other fanciful activity.

Katz compares Anne to Huck Finn as a child impatient with the limits of the adult world (196); however, unlike Huck, Anne not only transgresses herself but encourages women to transgress as well. Like Mary, Anne is temperamental, and she stamps her feet and scolds Mrs. Lynde when the matriarch criticizes her red hair (65). Anne's transgression releases a repressed girlishness in Marilla: after properly rebuking Anne for her temper, Marilla feels a desire to laugh at Anne's outspoken defense of ugly girls (69). Marilla enjoys Anne's conduct since as a child she silently submitted to an elder calling her a "homely" girl, although she was "every day of fifty before the sting had gone out of that memory" (68). Marilla later says of Anne, "It almost seemed to her that those secret, unuttered, critical thoughts had suddenly taken visible and accusing shape and form in the person of this outspoken morsel of neglected humanity" (83). After Anne apologizes, Mrs.

Lynde consoles her for having red hair by reverting to childhood herself, recalling a school friend whose red hair turned auburn over time. Similarly, Mrs. Allan laughs at Anne's liniment cake and reassures Anne when the girl blurts out her fears: "She'll think I tried to poison her. Mrs. Lynde says she knows an orphan girl who tried to poison her benefactor" (176). For Marilla, Mrs. Lynde, and Mrs. Allan, Anne's poisonings are not proof of the orphan girl's antisocial nature but an opportunity to readjust conventions that would label Anne bad. This is particularly true for Marilla since she participates in Anne's poisonings. Just as Anne (in part) recalls the woman poisoner by introducing external toxins into food, Marilla (in part) recalls the girl poisoner by creating noxious food accidentally and with good intentions. Marilla admits that it was she who broke the liniment bottle and poured the remaining liniment into an empty vanilla bottle, causing the mistake with Mrs. Allan's cake. Marilla also placed the raspberry cordial in the cellar, not the pantry as she told Anne, and is partly responsible for giving alcohol to Diana Barry, alcohol the Barrys criticized her for keeping in the first place. Through Marilla, Montgomery undermines the notion that women are naturally wise and domestic: womanhood has its errors as well as girlhood.[10] In addition, Marilla's desire to keep wine despite disapproval shows her own independence. Thus, the novel depicts not simply Anne's training in propriety but Marilla's (and Mrs. Lynde's and later Old Aunt

Barry's) relaxation of femininity's strict boundaries, encouraging readers to do the same. Only Mrs. Barry sees Anne's poisonings as malicious, but readers view her unsympathetically as too rigid. When Anne gives Minnie Barry ipecac (a most noxious remedy) to save her from choking, Mrs. Barry joins readers in realizing that a traditionally unfeminine girl may not be a villain but a heroine.

These iconic heroines date from the golden age of children's literature. While girls in late twentieth-century novels might not be expected to enact the same notions of femininity, Hermione Granger in the Harry Potter series is often a good girl in the same sense: obedient to authority and caregiving (especially to the marginalized, such as Neville Longbottom and Dobby).[11] Similarly, Hermione's poisonings in *Harry Potter and the Chamber of Secrets* (1998) emphasize her independence, resilience, and likability.[12] In this novel, Hermione illicitly brews "Polyjuice Potion" and "Sleeping Draught Potion" so that she, Harry, and Ron Weasley can impersonate members of Slytherin House and find the mysterious Heir of Slytherin who is threatening to kill Hogwart's Muggle-born students (students from nonmagical families). In her first poisoning, Hermione spikes two cupcakes with Sleeping Draught, and Harry and Ron give them to Slytherin House members Crabbe and Goyle. After the boys eat, they fall asleep so Harry and Ron put them in a broom closet and take pieces of their hair to complete the Polyjuice Potion. The second poisoning involves Hermione's own portion of the Polyjuice Potion.

Hermione's poisonings transgress many boundaries: she breaks school rules by fraudulently obtaining the potion book *Moste Potente Potions* with which to make the Polyjuice Potion and by stealing ingredients for it (215). She breaks social taboos when she brews it in a bathroom rather than a laboratory or kitchen, and she challenges gender norms when she chooses a girls' bathroom, since Harry and Ron do not usually enter girls' bathrooms. The haunted bathroom magically transgresses the boundary between life and death, and the potion itself magically crosses boundaries of identity. The transgressiveness of Hermione's conduct is emphasized by Ron, who says, "I never thought I'd see the day when you'd be persuading us to break rules" (166). In some sense, Hermione's deliberate poisoning of Crabbe and Goyle breaks with the girl poisoner tradition, where poisonings are unintentional and lighthearted in tone. At the same time, Hermione participates in a fairy tale tradition, as in the Grimm brothers' "The Peasant's Wise Daughter" and "The Two King's Children," in which the victim is drugged but unharmed. Moreover, Crabbe and Goyle are unsympathetic, described as bullies who are "thick" (meaning stupid) and "greedy" (213–14). Most importantly, this poisoning is designed less to harm the boys than to protect vulnerable Muggle-borns, an intentional poisoning but for noble purpose. As Hermione says, her serious tone reflected by J. K. Rowling's italics, "*I* don't want to break rules, you know. *I* think threatening Muggle-borns is far worse than brewing up a difficult potion" (165). Far from malicious, Hermione's poisoning of Crabbe and Goyle reflects her heroic defense of the marginalized, a powerful reconfiguration of the good girl's selflessness and caregiving.

Hermione's more traditional second poisoning is accidental and comedic. Hermione doses Ron and Harry with the hair from Crabbe and Goyle and herself with a hair plucked from the robes of Slytherin Millicent Bulstrode. Unfortunately, this hair is not Millicent's hair but Millicent's cat's hair. Hermione's unwitting use of cat hair transforms her into a cat-girl, with black fur, yellow eyes, and pointy ears. Unable to go with Ron and Harry to the Slytherin common room, Hermione lurks in the bathroom stall and emerges "sobbing, her robes pulled up over her head" (225), as ghost Moaning Myrtle laughs. She spends several weeks in the infirmary "to spare her the shame of being seen with a furry face" (227). Just as Anne cannot hold a grown-up tea party or Mary eat from the adults' table without the specter of poisoning, Hermione is not quite able to manage the Polyjuice Potion. That she herself is poisoned serves as both ironic punishment for drugging Crabbe and Goyle (through Millicent's cat, however, the Slytherins have their revenge!) and as comedic culinary mix-up, akin to Anne's liniment cake or Jo's salted strawberries. Despite the deliberate poisoning of Crabbe and Goyle, Hermione displays the same youthful enthusiasm and inexperience as earlier girl poisoners, as well as their overall good intentions, and, like them, she becomes more likable, and even heroic, because of her poisonings.

In contrast, Pixar's film *Brave* strains the likability of the girl poisoner. The film tries to challenge the stereotypes of Disney princesses by portraying Scottish princess Merida with unruly red hair and great skill at archery, although the symbolism of red hair and transgression recalls Anne Shirley.[13] Merida rejects her mother's advice to behave in a conventionally ladylike fashion and to submit to an arranged marriage. Instead, Merida seeks out a witch who gives her a cake to feed her mother in order to change her mother's mind. However, the magical cake transforms her mother's body into a bear, an animal enthusiastically hunted in the Scotland of the film. The comic relief is provided by Merida's treatment of the leftover cake: she leaves it in the kitchen and her three toddler brothers eat it and transform into baby bears. On one hand, Merida seems to draw upon the figure of the girl poisoner, where poisoning is unwitting mischief: Merida does not intend to transform her mother and brothers into bears. It also tries to depict poisoning as positive for women. After fleeing the castle, Merida and her mother embark on an adventurous exile in the woods during which her mother relaxes her usually rigid domestic rules about eating with a fork and fishing in the wild.[14]

On the other hand, Merida departs from the girl poisoner figure in several key ways. First, she deliberately feeds tainted food to her mother as part of a plot to further her own goals at her mother's expense, a purpose that strongly recalls the woman poisoner. Critics that praised Merida's feminist rejection of the marriage plot tend to gloss over her deliberate poisoning of her mother.[15] But the queen's poisoning did not sit well with some critics, who describe Queen Elinor's thrashings at realizing her new state and her frantic flight from her castle, hunted by her own husband, as horrifying rather than comic.[16] For these critics, the film's lighthearted tone seemed inappropriate to such dark events. As her mother doubles over with nausea during the transformation, Merida repeatedly asks whether she has changed her mind about the marriage, an unsympathetic and selfish reaction. Second, the plot involves a stereotypical witch figure, who provides the poisoned cake as well as the complicated remedy. It seems as if the film is trying both to subvert (in Merida) and to employ (in the queen and the Witch) anti-feminine stereotypes.[17] Third, the harm Merida inflicts is too severe to be called mere mischief. Unlike Marilla or Marmee, Queen Elinor cannot laugh at her situation because she is completely deprived of human speech. The bear-queen's wordless (and truly brave) attempts to maintain her humanity after her daughter poisons her are at times quite sad, more so since Merida ridicules her. Unlike Hermione, Merida does not poison herself, thereby gaining sympathy. Unlike Anne and the mouse-tainted sauce, Merida fails to warn her brothers about the cake. Unlike Anne, Hermione, and Jo, Merida causes life-threatening harm through deliberate poisoning for personal gain. Finally, Merida does not so much free her mother as degrade her to subhuman. In *Brave*, the girl poisoner *begins* the plot as likable, resilient, and independent, so the act of poisoning does not serve the usual rhetorical purposes and thus takes Merida on quite a different trajectory.

In some ways, the girl poisoner reinforces the hegemonic femininity of the golden age of children's literature by retaining the association between femininity and food sharing, just as in the good-girl heroines of Victorian and Edwardian literature. But the symbolism of food sharing is complicated by the specter of food poisoning, whether the food is actually noxious (as in Diana's cordial or Hermione's potion), potentially harmful (as in Mary's dinner or Jo's soured cream), intrinsically spoiled (as in Meg's undercooked biscuits), or externally tainted (as with Hermione's cupcakes). The specter of food poisoning is significant even if the victims do not eat it, as with Anne's mouse sauce and Meg and Jo's breakfast. In each case, the real or believed presence of poisoned food acts as a visible fault line in conventional femininity: it undermines the coding of cooking as naturally feminine, the notion of separate spheres, the safety of the domestic, and the self-abnegating ideology of Victorian/Edwardian womanhood.

Even in modern stories, the girl poisoner is associated with independence and adventurousness. The girl poisoner's naiveté may be read as undermining her subversiveness by making her transgressions seem mere childish ignorance. Conversely, readers may admire her all the more for acting independently and for coping with unexpected results. This resilience undermines the belief that a girl needs domesticity for her own protection, for her transgressions result in comedy, not tragedy. Moreover, her transgressions offer opportunities for adult women, such as Marilla, Marmee, and even Queen Elinor, to alter their relationship to food and thus to conventional femininity, even reconciling poisoning (surely a most extreme rejection of conventional femininity) and likability. In place of the woman poisoners' single, malicious purpose, girls *and* women in girl poisoner stories may enact a variety of rhetorical purposes, thereby transgressing conventions of both age and gender. Characters such as Mary, Jo, Anne, and Hermione are beloved *because* of their poisonings, although, as Merida exemplifies, the girl poisoner risks being subsumed into the unsympathetic woman poisoner figure. If beloved by readers, the girl poisoner is a more radical figure than the unsympathetic woman poisoner. While the latter's transgressions are repugnant (because tragic), the girl poisoner's transgressions reflect similar desires for self-assertion and independence but make these desires harmless, loveable, and fun.

Notes

1. Building on Katz, Kara Keeling and Scott Pollard argue, "Food is fundamental to the imagination, because food is fundamental to culture" (5). In addition, Carolyn Daniel places food at the heart of identity: "To be a proper (human) subject one must eat in a controlled manner, according to cultural rules. Eating, and specifically the cultural imperative to eat correctly, is a significant means by which society controls individual identity" (3).

2. Because self-will and independence are coded as masculine, Daniel argues that good girls in fiction do not eat to show that historically women had "controlled and modest desires; they were compliant and submissive to those with authority over them" (39).

3. Mary's transgressive nature is a vexed issue. Elizabeth Keyser argues that Mary's disagreeableness lies in her ugly looks, manners, and disobedience: ironically, these are what make her sympathetic to readers (1). Alison Lurie also finds Mary's independence subversive (142). Frances Dolan sees the novel as a taming of the shrew plot, thereby accounting for the reader's feeling of loss when feisty Mary is transformed into a well-behaved girl (206). In contrast, Seth Lerer finds her subversive to the end because of her authority over Colin (246). Humphrey Carpenter dismisses Burnett as a writer of saccharine children's novels and claims that Mary is too derivative (188–89). Daniel finds Mary not subversive in her investment in imperialism (26).

4. Andrew Mangham argues that stories about women murderers in sensation novels and in the press challenge "angel in the house" stereotypes and reveal "a ghastly, destructive energy lurking beneath female spaces and feminine graces" (9). Lyn Pykett suggests that sensation novels were sites of negotiation, not necessarily subversive or supportive of dominant norms (50). Winifred Hughes claims that sensation fiction offers a site of resistance to the dominance of domesticity in realist fiction (36), but only certain authors, such as Mary Elizabeth Braddon, subvert the feminine ideal (124).

5. Similarly, Lerer argues, "Such books teach many things (social decorum, personal care, moral virtue); but what they teach most of all is the cultivation of the imagination" (251). Lurie notes, "Most of the great works of juvenile literature are subversive in one way or another: . . . they make fun of honored figures and piously held beliefs; and they view social pretenses with clear-eyed directness" (4). Daniel claims, "Food narratives in children's stories are often 'grounded in playfulness' and transgressive of adult food rules, not just in terms of 'foodbungling tricks' but also timing, sequence, quantity, and quality" (12).

/ 167

6. All of the heroines in this essay are "girl poisoners" in that they are treated as *girls* in their respective texts (in other words, not as marriageable adolescents, adult spinsters, or married women) and prepare *noxious* food, whether to eat themselves or offer to others, whether accidentally or deliberately. In this, I am including under the umbrella term *noxious foods* food carrying potentially fatal toxins and bacteria (for example, cholera) and food causing potentially distressing gastrointestinal or other physical symptoms through natural food spoilage (such as undercooked eggs) or poor cooking technique (using salt for sugar, for instance). That girl poisoners appear in British, American, and Canadian texts highlights the international nature of children's literature, both in the golden age and in modern wide-release novels and films.

7. Carpenter views *Little Women* as transgressive in the questioning of parental authority but as ultimately conservative (95). Going further, Lerer calls the novel puritanical (242).

8. Blackford identifies Marmee as a divine figure: "The magic of divine mothers is not reproducible by humankind daughters, who are quite imperfect" ("Recipe" 45). I am arguing that this chapter shows Marmee's imperfections.

9. Similarly, Katz notes the emphasis in British texts on tea as a symbol of civility (193). To modern readers, wine may not seem noxious or poisonous, but in the contemporary temperance movement it was called both.

10. In contrast, Blackford argues that Marilla's mistakes indicate ambivalence in the older woman, destined to be displaced by the younger generation ("Recipe" 49). Lerer also reads Marilla as ambivalent but finds the novel subversive: "Such scenes reflect on Montgomery's own lessons to female readers: that there is a place for the female imagination" (239). Similarly, Katz says of Anne, "We are meant to approve of her spirited untamed state as well as her later surrender to convention" (195).

11. Lerer argues that Hermione is the inheritor of centuries of girls' fiction and embodies a variety of subject positions, from tomboy to student to maiden (229). Ximena Gallardo-C. and C. Jason Smith suggest that Hermione is a traditional figure because of her motherly caretaking of the boys; however, they also note her position as a "Mudblood" and claim that the novel champions the marginal (193, 202). Blackford reads Hermione as masculine, unlike Ginny Weasley and Moaning Myrtle who embody emotion (*Myth of Persephone* 190).

12. In *Harry Potter and the Sorcerer's Stone* (1998), Hermione solves a puzzle involving a series of potions, one of which is poisonous, in a forbidden area of Hogwarts castle. The incident emphasizes her evolution from prissy rule-follower to daring young woman.

13. Recent Disney films complicate the good-girl figure, including *Tangled* (2010), about a princess who escapes from her tower and witch/kidnapper, and *The Princess and the Frog* (2009), featuring a waitress/restaurateur. The former challenges the idea that girls belong in the domestic sphere but retains the vain witch figure. The latter challenges the idea that cooking is feminine (it's her father's gumbo recipe) and that marriage requires leaving the workforce but retains the connection between food, caregiving, and love.

14. Following Melanie Klein, Blackford argues that mother figures are either "divine sacrificial objects" or "evil witches," and the former "nurture with edible gifts," but the latter may be "cannibalistic inversions of mothers" ("Recipe" 43). Indeed, in one scene, Queen Elinor chases around baby Merida saying that she is going to eat Merida up.

15. Peter Travers's review simply says that a witch transforms Merida's mother. Louise Keller says that it is a "spell gone wrong." Manohla Dargis calls it a "quirky spell" and blames the witch.

16. Several critics find the scenes of Queen Elinor as a bear too violent or too ill-conceived to be humorous, including Melissa Anderson, James Berardinelli, Todd McCarthy, and Roger Ebert. Berardinelli and Kenneth Turan lose sympathy with Merida, calling her "spoiled" and "bratty" because of her poisoning.

Tasha Robinson calls her "flighty" and "selfish." Merida admits to many of these qualities in her final speech before the Scottish lords, highlighting how poisoning serves an educative purpose.

17. Several reviewers, including McCarthy, Robinson, and Ebert, note the stereotypical characters.

Works Cited

Alcott, Louisa May. *Little Women*. 1868. *Classics of Children's Literature*. Ed. John W. Griffith and Charles H. Frey. 3rd ed. Macmillan, 1992. 272–424.

Anderson, Melissa. Rev. of *Brave*, dir. Mark Andrews and Brenda Chapman. *Village Voice Movies* 20 June 2012. Accessed 7 May 2014.

Berardinelli, James. Rev. of *Brave*, dir. Mark Andrews and Brenda Chapman. *Reelviews* 22 June 2012. Accessed 7 May 2014.

Bilston, Sarah. *The Awkward Age in Women's Popular Fiction, 1850–1900: Girls and the Transition to Womanhood*. Clarendon P, 2004.

Blackford, Holly Virginia. *The Myth of Persephone in Girls' Fantasy Literature*. Routledge, 2012.

———. "Recipe for Reciprocity and Repression: The Politics of Cooking and Consumption in Girls' Coming-of-Age Literature." *Critical Approaches to Food in Children's Literature*. Ed. Kara K. Keeling and Scott T. Pollard. Routledge, 2009. 41–56.

Brave. Dir. Mark Andrews and Brenda Chapman. Perf. Kelly Macdonald, Billy Connolly, and Emma Thompson. Disney/Pixar, 2012.

Burnett, Frances Hodgson. *The Secret Garden*. 1911. Puffin-Penguin, 2010.

Carpenter, Humphrey. *Secret Gardens: A Study of the Golden Age of Children's Literature*. Houghton Mifflin, 1985.

Daniel, Carolyn. *Voracious Children: Who Eats Whom in Children's Literature*. Routledge, 2006.

Dargis, Manohla. Rev. of *Brave*, dir. Mark Andrews and Brenda Chapman. *New York Times Movies* 21 June 2012. Accessed 7 May 2014.

Dolan, Frances E. "Mastery at Misselthwaite Manor: Taming the Shrews in *The Secret Garden*." *Children's Literature* 41 (2013): 204–24.

Ebert, Roger. Rev. of *Brave*, dir. Mark Andrews and Brenda Chapman. *Roger Ebert* 20 June 2012. Accessed 7 May 2014.

Fromer, Julie E. *A Necessary Luxury: Tea in Victorian England*. Ohio UP, 2008.

Gallardo-C., Ximena, and C. Jason Smith. "Cinderfella: J. K. Rowling's Wily Web of Gender." *Reading Harry Potter: Critical Essays*. Ed. Giselle Liza Anatol. Praeger, 2003. 191–205.

Hughes, Winifred. *The Maniac in the Cellar: Sensation Novels of the 1860s*. Princeton UP, 1980.

Katz, Wendy R. "Some Uses of Food in Children's Literature." *Children's Literature in Education* 11.4 (Winter 1980): 192–99.

Keeling, Kara K., and Scott T. Pollard. *Critical Approaches to Food in Children's Literature*. Routledge, 2009.

Keller, Louise. Rev. of *Brave*, dir. Mark Andrews and Brenda Chapman. *Urban Cinefile (Australia)*. Accessed 7 May 2014.

Keyser, Elizabeth Lennox. "'Quite Contrary': Frances Hodgson Burnett's *The Secret Garden*." *Children's Literature* 11 (1983): 1–13.

Knelman, Judith. *Twisting in the Wind: The Murderess and the English Press*. U of Toronto P, 1998.

Knoepflmacher, U. C. "Little Girls without Their Curls: Female Aggression in Victorian Children's Literature." *Children's Literature* 11 (1983): 14–31.

Lerer, Seth. *Children's Literature: A Reader's History, from Aesop to Harry Potter*. U of Chicago P, 2008.

Lurie, Alison. *Don't Tell the Grown-Ups: Subversive Children's Literature*. Little, Brown and Company, 1990.

Mangham, Andrew. *Violent Women and Sensation Fiction: Crime, Medicine, and Victorian Popular Culture*. Palgrave, 2007.

McCarthy, Todd. Rev. of *Brave*, dir. Mark Andrews and Brenda Chapman. *The Hollywood Reporter* 10 June 2012. Accessed 7 May 2014.

Montgomery, Lucy Maud. *Anne of Green Gables*. 1908. Seal-McClelland-Bantam, 1990.

Pykett, Lyn. *The "Improper" Feminine: The Women's Sensation Novel and the New Woman Writing*. Routledge, 1992.

Robinson, Tasha. Rev. of *Brave*, dir. Mark Andrews and Brenda Chapman. *AV Club* 21 June 2012. Accessed 7 May 2014.

Rowling, J. K. *Harry Potter and the Chamber of Secrets*. Scholastic, 1999.

Ruskin, John. *Sesame and Lilies*. 1894. Project Gutenberg, April 1998 [e-text 1293]. Accessed 9 May 2014.

Stern, Rebecca. *Home Economics: Domestic Fraud in Victorian England*. Ohio State UP, 2008.

Travers, Peter. Rev. of *Brave*, dir. Mark Andrews and Brenda Chapman. *Rolling Stone* June 2012. Accessed 7 May 2014.

Turan, Kenneth. Rev. of *Brave*, dir. Mark Andrews and Brenda Chapman. *Los Angeles Times* June 2012. Accessed 7 May 2014.

12. BOXED WINE FEMINISMS: THE RHETORIC OF WOMEN'S WINE DRINKING IN *THE GOOD WIFE*

Tammie M. Kennedy

Alcohol is not a women's issue.

—Gloria Steinem, *Ms. Magazine* fortieth anniversary party

Alcohol is a socially acceptable, legal way to muscle through the post-feminist, breadwinning, or stay-at-home life women lead.

—Gabrielle Glaser, *Her Best-Kept Secret*

Two contending narratives about the drinking culture of women in the twenty-first century are represented by these opening quotations. On one hand, many feminists have distanced themselves from temperance rhetorics, opting instead to disrupt a traditional gender role associated with abstinence. On the other hand, the myriad of choices afforded by feminism and the increase in alcohol consumption among women have suggested that drinking practices are a reflection of the complexities of women's roles in the new millennium.[1] Some other critics go as far as blaming feminism for the increase in drinking. Regardless, drinking practices[2] function rhetorically, pointing to "questions about who drinks, when and where drinking occurs, what beverages are consumed," and how drinkers create and negotiate their identities in relation to their motives and relationships with others within social and ideological contexts (Rotskoff 11). Furthermore, drinking practices are inflected by gender ideologies that shape representations in popular culture.

By every quantitative measure during the first two decades of the twenty-first century, women are drinking more. In 2012, Gallup pollsters reported that nearly 66 percent of all American women drank regularly, a higher percentage than any other time in twenty-five years, and more than 52 percent of the women who drink prefer wine ("Majority"). More specifically, women purchase nearly two-thirds of the 856 million gallons sold and drink more than 70 percent of what they buy ("Wine Consumption"). Furthermore, women are more likely to drink wine to relax at home after work than men (Thach 139). Women's wine drinking shows no signs of slowing down. Between 2009 and 2013, women's wine consumption has continued to grow (Glaser 21).

The prevalence of women's wine drinking isn't just increasing because of college women's partying and binge-drinking practices. Instead, researchers reveal that it is "women in their thirties, forties, and fifties who are getting through their days of work, and nights with teething toddlers, trying teenagers, or sick parents," by consuming their beverage of choice—wine (Glaser 18). In fact, the middle-class female predilection for wine has become a hobby and socially endorsed identity for many educated and "successful" women who may or may not identify as feminists.[3] In addition, drinking habits correlate directly with socioeconomic status. The more educated and well-off a woman is, the more likely she is to imbibe (Johnston 51). If temperance was *the* women's issue of the nineteenth century, as Carol Mattingly argues in *Well-Tempered Women*, then the documented ubiquity of women's wine drinking in the twenty-first century presents an important artifact for feminist rhetoricians to study.

In this chapter, I provide a brief overview of women's wine-drinking practices in the last decade. Then, I perform a close reading of the wine-drinking habits depicted in *The Good Wife* (*TGW*). Although Olivia Pope's wine drinking in *Scandal* has been highlighted by mainstream media like the *New York Times*, *TGW* is one of the few prime-time series that passes the Bechdel test[4] and features a variety of strong women protagonists with a range of feminist philosophies, including the main character, Alicia Florrick (Julianna Marguilies). In order to understand the rhetorical nature of women drinking wine in media representations, I ground my analysis in Jacqueline Royster and Gesa Kirsch's notion of "social circulation," which examines how "traditions are carried on, changed, reinvented, and reused when they pass from one generation to the next" and are "expressed via new genres and new media" (101). Contemplating the social circulation of wine drinking as a rhetorical activity also disrupts the public/private binaries often associated with gender. This disruption is critical, especially when considering how wine drinking is equated with what sociologist Arlie Hochschild calls "emotion work," which "requires one to induce or suppress feeling in order to sustain the outward countenance that produces the proper state of mind in others" (7). Representations of wine-drinking practices on television shows, such as *TGW*, reflect how many women perform emotion work while navigating and managing their various roles.

Examining representations of women's wine-drinking practices, the spaces where these drinking rituals take place, and the politics of emotion inherent in these actions, reveals new ways of understanding how women "experience, negotiate, and perform shifting emotions, . . . including subjectivities that are multiple, emergent, diverse, and complex" (Jayne, Valentine, and Holloway 553). I argue that representations of women's wine-drinking habits in *TGW* dramatize the conflicts that emerge from women's changing roles in both the private and public spheres. More specifically, while wine drinking is equated with success (college education, independence, middle-class affluence and privilege, and "having it all"), it also functions as reward and respite from the emotional complexities of performing women's many roles. Kathryn Kueny calls wine an "ambiguous substance," evoking associations with religion, romance, health, pleasure, and affluence, as well as conjuring images of addiction and its effects on the idealized personal and professional life. This same ambiguity is exposed by *TGW*'s protagonist Alicia Florrick, who drinks wine as a means to navigate the freedoms and pressures gained from feminist and women's movements, as well as to manage her emotions and modulate her identity within these changing roles.

WOMEN'S WINE-DRINKING PRACTICES

Within the last ten years, wine as an ambiguous substance for women has foregrounded both the pleasure and harm in women's drinking practices and traced these issues to feminism and the need for women to self-medicate to deal with stress. The question of whether or not drinking is feminist has been discussed in a variety of publications. In "Libation as Liberation?," Barbara Ehrenreich argues that "going toe to toe with men is a feminist act; going drink for drink with them isn't." Although she focuses on the prevalence of binge drinking in her 2002 *Time* magazine article, Ehrenreich also examines the relationship between the women's liberation movement and alcohol consumption, arguing that feminist foremothers would not have believed that drinking was a form of female self-assertion. Later in 2008, *New York Magazine* published "Gender Bender," which profiles the increase in prominence and amount of women's social-drinking practices and argues that women's "drinking has become entwined with progressive feminism." Author Alex Morris supports the argument by describing an incident that happened with two editors of feminist website Jezebel, a website that Morris labels as "pro-alcohol":

> A well-respected media personality invited two of its writers onto her Internet show "Thinking and Drinking"—a typically classy, semi-Socratic affair—and the younger women got so visibly shitfaced and the conversation so disturbing that some critics referred to it as "the Night Feminism Died." (qtd. in Morris)

After the onslaught of reaction to the "Thinking and Drinking" show, as well as to the way the editors acted, Jezebel editor, Jessica Grose, tried to address the link between social drinking and feminism:

> I don't think that drinking in and of itself is feminist, but I do think that it comes from a feminist place, that it can bolster one's sense of herself as liberated . . . the whole point of Third Wave feminism is that individual choice should not be judged. (qtd. in Morris)

While many women rejected the charge that feminism is to blame for current drinking practices, they also recognized the need for more discussion about women's drinking in more nuanced, progressive ways. For example, in "Ladies! Liquor! Ladies and Liquor!" blogger Christen McCurdy examines "women's attitudes about drinking—and society's attitudes about women who drink" for *Bitch Magazine*, focusing particularly on third-wave feminism. She asserts that there needs to be more balanced discussions about the relationship between drinking practices and gender, as well as an understanding of how alcohol has fueled social justice efforts like the gay rights movement. In 2013, Ann Dowsett Johnston and Gabrielle Glaser, two highly respected journalists, both published books (*Drink* and *Her Best-Kept Secret*, respectively); the books focus on the dangers of women's drinking, especially how the normalization of women's wine drinking has made alcohol dependence a struggle for growing numbers of well-educated women. Their books were profiled in a wide variety of mainstream media outlets throughout 2013–14, raising new concerns about the pervasiveness of women's wine drinking. Certainly, many of these media discussions reflect gendered attitudes about sexuality and femininity that have circulated throughout history. However, these discussions also point to the importance of examining how the media's interest in and representations of women's wine-drinking practices in the twenty-first century expose the recapitulation of patriarchal ideologies in popular culture.

EMOTION WORK, FEMINISM, AND WINE DRINKING IN *THE GOOD WIFE*

Over the past decade, television programs featuring women in leading roles drinking wine in almost every episode have become part of the media landscape. Winemaker Stephanie Gallo, for example, credits the increase in wine consumption not only to the fact that the United States is making better wine but also that wine drinking has become a part of popular culture: "You can't turn on the TV, or look through a magazine without seeing wine" (qtd. in Schmitt). *New York Times* critic Alessandra Stanley even declares that "television has a drinking problem." From *Today*'s cohosts Hoda Kotb and Kathy Lee Gifford drinking wine at 10 A.M. to Bravo's Real Housewives franchise drinking wine as a part of every activity depicted on the series, to Jules and her suburban Cul-de-Sac Crew guzzling wine in *Cougar Town* to Olivia Pope downing lots and lots of red wine in *Scandal*, wine drinking in popular shows geared toward women is ubiquitous.

/ 175

Royster and Kirsch's notion of social circulation draws attention to wine drinking as a rhetorical activity, which enables scholars to "account for how identities and ideas form and become rhetorical," as well as how "language and ideas travel, create multiple circles of meaning, and engage multiple mechanisms for creating impact and consequence" (102). Royster and Kirsch's feminist rhetorical practices also point to the importance of examining what Hochschild calls the emotion work that women perform in these representations. Hochschild argues that all of us manage emotion; however, women in particular are required to perform more emotional work, which creates a "commercialization of feeling" that is required in public and private positions (14). Emotion work is grounded in "feeling rules" that prescribe what to feel, when to feel, where to feel, how long to feel, and how strong our emotions can be, which are dictated by gender-based notions of normality (56–57). Feeling rules also establish expectations about emotional exchanges in various situations—both what a woman thinks she *should* feel and what others expect her to feel and how she should act on those emotions. Furthermore, as Sara Ahmed argues, emotions are part of larger material and discursive structures. It is important to understand "how emotions work, in concrete and particular ways, to mediate the relationship between the psychic and the social, and between the individual and the collective" (119). An analysis of the wine-drinking practices on *TGW* dramatizes how drinking practices intersect with gendered emotion work.

CBS's drama premiered in 2009 and offers one of the most feminist programs on broadcast television. The show appeals to a cross section of women—more than ten million viewers for season 5—and evokes much discussion, ranging from the *New York Times* to *Glamour* to *Feminist Spectator* to other blogs and fan fiction sites (O'Connell). The series focuses on Alicia Florrick, an educated, middle-aged white woman with two teenaged children and a husband who has been jailed following a very public sex and corruption scandal. While her husband sits in jail, Alicia returns to work as a lawyer after thirteen years of staying at home with the children and a last name that draws mixed attention to her. Viewers watch Alicia navigate the challenges of a hectic professional career, two teenagers, a meddling mother-in-law, a boss she has feelings for, a law firm in bankruptcy, and a husband who betrayed her but wants her back, all while successfully managing a difficult caseload. Although at first glance the program may seem to be a typical legal drama filled with romance and intrigue, it actually depicts the emancipation of its main character from gender stereotypes and tired tropes about women "having it all" or "love conquers all": Alicia is

176 /

> fascinating because we're witnessing a shift in her life that echoes the major social changes of the last decades, a shift from her *bourgeois* identity to an independent lifestyle she would've never taken on her own—and that she wouldn't give up for anything anymore. (Morin 45)

Furthermore, the complexity of the character illuminates the conflicts and contradictions that still exist for many women who endure harsh scrutiny and internal turmoil in whatever roles they perform in their homes and workplaces.

Alicia is portrayed as not only intellectual and brave but also as empathetic, a skill that is put to good use with her clients who she keeps calm and listens to in ways that often help her win cases. But beneath this calm, self-contained composure, viewers often witness Alicia doing the emotion work that keeps her effective in both her personal and professional lives. As Hochschild argues, "women often do extra emotion work—especially emotion work that affirms, enhances, and celebrates the well-being and status of others" (165). Alcohol infuses this emotion work and signifies what Ahmed calls "an object of feeling," which both shapes and is shaped by emotion (4). Drinking practices involve an interweaving of the personal with the social and allow for interactions with others and self-reflection in a way that might not happen if one was not drinking (28). The interaction between emotion work and drinking practices is pivotal to the depiction of Alicia's character in *TGW*.

In *TGW*, wine serves as one "object of feeling" that symbolizes the emotion work Alicia performs in various spaces. Although Alicia drinks with colleagues and clients—beer with her boss and Georgetown friend, Will (Josh Charles); tequila with the firm's investigator and friend, Kalinda (Archie Panjabi); martinis with her other boss, Diane (Christine Baranski); champagne to celebrate court victories with her colleagues; and wine at political functions with her husband, Peter (Chris Noth), it is Alicia's wine drinking at home, alone or with her immediate family, that best demonstrates the rhetorical function of wine drinking and how it shapes emotion work and its circulation.[5] In the pilot episode, after a long, stressful day at her new job, viewers see Alicia pour herself a large glass of red wine ("Pilot"). Just as movies often reveal the themes of the film in the first five minutes, the series establishes red wine as an important object of feeling for Alicia. Red wine provides Alicia respite from the stresses of her professional life; it also offers her the lubricant needed to do the emotion work that helps her critically self-reflect about her values and actions, as well as find a way to her more authentic self, the "Alicia" out of the public eye and beholden to her family and colleagues.   / 177

Alicia's wine drinking at home during the first season is meager until her husband is released from prison on electronic monitoring and returns home ("Hi"). Once Peter is home, Alicia's emotion work shifts. While he was incarcerated, Alicia could maintain both her anger at Peter's affair and her focus on succeeding at work as a new associate in a law firm. However, once he returns home, Alicia is confronted by the realities of her transition from housewife to attorney and the fallout involving her previous friends and lifestyle. Peter often uses red wine as a token of their past marriage that he wants to reestablish, offering her wine when she gets home from work ("Bang"; "Heart"), during family dinners ("Hybristophilia"), or later in the series when they make amends and Alicia joins him on the campaign bus ("A More Perfect Union"). Drinking wine with Peter in these situations represents the tension between Alicia's past when she sacrificed her career for Peter's political aspirations and an evolving sense of self that questions those choices and what she wants for her life going forward. However, no matter how much pressure she gets from her family, Alicia inevitably can't feel what Peter wants her to feel. For example, in "Heart," Alicia is torn between her feelings for her boss Will and her duties as a "good wife" to Peter. When she returns home from work after allowing herself to act on her attraction to Will by kissing him, she and Peter have sex in his bedroom. While Peter interprets the act as hopeful for their relationship, the viewer senses that it was a mere act of sublimation and guilt on Alicia's part. Before their sexual encounter, Peter had offered Alicia a large glass of red wine. However, once they are finished having sex, the viewer witnesses Alicia's confusion underneath her cool reserve. She leaves the red wine on the counter and goes to bed alone in her room. Leaving the wine is symbolic of her ongoing transformation in which she questions what a good mother and wife means to her rather than how others define it. She can no longer perform her previous role of wife. But she has yet to assert what she does feel and how those feelings fit with both her professional and personal life.

Although Alicia is represented as a fairly typical social drinker in public, Alicia and her family members comment on her domestic wine-drinking practices throughout the various seasons. Her daughter, Grace (Makenzie Vega), who has been exploring religion and comes out as a Christian, an identity that Alicia finds very surprising given her views on religion, comments on Alicia's drinking. In "Silver Bullet," Grace worries about her mother's *need* to have wine when she gets home, especially when discussing religion. Alicia coolly replies: "I don't need wine. I like wine. I like a glass of wine after work." When Grace presses the point—"You talk to me all the time about drugs. Wine is a drug."—Alicia chugs down the whole glass. And when Grace goes into a rant about science not taking prayer seriously, Alicia pours another glass. "Just taking another hit off the crack pipe," she tells her daughter, ending the contentious conversation. Later, in "Ham Sandwich," Alicia confesses to Kalinda that Grace thinks she drinks too much wine. Kalinda comforts Alicia's concern by replying, "This is tequila." The two continue drinking together, the scene reinforcing the intimate friendship they are developing. In a later episode, Kalinda, knowing her friend's basic needs, brings Alicia provisions because she's been stuck in a remote hotel in Minnesota for two days to complete a deposition. In addition to clean clothes, Kalinda brings a bottle of red wine. As the two women share the wine and chat, Alicia admits what she misses about being an "opt-out" wife and mother:

> You know what I miss about my old life, before the glamour of the law? The quiet. At home in the afternoons, I would drink every day at three o'clock a glass of red wine, waiting for the kids to come home. I miss the silence in the house at three. ("Boom De Yah Da")

At the end of season 5, Alicia's mother, Veronica (Stockard Channing), and mother-in-law, Jackie (Mary Beth Peil), prepare lasagna for Zach's (Graham Phillips) graduation while Alicia is at work because they didn't think Alicia should serve catered food for such an important event. As the two women cook, they drink red wine and bicker about whose fault it is that Alicia and Peter's marriage has crumbled into a union of convenience. As Alicia's mom guzzles red wine, Jackie says, "I see where Alicia's drinking comes from" ("A Weird Year").

The comments about Alicia's drinking focus on her wine-drinking practices at home. Like so many of the women profiled in Johnston's and Glaser's books, wine drinking denotes the shift from work to home—a much-needed break, reward, and way to relax, which Johnston describes based on her personal experience: "[When I was drinking wine,] my first instinct was to shed some stress as quickly as I shed my coat. . . . Alcohol smoothed that switch from one role to the other. It seemed to make life purr" (160). Peter notes this same habit, pointing out that Alicia has poured herself a glass of wine before she has even taken off her coat ("Great Firewall"). Although Alicia's wine-drinking habits fit Johnston's observation on a couple of occasions, mostly she appears to drink red wine at home as a way to transition between her work life and family life. She even changes into a beige cardigan, her "wine cardigan," when she's at home. The cardigan, like the wine, denotes a space change (think Mr. Rogers) but also symbolizes her emotional state. She wraps it tightly around her body as she curls up with a glass of wine, reflective, angst-ridden, and trying to unwind from the stresses that threaten to engulf her. When she's not alone at home, viewers see Alicia drink wine with her arm around her daughter while watching television ("A New Day"; "Two Girls, One Code"). She also drinks wine at home when she is working, such as conducting Internet searches ("Unorthodox") or paying bills ("Unplugged").

While the wine drinking appears to be her way of soothing her stress, viewers also see that it serves as an object of emotion, which signifies self-doubt. For example, Alicia laments her failings to her daughter with a wineglass in hand: "I wish I was a better mom. I was, but things are out of control" ("Pants on Fire"). Psychologist Pamela Stewart explains the gendered nature of the emotion work behind some women's wine drinking: "Typically, men drink to heighten positive feelings or socialize. Women are more likely than men to drink to get rid of negative feelings" (qtd. in Johnston 108). Furthermore, these "negative emotions" often stem from what Jan Bauer calls the "perversion of feminism," which is rooted in the need to be perfect in all aspects of one's life (qtd. in Johnston 162). Viewers see Alicia drink when she feels jealous of Will's new relationship even though she's still married to Peter ("Blue Ribbon Panel"), when she might not be winning a case ("Parenting Made Easy"), when she's not sure how to talk to her son about interracial dating ("Bitcoin for Dummies"), when she doesn't know what to write to the owner of her old house, which is now up for sale ("Blue Ribbon Panel"), or when she doesn't understand one of her kids' favorite television shows ("The Seven Day Rule"). The heart of Alicia's wine drinking in these circumstances is her entanglement in the feeling rules by which she has been indoctrinated and recognizing on some level that these rules stunt her from honoring what she truly wants and feels is right for her present life.

Navigating feelings of insecurity and self-estrangement are apparent when Alicia drinks wine in more intimate settings with her family. The viewer witnesses Alicia's fatigue from working so many hours at the firm and at home and trying to do both jobs perfectly, creating more stress. Hochschild considers the complexity of such self-estrangement:

> Estrangement from aspects of oneself are, in one light, a means of defense between the "real self" [and the work self]. . . . But this solution also poses serious problems. For in dividing up our sense of self, in order to save the "real" self from unwelcome intrusions, we necessarily relinquish a healthy sense of wholeness. We come to accept as normal the tension we feel between our "real" and our "on-stage" selves. (183–84)

Often, when Alicia reaches an uncomfortable level of estrangement from her most authentic needs, she and her brother, Owen (Dallas Roberts), process her life so that she can gain a more realistic perspective. Although Owen is mischievous, he also loves Alicia and functions as her truth-teller because he's not afraid to say what needs to be said. This emotional processing, however, is always accompanied by wine ("Breaking Fast"; "Poisoned Pill"; "Net Worth"; "Tying the Knot"). These conversations often reveal a more a poignant truth about Alicia's more genuine self, the one not so bound up in prescriptions about how she should feel about her husband, lover, work, or children. These emotional talks also disrupt what Owen calls Alicia's "facade of perfectionism," which is often steeped in tamped-down anger or overly intellectual rationalizations of her unsettled feelings ("Tying the Knot").

The show argues that drinking wine helps Alicia to drill down to the truth of what she really needs and what action she should take to secure this goal. The excavation process is evident when Alicia drinks wine with her mother. Although Alicia rebelled against her free-spirited mother when she was younger by being "perfect," maintaining a steely exterior that hides her fears, disappointments, and anger and shackled her to the "curse of competence," drinking wine with her mother allows Alicia to let down her guard and embrace some of the qualities in her mother that might serve her better now. In "The Deep Web," for example, Alicia is no longer able to maintain her poise after the death of her boss and former lover, Will. Alicia's new legal partner, Cary (Matt Czuchry), demands that she take a day off. Alicia, now unaccustomed to being at home, is hobbled by depression that keeps her hidden under the covers and by anxiety that makes being awake and in the world almost unbearable. Her mother comes to check on her. As they drink their red wine, Alicia confesses that she's not handling Will's death well even though she and Peter are "engaged" to renew their marital vows—a choice that was more pragmatic than romantic on Alicia's part. Alicia admits that she's always tried to be the "good" one, but she's lost: "I don't know what I am anymore. I'm spinning, Mom, and I can't stop." While earlier Alicia had worried that she made a mistake by being a lawyer, a deeper truth emerges during her wine consumption: "I shouldn't have stopped working."

Wine-soaked chats with Owen and Veronica and cardigan-wrapped wine drinking alone at home help Alicia excavate her emotions in more productive ways. As Ahmed argues, "emotions are the very 'flesh' of time. They show us the time it takes to move, or to move on, is a time that exceeds the time of an individual life" (202). Once Alicia's emotions materialize through her wine-drinking practices, she is empowered to make the kinds of deep-seated changes that gird her ongoing transformation. Although she and Peter stay together, Alicia refuses to play the "good wife" in the ways she did before she returned to work. As Peter celebrates his gubernatorial victory, Alicia quietly leaves the celebration and goes home. She pours a large glass of red wine, waiting for her colleague Cary to meet her at her apartment. When Cary arrives, Alicia agrees to start a firm with him, thereby embarking on a major professional and personal risk. She will leave Lockhart and Gardner, the one firm willing to hire her after a thirteen-year absence from the workplace, to start her own firm with Cary. Such a move certainly obliterates any semblance of a relationship she might maintain with Will before his character is killed ("What's in the Box?"). However, Alicia has been transformed; she is no longer defined by her love interests or beholden to Will who advocated on her behalf. This transformation comes to fruition in "The One Percent," the penultimate show of season 5. Peter's campaign manager, Eli Gold (Alan Cumming), meets with Alicia to try to figure out the state of Peter and Alicia's marriage, which is a question that haunts Peter's political career. Alicia pours the red wine and makes her most honest confession: "I'm tired. I'm just done. We are staying together, but that is it." The last season ends with Alicia drinking red wine after her son leaves home after his high school graduation, marking another major shift for her.

CONCLUSION

Analyzing the wine-drinking practices of women on television shows such as *TGW* helps feminist scholars to investigate how gendered ideologies are recapitulated, recognized, and managed in women's lives. These powerful television representations normalize drinking wine as a way for women to navigate the tensions of their personal and professional choices, and this message is reinforced as it circulates throughout various spaces—social media, television/film, gender-based social activities, and domestic drinking practices. Since the emotions connected with women's wine-drinking habits "should not be regarded as psychological states, but as social and cultural practices" (Ahmed 9), it is imperative to critically examine how emotions "stick" (11) in terms of the effect on women and their ways of navigating gendered ideologies. While gender equality correlates with parity in drinking practices, it is also important to understand what this link contends about personal and professional success and happiness for many women. As Caroline Knapp chronicles in her book *Appetites*, freedom is not the same as power: "The ability to make choices can feel unsettling and impermanent and thin if it's not girded somehow with the heft of real economic and political strength" (35). Representations of women on television shows like *TGW* draw from the liminal space between choice and power, depicting high-functioning professional women who drink wine to "fend off the discomfort, to dilute inhibition, and wash away anxiety." A woman may experience these issues when

> teased with freedom—to define herself as she sees fit, to attend to her own needs and wishes, and to fully explore her own desires . . . she may not quite feel . . . in her bones or believe will last. (Knapp 33)

Just as the temperance movement promised women more agency by abstaining from drinking, many twenty-first-century women seek empowerment and balance through their wine-drinking practices. However, the history of women's drinking habits has shown that the freedom to choose and the power to transform oneself and others is modulated by gendered ideologies often constrained by the emotion work assumed by many women. Analyzing how wine-drinking practices are represented in popular culture offers a tangible object of emotion that helps feminist rhetoricians better locate both potential spaces of transformation and potentially dangerous consequences for women who drink wine as a way to navigate the pressures they feel when performing various roles at home and in the workplace.

Notes

1. Noted alcohol researchers Richard Wilsnack and Sharon Wilsnack point out that increased drinking among females might be a result of the women's movement and changes in women's roles, especially changes that involve exposure to formerly masculine environments and roles. They suggest that changes in sex roles might increase women's exposure to alcohol and opportunities to drink; might modify traditional norms against female drinking, thereby making drinking more permissible; and might offer females new goals and aspirations, thus causing stress that alcohol might be used to reduce.

2. For the purposes of this chapter, I will be looking at "social drinking" or "moderate drinking" rather than alcoholism or binge drinking. The Betty Ford Center defines "social drinking" as follows:

> Social drinking may be that drink or two that soften the harsh events of the day or release one to relaxed sociability or just allow you to see the humor of it all. How many drinks do social drinkers drink? It probably varies. Whatever they do . . . , social drinkers do not chase after good feelings by drinking more and more until they lose control. To social drinkers, alcohol is not important. Some wise person said, "If you have to drink to be social, that's not social drinking." ("How")   / 183

According to the *Dietary Guidelines for Americans*, moderate alcohol consumption is defined as having up to one drink per day for women and up to two drinks per day for men. Five ounces of wine (12 percent alcohol content) is equivalent to one drink (US Department of Agriculture). Furthermore, this chapter and many of the statistics cited focus on what Karen MacNeil calls "beverage wine," wine purchased at the supermarket (typically less than fourteen dollars per bottle) for daily consumption instead of more expensive, collectible wines.

3. The prevalence of wine drinking is apparent in a variety of media and social activities. Clothing designer Kate Spade created a necklace that spells out "Pop the Cork." More than 650,000 women follow "Moms Who Need Wine" on Facebook. Another 131,000 women are fans of "OMG I So Need a Glass of Wine" or "I'm Gonna Sell My Kids." "OMG I Need a Glass of Wine" has more than 180,000 likes. "Wine Sisterhood" puts out daily "wine notes" that endorse drinking wine and has more than 371,000 followers. Newly conceived "paint-bars" pair wine drinking and painting instruction as a social event for women.

4. The Bechdel test was created by American cartoonist Alison Bechdel. The test was originally used to judge the feminist qualities of films. Now the test is used to assess a variety of media for gender bias: (*1*) It has to have at least two women in it; (*2*) who talk to each other; and (*3*) about something besides a man. Despite the simplicity of the test, very few television shows or films meet these minimum requirements.

5. The women's drinking practices on *TGW* are significant. Bisexual investigator Kalinda is never shown drinking at home or when she is with her lovers in a domestic space; instead, she drinks hard liquor with both men and women at bars. She and Alicia usually do shots of tequila. Diane, senior partner and comanager at the Lockhart and Gardner Firm, drinks bourbon with her legal partner, Will, often in the office at the end of the day as they confer about case strategy or office politics. When Cary and Alicia leave Lockhart and Gardner to start their own firm, they swear not to drink bourbon like Diane and Will. Diane often drinks white wine when she is on a date or in the company of women outside of the office. Viewers don't see her drinking at home. After Will's death, Alicia and Diane get drunk on martinis after the funeral, which is symbolic of their attempt to distance themselves from Will's memory. Jackie, Alicia's mother-in-law, often judges Alicia and her mother Veronica's wine drinking. An exchange between the mothers represents this difference—Jackie: "You should drink less." Veronica: "You should drink more to get that bug out of your ass" ("Battle of the Proxies"). However, after Jackie admits that her husband, too, carried on a long-term affair with a staff member, she starts to "loosen up," enjoying wine at family dinners and during social occasions. Alicia's mom, Veronica, mostly drinks wine and asks if Zach can have wine on his eighteenth birthday because she allowed Alicia to drink at sixteen years old. While Veronica also drinks margaritas, she only drinks red wine with Alicia.

Works Cited

Ahmed, Sara. *The Cultural Politics of Emotion*. Routledge, 2004.

"Bang." *The Good Wife*. CBS. 2 March 2010.

"Battle of the Proxies." *The Good Wife*. CBS 2 December 2012.

"Bitcoin for Dummies." *The Good Wife*. CBS. 15 January 2012.

"Blue Ribbon Panel." *The Good Wife*. CBS. 25 March 2012.

"Boom De Yah Da." *The Good Wife*. CBS. 6 January 2013.

"Breaking Fast." *The Good Wife*. CBS. 12 October 2010.

"The Deep Web." *The Good Wife*. CBS. 4 May 2014.

Ehrenreich, Barbara. "Libation as Liberation?" *Time* April 2002. Accessed 23 May 2014.

Glaser, Gabrielle. *Her Best-Kept Secret: Why Women Drink—and How They Can Regain Control*. Simon and Schuster, 2013.

"Great Firewall." *The Good Wife*. CBS. 1 March 2011.

"Ham Sandwich." *The Good Wife*. CBS. 22 March 2011.

"Heart." *The Good Wife*. CBS. 16 March 2010.

"Hi." *The Good Wife*. CBS. 9 February 2010.

Hochschild, Arlie Russell. *The Managed Heart: Commercialization of Human Feeling*. 1983. U of California P, 2012.

"How Do You Define Social Drinking?" *Betty Ford Center* 19 October 2010. Accessed July 2014.

"Hybristophilia." *The Good Wife*. CBS. 18 May 2010.

Jayne, Mark, Gill Valentine, and Sarah L. Holloway. "Emotional, Embodied, and Affective Geographies of Alcohol, Drinking, and Drunkenness." *Transactions of the Institute of British Geographers* 35.4 (October 2010): 540–54.

Johnston, Ann Dowsett. *Drink: The Intimate Relationship between Women and Alcohol*. HarperCollins, 2013.

Knapp, Caroline. *Appetites: Why Women Want*. Counterpoint, 2003.

Kueny, Kathryn. *The Rhetoric of Sobriety: Wine in Early Islam*. State U of New York P, 2001.

MacNeil, Karen. *The Wine Bible*. Workman, 2000.

"Majority of U.S. Drink Alcohol." *Gallup* 17 August 2012. Accessed 15 June 2014.

Mattingly, Carol. *Well-Tempered Women: Nineteenth-Century Temperance Rhetoric*. Southern Illinois UP, 1998.

McCurdy, Christen. "Ladies! Liquor! Ladies and Liquor!" *Bitch Magazine* 1 November 2012. Accessed 6 June 2014.

"A More Perfect Union." *The Good Wife*. CBS. 21 April 2013.

Morin, Céline. "How to Love When You're a Good Wife." *"The Good Wife" and Philosophy: Temptations of Saint Alicia*. Ed. Kimberly Baltzer-Jaray and Robert Arp. Open Court, 2013. 39–50.

Morris, Alex. "Gender Bender." *New York Magazine* 7 December 2008. Accessed 17 May 2014.

"Net Worth." *The Good Wife*. CBS. 15 February 2011.

"A New Day." *The Good Wife*. CBS. 25 September 2011.

O'Connell, Michael. "TV Ratings: *The Good Wife* Continues to Climb." *Hollywood Reporter* 31 March 2014. Accessed 5 July 2014.

"The One Percent." *The Good Wife*. CBS. 11 May 2014.

"Pants on Fire." *The Good Wife*. CBS. 15 April 2012.

"Parenting Made Easy." *The Good Wife*. CBS. 4 December 2011.

"Pilot." *The Good Wife*. CBS. 22 September 2009.

"Poisoned Pill." *The Good Wife*. CBS. 9 November 2010.

Rotskoff, Lori. *Love on the Rocks: Men, Women, and Alcohol in Post–World War II America*. U of North Carolina P, 2002.

Royster, Jacqueline Jones, and Gesa E. Kirsch. *Feminist Rhetorical Practices: New Horizons for Rhetoric, Composition, and Literacy Studies*. Southern Illinois UP, 2012.

Schmitt, Patrick. "US Wine Sales: 'Nowhere to Go but Up.'" *The Drinks Business* 7 October 2103. Accessed 10 January 2014.

"The Seven Day Rule." *The Good Wife*. CBS. 27 January 2013.

"Silver Bullet." *The Good Wife*. CBS. 22 February 2011.

Stanley, Alessandra. "Where Alcoholism Drinks in the Laughs." *New York Times* 2 December 2010. Accessed 10 January 2014.

Thach, Liz. "Time for Wine? Identifying Differences in Wine-Drinking Occasions for Male and Female Wine Consumers." *Journal of Wine Research* 23.2 (July 2012): 134–54.

"Two Girls, One Code." *The Good Wife*. CBS. 14 October 2012.

"Tying the Knot." *The Good Wife*. CBS. 27 April 2014.

"Unorthodox." *The Good Wife*. CBS. 10 November 2009.

"Unplugged." *The Good Wife*. CBS. 11 May 2010.

US Department of Agriculture and US Department of Health and Human Services. "Food and Food Components to Reduce." *Dietary Guidelines for Americans*. 7th ed. US Government Printing Office, 2010. 30–32.

"A Weird Year." *The Good Wife*. CBS. 18 May 2014.

"What's in the Box?" *The Good Wife*. CBS. 28 April 2013.

Wilsnack, Richard W., and Sharon C. Wilsnack. "Sex Roles and Drinking among Adolescent Girls." *Journal of Studies on Alcohol* 39 (1978): 1855–74.

"Wine Consumption in the U.S." *Wine Institute* 14 March 2013. Accessed 21 June 2014.

PART IV

RHETORICAL REPRESENTATIONS
OF BODIES AND CULTURES

13. THE COMMODIFICATION OF MEXICAN WOMEN ON MEXICAN FOOD PACKAGING

Consuelo Carr Salas

Walking into my neighborhood grocery store one evening, I frantically began looking up to the aisle markers with the list of products available in
each aisle. I was in a rush looking for premade salsa. I generally don't buy
premade salsa as I usually make it myself, but this time I needed to buy it. I
zigzagged through the aisles when suddenly I stopped in my tracks. There it
was, aisle 4b "Mainstream Salsa." "Mainstream Salsa?" I thought to myself.
"What exactly is that supposed to mean?"

I live in El Paso, Texas—a border city that sits directly next to Ciudad
Juárez, Chihuahua, Mexico. According to US census data, El Paso is 80 percent Hispanic, and it is commonplace to see an aisle dedicated to Mexican
premade food products, even in national chain grocery stores. The Mexican
premade foodstuffs found in this aisle expands what can generally be found
in the "Ethnic" or "Mexican" aisle of grocery stores in other locations. In
this aisle, you can find Mexican Coca-Cola, packaged in the same red and
white label but made with real sugar instead of high fructose corn syrup;
Jarritos, Mexican flavored sodas, packaged with three different sized *jarros*
(jugs) aligned in order from small to medium to large; Las Palmas red and
green enchilada sauces, featuring images of plump red or green enchiladas
perfectly plated; Doña María's mole, a *chile* chocolate sauce, always sold in
a short glass container with the image of a plate of mole; and El Mexicano
nopales, with a label that shows strips of dethorned cactus pads. This aisle is a

familiar space for shoppers as most common Mexican premade foodstuff can be found here, but off to the side of that aisle was aisle 4b, "Mainstream Salsa."

I walked into the aisle and looked to see what exactly was stocked in "Mainstream Salsa." I found Hatch Green Chile, from the Hatch Valley of New Mexico, with its iconic "Hatch" typography; Pace *Picante* Sauce with a bright orange-and-yellow sun; and Cholula hot sauce with the image of a woman dressed in white sitting beneath the archway of an adobe house. I was puzzled by the power dynamic being enacted in aisle 4b in classifying certain types of salsa as "mainstream" and was curious about what the use of the word as an adjective with salsa really meant.

It was after critical reflection on this moment that I began examining how Mexican foodstuffs are packaged and presented to customers. After speaking with food studies scholar Meredith E. Abarca, I began noticing that images such as the "sleeping Mexican man," the sombrero, and the *zarape* are prevalent on numerous Mexican food product labels (see Salas and Abarca for further discussion of these images). These stereotypical representations are not isolated to the male gender; they are also seen with the female gender.

Join me as I return to the "Ethnic" or the "Mexican" food aisle of the grocery store and study the packaging. Examining tostada chip bags, tortillas, or salsa reveals several stereotypical images commonly used, but for now, let us concentrate on the images representing women. You may see a woman wearing an elaborately designed, traditional Mexican *folklórico* dress, a woman that is wearing a more simplistic blouse and skirt and perhaps a scarf over her head, or a woman in a traditional kitchen setting. Several of these images can be seen in figure 13.1. However, you may also find that there are some Mexican foodstuffs that do not have such representations. Perhaps you will find a chile or no image at all but instead just the brand's name, such as in figure 13.2. The differences in these representations spark numerous questions. Why do some companies choose to sell their product using a stereotypical image? What is the purpose of the image? Who is the audience for these images? What is communicated by these images?

This chapter examines the stereotypical representations of Mexican women found on the packaging of Mexican foodstuffs. Even though the use of a clichéd portrayal of a Mexican woman on a single jar of salsa is not the only identifier of Mexican women, such representations can become problematic. Each image becomes one more stereotypical portrayal and continuously adds to the collective idea of who Mexicans are. These images provide a site where visual rhetoric can expand and account for the "mundane practices [of the everyday], no one of which is crucial, but each of which, taken together, are

Women on Mexican food products

Mexican food products

the concrete materials of which we constitute our selves" (Dickinson 24). By looking at the constellation of "mundane practices" and what cultural rhetorics call the "meaning making practices and the things produced by those practices," cultural rhetorical critics have the potential to dissect how rhetoric is enacted in quotidian things, such as images paired with food packages, and they can begin to break down the messages being presented ("Call").

I look at food-related images promoting Mexican food for two reasons. First, I chose Mexican food because of its current prevalence in mainstream US consumption habits. According to food historian Jeffrey Pilcher, "Mexican is one of the top three ethnic foods in the United States" (xiii). Second, I am concerned with the translation of Mexican culture in the United States. In *Planet Taco*, Pilcher argues that Mexican food sold in the United States is not food that would be found within the country of Mexico, but instead, it is an Americanized version of Mexican food (20). Therefore, I am interested in the way food packaging depicts Mexicans from a US perspective to a US-based and international audience.

The food aisle is a space where "presence," as discussed by Chaim Perelman and Lucie Olbrechts-Tyteca, is on display for visual rhetoricians. According to Perelman and Olbrechts-Tyteca, "by the very fact of selecting certain elements and presenting them to the audience, their importance and pertinency to the discussion are implied. Indeed, such a choice endows these elements with a *presence*" (116). Therefore, what the marketing team for food products decides to present their customers is a form of what they would like to give "presence" to in their product. The images on the label present a strategic argument that advertisers hope resonates with the consumers.

Product packaging plays an enormous role in consumer attraction and influencing purchases. Foods labels are spaces where issues of class, gender, and ethnicities are created and reinforced. According to Davide Girardelli, "a package not only functions as a protection of the food, but it also acts as a symbolic vehicle in the process of attributing symbolic values to the food contained in the package" (311). Additionally, in the National Geographic Channel television series *Brain Games*, Susan Carnell, a professor of psychology at Johns Hopkins University, asserts:

> The bright vibrant colors in the supermarket are all a part of the allure of making food more attractive to your brain. Before any food has entered your mouth or your stomach, in a way you've already begun to eat it with your eyes. How food looks is as, if not more, important than how the food actually tastes. In many cases the different brands you see all taste

the same with the same ingredients and the same cooking methods. All you're really buying is the packaging. The brain is already hard wired to have an association with the foodstuff being sold, and so what is being sold is not necessarily the foodstuff itself but instead the packaging.

Given the power of packaging, what are static, stereotypical images of Mexican women communicating to consumers of Mexican foodstuff?

The packaging itself communicates with its audience, but it is both the advertisers' and the consumers' previous knowledge and experiences that help mold how the packaging is received and what it communicates. Judith Williamson in *Decoding Advertisements* succinctly states, "Advertisements' role is to attach meaning to products, to create identities for the goods (and service providers) they promote" (iv). While Williamson presents a valid point, several scholars align themselves with the notion that consumers are not simply recipients of advertisers' messages but, instead, active participants in creating the meaning of advertisements (see Olson, Finnegan, and Hope; Niblock; Pajaczkowska; Faigley). Lester Faigley argues, "Advertisers enact a conversation of images with their audiences. Advertisers are both manipulators and manipulated because they must interject their product into an ongoing system of signs. Their effect depends on extending a set of cultural associations" (191). Therefore, the advertisement is only successful if the sign system inherent within the viewer allows it to be so.

The issue becomes whether the static stereotypical representations of Mexican women on food labels resonate with consumers. Stereotypes of Mexican men and women have been used for close to a century in different mediums and contribute to the "cultural logic" of perceived Mexican identity (Enfield). Mexican American literature professor William Anthony Nericcio archives the trajectory of representations of Mexican Americans in the United States in postcards, films, photos, and advertisements. In *Tex[t]-Mex*, Nericcio demonstrates that stereotypical representations of Mexicans have a long and complex history. Additionally, Nericcio unveils how *representations* of Mexicans are, in fact, nothing more than a *presentation* of Mexican via American cultural creators (24–25). (Stuart Hall argues that mass media does not simply *reflect/ represent* characteristics of groups but instead *creates/presents* an idea of them [*Representations*]). Nericcio does an excellent job of creating an archive and analyzing the plethora of images that have been used to portray Mexican and Mexican Americans. His work allows readers "to understand the series of events (historical and aesthetic) that rendered our contemporary 'Mexican' and Latino hallucinations meaningful" (24). Nericcio argues that

"Mexicans," in the imagination of the Americas—North, Central, and South—are less a *raza* than a seductive ruse and maintain that the peculiar and particular apparitions of "Mexicans," "Mexican Americans," "Mexican-Americans," "Hispanics," "Chicanas/os," and "Latinas/os" in the U.S. marketplace are overdue for patient scrutiny. (28)

It is in the aisles of grocery stores where the ultimate test of whether the images used by advertisers to sell Mexican food either resonates or not with the consumers.

Scholars in various fields have conducted numerous studies of the binary, static, and stereotypical representations of women in advertisements. While it can be argued that representations of women in advertisements have become more pluralistic in the last fifty years and that women have begun to be represented in more diverse roles, there are still areas within the advertising industry—especially food advertising—where women are cast in static, stereotypical representations. While much critical attention has been given to food advertisements in other fields, such as visual communication, visual culture, anthropology, and food studies, not much attention within rhetoric has been given to rhetorically analyzing the representations of women on food packages themselves.

My analysis asks us as consumers and visual rhetoricians to look carefully at *presentations* of certain cultures and to consider the ways stereotypes are created and perpetuated. When discussing issues of cultural representation, there are always issues of power. Who is being represented and who is doing the representation is a conversation wrapped up in issues of power. Marie Sarita Gaytán argues a similar point when she states, "Practices of authenticity have real-world implications that illustrate the limits and constraints that less powerful populations face in the marketplace—especially when it comes to accessing the conditions that enable the production and consumption of their identities" (338). Female Mexican identity is constantly being commodified and consumed, and yet Mexicans, Mexican Americans, and Latinas/os have very little say in how they are portrayed by advertisers.

Images using stereotypical representations of Mexican women, such as figure 13.1, communicate what Chimamanda Adichie calls a "single story" of Mexican people, culture, and food. With enough repetition and continual use, these "single stories" ultimately transform into *acceptable* stereotypes by dominant cultures. Merchandisers package these single-story stereotypes on food products and create a "commodified perception of culture" (CPC). According to myself and Abarca, "commodification of culture is a result of mass production, which is the very process by which Mexican food has been accepted into the American palate and beyond" (207–8). I look to expand this definition and present CPC as a framework for visual rhetoricians. A CPC framework of visual analysis puts issues of "authenticity," nostalgia, and "global memoryscapes" into conversation to analyze the multiple dynamics involved in creating a single story of certain cultures or groups by being attuned to the ethnic stereotypes used by mass merchandisers.

To put this framework into practice, let us look at the single story presented in figure 13.3. In the first half of the diptych, there is a two-story adobe home with a terra-cotta roof. This image attempts to situate the consumer in a past rural setting, perhaps in the US Southwest or northern Mexico. Additionally, there are images of chickens roaming in front of the home. This image suggests an agrarian lifestyle, one in which individuals raise/grow their own foods. In the second half of the diptych, there is a woman wearing a yellow blouse that is undecorated and tucked into her purple skirt that ends just at the ground. Complementary colors are used in the woman's clothing to attract the consumer's eye. On her head is a brown-red *rebozo*, a folkloric Mexican shawl, which exposes just a bit of her hair. She stands on a brown ground, signifying dirt, with a few opuntia, prickly pear, cacti in the background. The woman is bunching presumably just-picked flowers by a water fountain.

/ 195

Mexican woman in headscarf

The *presentation* of the Mexican woman on the salsa label may not immediately cause concern in consumers because the image appears to be a "natural" *representation* of Mexican women. Sue Hum's germinal theory of the "racialized gaze" is useful to this analysis of the appeal to authenticity within food advertisements. The racialized gaze

> construct[s] a racial identity that replicates the cultural value systems of the status quo; as a result of the racialized gaze, spectators accept this racial configuration as "real" and "natural." Central to that racialized gaze is the dynamic of authenticity—the compulsion to accept what one sees as pure and truth. (114)

In other words, the sign system being used may resonate with the consumer due to the consumer's previous experience with other representations of Mexican women dressed in this way and in this setting. The marketers have given "presence" to the stereotypical portrayal of a Mexican woman to create the idea that this scene is "authentically" Mexican and, consequently, the food is authentically Mexican. Arlene Dávila argues that this pattern of advertising is commonplace, "Latinos are continually recast as authentic and marketable, but ultimately as a foreign rather than intrinsic component of U.S. society, culture, and history" (4). Analyzing Mexican food product packaging and its portrayal of Mexican women brings to light the attempt to authenticate the contents. However, it must be asked: who is the audience for such portrayals of Mexican women?

Taking a look at the context of the setting, it becomes apparent that the image is attempting to sell "Double Roasted Salsa" to several different groups: (1) non-Latina/o communities; (2) Latina/o communities who have no ties to Mexico, but have connections to the country through cultural affiliation and US "hallucinations" (Nericcio); and (3) Latina/o communities who have connections to Mexico. To non-Latina/o communities, the representation of the woman, her dress, and the home is yet another example of a "seductive ruse" of Mexico and Mexican people created and understood through previous "cultural logics." While US Latina/os may also be drawn to the ruse, through the icon of the home and the agrarian setting the image attempts to create a nostalgic feeling of "home," what Arjun Appadurai calls an "imagined nostalgia," a "nostalgia for things that never were" (76), even though many may never have lived in a rural agrarian community or in an adobe home. The rural past setting both in the location and in the portrayal of the Mexican woman could appeal to some "cultural logic" of an "authentic"

Mexico. By attempting to evoke "authentic Mexico," this is an example of what Appadurai defines as "ersatz nostalgia," "the simulacra of periods that constitute the flow of time, conceived as lost, absent, or distant" (78). The appeal to an "authentic" Mexico through an "authentic" representation of Mexican women then translates into an "authentic" salsa. Jean Baudrillard's "simulation" and "simulacra" can also be applied to the second audience interpretation. Baudrillard defines "simulation" as "no longer that of a territory, a referential being or substance. It is the generation by models of a real without origin or reality: a hyperreal" (2). Baudrillard argues that due to simulation all that remains is nostalgia, the longing for something that is now gone. A simulacrum is the static image that is a result of simulation. The image we see on the jar of salsa is a simulacrum of a period of time that is now gone.

When discussing imagined nostalgia, Appadurai highlights the phenomena that mass merchandisers have actually created nostalgias because they do "not principally involve the evocation of a sentiment to which consumers who really have lost something can respond. Rather, these forms of mass advertising *teach* consumers to miss things they have never lost" (76, emphasis mine). Kendall Phillips and Mitchell Reyes's "global memoryscapes" demonstrate that memories, much like nostalgias, have become socially   / 197 constructed concepts that have moved/been sold beyond local and national boundaries. "Global memoryscapes" are "a complex landscape upon which memories and memory practices move, come into contact, are contested by, and contest other forms of remembrance" (5). The notion that mass merchandisers can "teach" consumers to miss something that they never lost is integral when considering the selling of cultural representations on a national and global scale.

I do not wish to advocate for a "real" representation of Mexican women, as no such thing exists. However, I do wish to demonstrate that stereotypical images of Mexican women are being used in an attempt to signify that the contents of a package are authentically Mexican. We, as visual rhetoricians, need to examine food packaging in order to recognize how attempts to appeal to the authenticity of a food product can create an essentialized stereotype of certain groups and cultures. Pausing when we encounter food products in the aisles of the grocery store and allowing ourselves to question audience and purpose in conjunction with an analysis of appeals to authenticity will allow for deeper understandings of what these images attempt to do—and allow consumers to question whether they are buying just a product or also stereotypical images of others.

Works Cited

Adichie, Chimamanda. "The Danger of the Single Story." *YouTube* July 2009. Accessed 7 February 2016.

Appadurai, Arjun. *Modernity at Large: Cultural Dimensions of Globalization.* U of Minnesota P, 1996.

Baudrillard, Jean. *Simulacra and Simulation.* Trans. Sheila Faria Glaser. U of Michigan P, 1981.

"Call for Proposals." *Cultural Rhetorics Conference.* 7 July 2016. Cultural Rhetorics.

Dávila, Arlene. *Latinos, Inc.: The Marketing and Making of a People.* U of California P, 2001.

Dickinson, Greg. "Joe's Rhetoric: Finding Authenticity at Starbucks." *Rhetoric Society Quarterly* 32.4 (2002): 5–27.

Enfield, Nick J. "The Theory of Cultural Logic: How Individuals Combine Social Intelligence with Semiotics to Create and Maintain Cultural Meaning." *Cultural Dynamics* 12.1 (2000): 35–64.

Faigley, Lester. "Material Literacy and Visual Design." *Rhetorical Bodies.* Ed. Jack Selzer and Sharon Crowley. U of Wisconsin P, 1999. 171–201.

"Food." *Brain Games.* National Geographic Channel. Amazon Video, 2004.

Gaytán, Marie Sarita. "From Sombreros to Sincronizadas: Authenticity, Ethnicity, and the Mexican Restaurant Industry." *Journal of Contemporary Ethnography* 37.3 (2008): 314–41.

Girardelli, Davide. "Commodified Identities: The Myth of Italian Food in the United States." *Journal of Communication Inquiry* 28.4 (October 2004): 307–24.

Hum, Sue. "The Racialized Gaze: Authenticity and Universality in Disney's *Mulan.*" *Ways of Seeing, Ways of Speaking: The Integration of Rhetoric and Vision in Constructing the Real.* Ed. Kristie S. Fleckenstein, Hum, and Linda T. Calendrillo. Parlor P, 2007. 107–30.

Nericcio, William Anthony. *Tex[t]-Mex: Seductive Hallucinations of the "Mexican" in America.* U of Texas P, 2007.

Niblock, Sarah. "Advertising." *Feminist Visual Culture.* Ed. Fiona Carson and Claire Pajaczkowska. Routledge, 2001. 295–307.

Olson, Lester C., Cara A. Finnegan, and Diane S. Hope. "Commodifying and Consuming." *Visual Rhetoric: Reader in Communication and American Culture.* Ed. Olson, Finnegan, and Hope. SAGE Publications, 2008. 273–78.

Pajaczkowska, Claire. "Issues in Feminist Visual Culture." *Feminist Visual Culture.* Ed. Fiona Carson and Pajaczkowska. Routledge, 2001. 1–21.

Perelman, Chaim, and Lucie Olbrechts-Tyteca. "The Choice of Data and Their Adaptation for Argumentative Purposes." *The New Rhetoric: A Treatise on Argumentation.* Trans. John Wilkinson and Purcell Weaver. U of Notre Dame P, 1969. 115–20.

Phillips, Kendall R., and G. Mitchell Reyes, eds. *Global Memoryscapes: Contesting Remembrance in a Transnational Age*. U of Alabama P, 2011.

Pilcher, Jeffrey M. *Planet Taco: A Global History of Mexican Food*. Oxford UP, 2012.

Representations and the Media. Dir. Sut Jhally. Media Education Foundation, Documentary Films, Challenging Media, 1997.

Salas, Consuelo Carr, and Meredith E. Abarca. "Food Marketing Industry: Cultural Attitudes Made Visible." *Latin@s' Presence in the Food Industry: Changing How We Think about Food*. Ed. Abarca and Salas. U of Arkansas P, 2016. 202–22.

Williamson, Judith. *Decoding Advertisements: Ideology and Meaning in Advertising*. Marion Boyard, 1994.

14. FEEDING THE SELF: REPRESENTATIONS OF NOURISHMENT AND FEMALE BODIES IN HOLOCAUST ART

Alexis Baker

In June 2013, I visited the *Women and the Holocaust* exhibit at the Maltz Museum of Jewish Heritage in Beachwood, Ohio. As I looked at the photos, letters, and artifacts, I came across a handmade bra that had been sewn by a woman in one of the concentration camps. It was made from scraps of material collected over time. No matter that it was piecemeal and primitive, it was beautiful. The narrative that accompanied the bra explained that she made it to maintain the modesty she was used to before the camps. When other women learned of her bra, they begged her for one, all of them wishing for this small reminder of their lives before the Holocaust.

As I stood in front of this exhibit, I began to see women who experienced the Holocaust not as a homogenous group with one grand narrative experience but, rather, as individuals who experienced such atrocities in unique and complex ways. As a result, I wanted to examine how women represent their ethoi within art that depicts a Holocaust experience. In this application, ethos refers specifically to the women's experiential authority to represent their cultural, spiritual, and physical identities through art and to link those identities to their bodies. Throughout this chapter, I also use the term "self," defined by Elinor Ochs and Lisa Capps, as a sense of being in the world, a conscious understanding of one's past, a connection to the present, and the ability to envision a viable future (21). I combine these concepts to form the basis of my claim that the art examined here is the product of rhetorical choices, specifically visual metaphors of health, strength, and nourishment that represent women as having selves that transcend and resist the reality of the camps.

Artwork by women, representing women, in the Holocaust frequently depicts healthy, well-nourished, fully functioning female bodies, as if there was plenty of wholesome food available in the camps. Feminist scholars, such as Joy Ritchie, Kate Ronald, and others, explain that women must find available means to speak, especially under conditions as brutal as the Holocaust. Thus, art and, more specifically, the visual representations of nourishment and health within that art become formidable avenues for power and agency by creating metaphors for well-fortified Jewish female identity and ethos. If, as Sara Horowitz claims, the treatment and functions of a woman's body can be read rhetorically as metaphors for experiencing and remembering the Holocaust in specifically female ways, then artistic representations of the body can act in similar ways. In Holocaust art, women are often represented as they might have appeared before the travesties of genocide (264). No matter how starved their actual physical bodies may have become, the visual metaphors suggest that a cultural and spiritual sense of self remained intact.

Such an interpretation is not an attempt to reify the practice of turning complex and painful experiences into something positive and palatable. Instead, this perspective demonstrates that representing the women with well-nourished bodies suggests a strong ethos that is closely linked to identification with their pre-Holocaust selves. Of course, the self is not a static thing, it is influenced by experience, intention, and perception, but it ultimately tries to square "truth" with these things (Martin 76). By analyzing these visual statements rhetorically, my study shows that women's Holocaust art is shaped by forces other than material conditions and is an attempt to square the truth of the self with the reality of the atrocity. In this case, images of fortified, well-sustained women reveal that identity is not strictly linked to physical conditions.

/ 201

HISTORICAL AND SCHOLARLY BACKGROUND

Because there were a disproportionate number of women who died during the Holocaust, there are relatively few female survivor stories. As a result, the corpus of female survivor stories is small and the diversity of women's Holocaust experiences largely missing from public memory. Jessica Enoch explains the importance of hearing "histories that recover the work of female rhetors and rhetoricians" (58). The work of female rhetors shapes how women's experiences are told and held in the public's memory. Enoch argues that rhetorical work also shapes group identity, that "there are dominant public memories that fortify the status quo, and there are counterpublic memories that disrupt visions of life as it was, is, and will be" (62).

Zoë Vania Waxman argues that the majority of published women's Holocaust narratives uphold gendered approaches to the texts by celebrating women who nobly maintain their roles as wives and mothers during internment. Waxman notes that "assumptions about appropriate gender behavior obscure the diversity of women's Holocaust experiences" (124). She contends, however, that focusing solely on noble representations simplifies and misrepresents female Holocaust experiences. Privileging the perspective of the noble woman also strips the power from those who actually went through the trauma by reappropriating their stories to make them easier for audiences to digest.

Waxman also comments that outside forces influenced how women of the Holocaust used narratives to represent their ethoi in ways that depart from the physical realities of their bodies. Waxman cites Sara Zyskind's *Stolen Years* as an example. Zyskind describes just how deplorable the situation

was, especially in terms of food and nourishment:

> In the ghetto we had no need for a calendar. Our lives were divided into periods based on the distribution of food: bread every eighth day, the ration once a month. Each day fell into two parts: before and after we received our soup. In this way the time passed. (qtd. in Waxman 26)

Instead of the problems with food, the publisher reappropriates her experiences and focuses on aspects of "love and courage" (Waxman 129). Waxman suggests that the publisher is playing to the value the public places on positive narratives, narratives that sometimes even erase suffering. My analysis depends on and complicates Waxman's perspective.

Yitzhak Buxbaum suggests that some Jewish women make rhetorical choices that represent the belief in the teaching that the soul, not the body, is the foundation of identity. For example, Buxbaum cites Rebbetzin Devorah Cohen's remembrances of Auschwitz, where she lost her parents and sisters to the gas chambers and was the subject of experiments performed by the notorious Dr. Mengele:

> On that first night in Auschwitz, a veteran inmate had pointed to the smoke issuing out of the chimney of the crematoria and told her, "That's your parents." Nevertheless, she asserted, "Auschwitz was not a bad place

... there was a group of religious Hungarian girls. We stuck together. And all the mitzvot[h] [commandments] we could do, we did do.... A bad place is a place where Jew can do mitzvoth but don't do them." (39)

The story shows Cohen's belief that the body's physical condition and location do not determine a person's identity, even in times of horrific suffering. The physical space that the women in Cohen's narrative occupy does not erode their understanding of themselves as Jewish women. Location and other physical realities are not the locus of their identities. Their memories are centered on their connection to mitzvoth and the sense of self that results from its practice, not on physical suffering. Thus, it becomes significant that women's bodies are often drawn as they were before the women's internment, as if to argue that the essence of these women remains unchanged, regardless of their physical condition.

Many people are familiar with images of the horrific state of the concentration camps, particularly the emaciated bodies of those who occupied them. Food was scarce and sanitation deplorable. These deprivations quickly took their toll on prisoners. Even the most robust suffered. According to Rochelle Saidel's article "Ravensbruck Women's Concentration Camp," conditions were especially poor in the camps designed for women, such as Ravensbruck, which stood about fifty miles outside of Berlin. Rations were low and women and their children, including newborn infants, starved and died at astounding rates. The conditions worsened over the years as the population of the camp swelled. In 1944, for instance, thousands of Hungarian women arrived at the already bursting camp. To "house" the overflow, a small tent was erected. Food supplies did not increase and over three thousand women died from starvation, exposure to the freezing temperatures, and disease.

Interestingly, the women eased their suffering by composing recipe books based on their lives before the Holocaust. Clearly, "this was a form of resistance unique to women because it enabled them to use their homemakers' skills to cook in words and remember better times at home" (Saidel). Two such cookbooks survive. In them, the women used food as a remembrance of safer, healthier, happier times. Their ability to "cook with words" enabled them to locate themselves, however briefly, outside of the realities of Ravensbruck and in an imaginative realm.

From these examples, we see that Holocaust art frequently represents women as healthy and well fed. Despite the conditions in the camps, women are often drawn with full hips and breasts or as pregnant or nursing mothers. Thus, it is clear that art and its representation of identity is shaped not only by reality but by other, less tangible elements. Women are shown as able to continue performing the roles they have always held within their community. Their cultural and spiritual identities appear to continue to thrive, even as their bodies starve, because the soul transcends physical hunger and presents identities not of victims but of strong Jewish women.

MY APPROACH TO THE ART

Following David Birdsell and Leo Groarke, I hold that words are no more or less effective than visuals at making arguments, although they are clearly based on different conventions. Words are arbitrary and associated with particular cultures. Visuals may be linked to a specific culture, but their forms are more universally recognized (hence, international symbols are used where words would confuse, such as using an *X* to indicate that something is prohibited). Because of these differences, Birdsell and Groarke note that it is especially important to understand visual arguments, with as many subtleties as possible, in context: "'Context' can involve a wide range of cultural assumptions, situational cures, time-sensitive information, and/or knowledge of a specific interlocutor" (314).

In this analysis, I consider the art in terms of visual metaphor; I also consider how those rhetorical moves express certain aspects of Jewish female identity. When examining the metaphors, I sought comparisons contained in the images. For example, when a work depicts a pregnant body, it compares the healthy woman, capable of sustaining pregnancy, with the woman in the camp, who wouldn't be likely to endure pregnancy, and represents her as healthy. Similarly, the images use space and content to tell stories. Depictions of mothers with their children indicate that women and their children are together in the camps rather than separated. In what follows, I offer one way to understand representations of Jewish women in the Holocaust.

THE ANALYSIS

This analysis is not meant to essentialize Jewish women or to downplay the tragedy of their suffering. This chapter does, however, rely on the fact that many of the Jewish women in the camps would have identified with clearly defined rules of modesty, marriage, and motherhood, and perhaps have found strength in these traditions. *Nefesh Chaya: The Unique Avodas Hashem of the Jewish Woman* by Rav Shimshon Dovid Pincus explains that motherhood is an especially important aspect of a traditional Jewish woman's identity.[1] Her "main task in the partnership of marriage is the rearing of the children. . . . Her whole life [is dedicated to this] and [to] shaping the Jewish home" (4). An observant Jewish woman does everything "for the sake of Heaven alone . . . it is all inside of [her]" (19). In other words, for many Jewish women identity is not defined by bodies or physical existence or experiences but rather by the work they do for God, which is sometimes linked to the roles they play within their families. Birdsell and Groarke point out that visuals expand the arguments made by written and verbal texts; "when we incorporate conventionalized, situation-specific meanings within the process of interpreting visual arguments, we effectively extend the traditional verbal enthymeme," that is, the traditional rhetorical syllogism (315). Much Holocaust art shows motherhood as one of the most essential facets of a Jewish woman's identity, revealing this role's importance. In this way, depictions of motherhood in Holocaust art function as extended metaphors for traditional Jewish women's identity.

Halina Olomucki's work *Mother and Child* (figure 14.1) shows a mother acting out her traditional role of protector and nurturer. The woman and her child are represented as being together, even though most women were

Mother and Child, by Halina Olomucki. Art Collection, Beit Lohamei Haghetaot, Ghetto Fighters' House Museum, Israel.

/ 205

separated from their children in the camps. The mother also has her hair, despite the fact that one of the first degradations women suffered in the camps was having their heads shaved. Her thick, wavy hair is healthy, as if she is not a prisoner in the camps and as if her body has enough nutrients to produce such beautiful tresses. In fact, both mother and child appear relatively robust. They have rounded cheeks and full upper arms. The child's body is slightly plump, indicating good nutrition. Interestingly, there is nothing to hint at their location, no buildings or landscape. The only background is a vague swirl around them, indicating that place is inconsequential. We simply see a well-nourished woman holding her child, not a person suffering in a camp. The picture, a classical mother and child pose, is a metaphor for the woman's ability to protect and care for her child as she normally would have before the Holocaust.

The other important point is the woman's expression. Unlike her child, she does not look at the viewer but rather at some unseen point beyond. This gives the impression that she is somehow removed from the moment, as if her focus is on the realities of some other place and time, perhaps the better past, perhaps the future she hopes to see. Like the women who produced the Ravensbruck cookbooks, this woman could be in a different time and place when she pursued her life as a well-nourished Jewish woman. Her expression makes her seem untouched by what is happening around her, and it creates a powerful sense of ethos, suggesting that this woman, regardless of her current situation, consciously connects to another place that has nothing to do with her present circumstance. The depiction of her well-fed body implies that she is not defined by the physical conditions of the camp and that her identity transcends her material environment.

The next image, *Women and Children Being Sent on a Transport from the Terezin Ghetto* by Helga Weissová-Hošková (figure 14.2), shows the importance of motherhood to Jewish female identity in specific terms of pregnancy. A heavily pregnant woman holds the hand of a child. She is accompanied by a second person holding another child. The star on the child's chest indicates that this is a group of Jewish women and children. The title clearly states that they are being transported from a ghetto to either a camp or their deaths; however, the representation constructs a metaphor of survival and strength. The image focuses on the woman's heavily pregnant belly, which emerges from the negative space behind the group and stands in sharp contrast to the rest of her emaciated frame. The child within her body, and her body's ability to sustain that child, acts as a metaphor for potential life, a future, as does the child, whose hand she so tightly grips.

Women and Children Being Sent on a Transport from the Terezin Ghetto, by Helga Weissová-Hošková. Courtesy of the artist and DILIA Theatrical, Literary, and Audiovisual Agency, Czech Republic.

This image of healthy motherhood creates a metaphor of endurance and defies the reality most women experienced during the Holocaust. Her advanced-stage pregnant belly sharply contrasts with the rest of her body, which displays the ravages of extreme malnutrition: her eyes are sunken, her cheekbones jut from her skin, the sinews in her neck are visible, and her shoulder bones stick out sharply from her body. A woman this malnourished is at high risk for miscarriage, yet this woman's ability to carry a baby appears unaffected by the lack of food, and her baby seems to be growing well, as indicated by the size of her belly. The presence of the three children suggests hope for survival and the continuation of the Jewish culture.

There are yet other prominent aspects of her body that suggest that she receives proper nutrition. Her muscular calves and large hands show physical strength. Her large breasts imply she has nursed her children, and they will survive as the result of the nourishment they receive from her. Her feet are disproportionately large and appear to root her firmly in place, lending a sense of permanence and maternal power. Through her solid, grounded presence, this image suggests that woman's identity, and thus her children's and that of all future generations, has a deep and solid foundation. Moreover, because her physicality is not the only source of her identity, her poorly fed body is inconsequential.[2]

Weissová-Hošková's picture suggests complex metaphorical connections between food, nutrition, and women's bodies. Customs involving food are an integral part of cultural identity; this is especially true when they intersect with religious beliefs. Pincus tells us that a Jewish woman's role is keeping a proper household, which includes cooking for her family and keeping a kosher home (24). Couple this with the food deficit in concentration camps, and it makes sense that nutrition and motherhood become powerful metaphors in Holocaust art. They are rhetorical choices that indicate a sustained sense of self and identity and resistance against annihilation.

These two images offer compelling depictions of women's bodies. Regardless of their actual nutrition levels, the art shows healthy and well-nourished female bodies that function as they would outside of the camps. Metaphorically, mothers continue to feed and protect their children. As the first picture shows, women are often portrayed as looking beyond the material world and remaining grounded in their maternal roles. Pincus writes,

> The daily schedule of a wife and mother in a Torah home today is quite the same as that of a Jewish woman a hundred or a thousand years ago. She gets up in the morning, [prays], cleans the house, cares for her children, and so on. (24–25)

Such routine tasks become difficult, nearly impossible, without the good health that results from proper nourishment. Yet the tasks that define women's roles are clearly present in both the visual representations of women's bodies and in the written and oral narratives of female survivors.

Judith Liberman's *Women in the Holocaust* (figure 14.3) starkly depicts the significance of these routine tasks. Unlike the other two, this piece presents multiple women; yet, like the other two, these women are physically depicted in a way that would have been impossible in the reality of the camps. The women in Liberman's picture are robustly healthy, with wide hips, full breasts, and gorgeous heads of hair. Fully aware of the Schutzstaffel men behind them, the women try to maintain their modestly by crossing their legs, standing sideways, and hiding behind one another, yet the power and health of their bodies

Figure 14.3. *Women in the Holocaust*, by Judith Liberman.
Florida Holocaust Museum.

are fully displayed and work metaphorically to create a sense of community
and support despite the very real threat posed by the presence of Nazi guards.

The space and place of the painting is clearly defined by the bars enclos-
ing the women. They show that the women are trapped and at the mercy of
the guards. They also place a barrier between the women and the viewer.
Moreover, the bars indicate that, as with the other drawings, the women have
once again maintained a connection to their former identities regardless of
their present imprisonment and vulnerability. Metaphorically, their selves
are essentially the same, healthy and robust, as before the Holocaust.

The composition creates a group identity that functions on a separate
plane than the threat represented by the men behind the women. This representation of women's physical vitality indicates that they are sustained
by something beyond whatever meager food they are given. The reality of

their vulnerability is clear, but they are depicted as physically healthy and strong. Their well-nourished bodies symbolize a strong sense of self, even at a moment of extreme vulnerability.

CONCLUSIONS AND IMPLICATIONS

These visual metaphors suggest that the Jewish women's malnourished bodies do not define their ethoi. The realities their bodies likely endured are not represented; rather, representations of motherhood and community show that identity is not determined by physical realities. A dear Orthodox Jewish friend once explained to me that a Jewish woman is *always* a Jewish woman. It does not matter what you do to her body or where you put her. While the art frequently depicts female bodies as they were before their internment, it also reflects the strong sense that the self remains intact, regardless of physical conditions of starvation.

Waxman argues that the published accounts of Holocaust survivors negate narratives that do not adhere to traditional constructions of gender (124) to feed the public palatable, simple accounts of the Holocaust. While Waxman is absolutely correct, the images do uphold traditional gender roles but not as mere stereotypes. As such, these pieces are complex statements about cultural and spiritual identity, which we should not underestimate.

These representations of strong, fully functioning female bodies operate as visual metaphors about the survival of women's cultural and spiritual identity—despite the horrors of the Holocaust. While I do not at all wish to claim that this was every woman's experience, the metaphors within the art do open a space where viewers can imagine strong women who say, *this is who I was; this is who I still am.* Before the Holocaust, many Jewish women lived lives rooted in the essential tenants and traditions of their faith; they were, above all, wives and mothers. As feminist scholars, this may be difficult for us to swallow, but neither is it in keeping with modern feminism to apply a label to an individual who claims another identity for herself.

Food and sustenance are integral elements of this identity. Often, the conventions surrounding food are the signs of culture that survive long after language, dress, and other customs disappear. The art serves as a means of survival and resistance because the ability to make rhetorical choices brings a power and dignity to our lives, a concept that becomes especially meaningful in a situation like the Holocaust. Representations of healthy bodies symbolize nourished souls and demonstrate identity may be sustained by rhetorical agency, even under the most appalling circumstances.

Notes

1. "Avodas Hashem" in Pincus's title refers to one's loving duty to God or to working hard in a holy task for God. For women, it refers to such tasks as celebrating *Shabbos*, raising children, and helping others.

2. Yet it is interesting that the female body is necessary to pass Judaism on to future generations, essentially the female body is the threshold for a person's Judaism.

Works Cited

Birdsell, David S., and Leo Groarke. "Toward a Theory of Visual Argument." *Visual Rhetoric in a Digital World: A Critical Sourcebook*. Ed. Carolyn Handa. Southern Illinois UP, 2004. 309–20.

Buxbaum, Yitzhak. *Jewish Tales of Holy Women*. Jossey-Bass, 2002.

Enoch, Jessica. "Releasing Hold: Feminist Historiography without the Tradition." *Theorizing Histories of Rhetoric*. Ed. Michelle Ballif. Southern Illinois UP, 2013. 58–73.

Horowitz, Sara R. "Memory and Testimony of Women Survivors of Nazi Genocide." *Women of the Word: Jewish Women and Jewish Writing*. Ed. Judith R. Baskin. Wayne State UP, 1994. 258–82.

Judith Liberman Art Works. Center for Holocaust and Genocide Studies. University of Minnesota. Accessed 21 November 2013.

Martin, Wallace. *Recent Theories of Narrative*. Cornell, 1986.

Ochs, Elinor, and Lisa Capps. "Narrating the Self." *Annual Review of Anthropology* 25 (1996): 19–43.

Olomucki, Halina. *Mother and Child*. Ghetto Fighters' House Archives. Accessed 21 November 2013.

Pincus, Rav Shimshon Dovid. *Nefesh Chaya: The Unique Avodas Hashem of the Jewish Woman*. Feldheim, 2011.

Ritchie, Joy, and Kate Ronald, eds. *Available Means: An Anthology of Women's Rhetoric(s)*. U of Pittsburgh P, 2001.

Saidel, Rochelle G. "Ravensbruck Women's Concentration Camp." *Jewish Women: A Comprehensive Historical Encyclopedia*. 1 March 2009. Jewish Women's Archive. Accessed 25 June 2014.

Waxman, Zoë Vania. *Writing the Holocaust: Identity, Testimony, Representation*. Oxford UP, 2006.

Weissová-Hošková, Helga. *Women and Children Being Sent on a Transport from the Terezin Ghetto*. Ghetto Fighters' House Archives. Accessed 21 November 2013.

15. EVOLVING ANA: INVITING RECOVERY

Morgan Gresham

In describing their work with food, Jennifer Cognard-Black and Melissa A. Goldthwaite explain how teaching the literatures of food is often received by colleagues:

> [In] talking about Books That Cook with our colleagues, we have often received what we've come to call the "arched-eyebrow response." While there is no dictionary to define it, the connotation of the arched eyebrow is "You English folk will teach anything and call it literature." We have discovered that there is an inherent distrust of a class in which food is taken seriously—read, discussed, written about, cooked, and consumed. The carnivalesque comes to mind, as well as the notion of education packaged and sold as "entertainment." (421–22)

Although I don't teach food-based literature, I understand Cognard-Black and Goldthwaite's experiences with others' views of their subject matter. I research pro-ana websites, sites that advocate for anorexia. Similar to feminism, pro-ana has many definitions and has undergone multiple phases; however, at its simplest, pro-ana means taking a stance that promotes or supports behaviors and attitudes associated with anorexia. Upon hearing about the pro-ana movement or learning about pro-ana websites, the typical response is disgust or disbelief. Still, I believe it is important to study these sites because they are essential acts of communication from a group of mostly young women who often feel marginalized yet attempt to communicate their worldview with hope for change.

Pro-ana sites often provoke a series of questions to which researchers must respond either implicitly or explicitly:

- Why do these spaces exist?
- Why should we study these online spaces?
- If we study these spaces, is it because we have a "sick fascination" with (dis)eased bodies?
- Are you one of them?

There has been significant backlash against these sites and their authors and expressions of concern that pro-ana and pro-mia (that promote bulimia) sites teach mostly young girls and women how to have, how to develop, how to live with an eating disorder. Here is an excerpt from one website:

> The Internet can be a valuable medium for educating the public about anorexia nervosa and for helping people with eating disorders find 24-hour support. But the online world also holds dangers for girls and young women who are struggling with a distorted body image. Pro-ana blogs, message boards and communities advocate a lifestyle that revolves around a pathological obsession with getting thin. Some online social media platforms have even banned pro-ana sites for portraying self-destructive behavior as glamorous or desirable. ("Dangers")

/ 213

Critics such as these see pro-ana sites as inherently dangerous and often seek to silence the views represented. Rather than trying to quiet the authors of pro-ana sites, I am interested in understanding the complexity of the discourse that happens on such sites. To do so, I look closely at the conversations created by participants willing to transgress discourse community borders enough to have conversations rather than merely post antagonistic rants on the opposing sites. Invitational rhetoric is a rhetorical stance, one that demonstrates a willingness to seek a richer understanding, to open spaces for potential conversation, and to offer the potential for evolution of positions from one identity to another. Identity construction is vital to feminist action, and it is important that feminist scholars and researchers have a clearer understanding of the kinds of websites that reveal and shape the experience of many young women, especially if we hope to offer alternative identity categories.

Recent scholarship on the pro-ana movement shows how responses to pro-ana websites, Tumblr sites, Instagram posts, and other social media sites can be read as potentially feminist. My research reports on the change in pro-ana websites since 2001 and looks specifically at House of Thin, which identifies itself as a primary shaper of the pro-ana evolution:

> The evolution is for the people who NEED this as a support system, realize that living with an eating disorder is not healthy, do not tell others how to become anorexic (because you can't . . . it's not something you learn), and want to get help in getting out of all this disordered mess.

In this chapter, I extend Nick Fox, Katie Ward, and Alan O'Rourke's research on pro-ana sites, and I consider the ways in which House of Thin is indeed an evolution of pro-ana that invites more pro-ana women into the conversation about recovery.

Fox, Ward, and O'Rourke speak to the concerns of those who see pro-ana sites as only negative and destructive. They explain,

> What from the outside appears a bizarre and pernicious sect, can be understood as a reasoned world-view. Pro-anorexia is not a diet, nor is it a lifestyle choice. It is a way of coping and a damage limitation that rejects recovery as a simplistic solution to a symptom that leaves the underlying pain and hurt unresolved. . . . [W]hile the routines and rituals of pro-ana appear extreme and risky, they are normalised, controlled, justified and legitimated through the sharing of information, risk management and support. (967)

House of Thin is a website created in response to the conversations surrounding pro-ana and pro-mia websites. It neither justifies nor judges those who identify as pro-ana. Rather, it seeks to provide a supportive environment for those who may wish to recover from an eating disorder.

HISTORY OF PRO-ANA WEBSITES

In the late 1990s and early 2000s, girls with a range of programming skills began creating websites that were dedicated to inspiring thinness, sometimes at great bodily cost. As these women self-identified as anorexic or bulimic or with an unspecified eating disorder, these websites became known as pro-ana or pro-mia sites. In broad strokes, these sites contained:

- thinspiration quotations and images
- strategies for losing weight or maintaining weight loss
- methods of hiding emotions/hiding food
- ways to manage emotions via other potentially self-harming techniques, such as cutting, vomiting/purging, excessive exercise

Pro-ana sites serve as a means of creating an identity around the disease: "From the pro-ana perspective, recovery was not an option for most anorectics. Unlike other anorexia EMs [explanatory models], the main objective of management in pro-ana was not treatment but the safe management of a dangerous condition" (Fox, Ward, and O'Rourke 959). When I first began studying these sites during the academic year 2000–2001, there were approximately five hundred pro-ana websites (Reaves). Some researchers recognized the value of these sites. In "Pro-anorexics and Recovering Anorexics Differ in Their Linguistic Internet Self-Presentation," Elizabeth Lyons, Matthias Mehl, and James Pennebaker explain that by creating pro-ana websites, "pro-anorexics may use a coping strategy that stabilizes them emotionally and allows them to experience a sense of control over their illness" (256). Not everyone, however, saw value in such sites. In 2001, as the public first started to learn of the existence of pro-ana sites, the National Association of Anorexia and Associated Disorders and the National Eating Disorders Association spearheaded a movement to have Internet service providers (ISPs) like Yahoo!, GeoCities, and Angelfire take down the pro-ana sites. By 2004, many sites existed, primarily on private ISPs, but were often ephemeral. Further, because of the number of complaints and threats to remove pro-ana sites from hosting ISPs, almost all sites now display some type of "triggering" disclaimer, suggesting that the interior pages may trigger those in recovery to have disordered responses. Many of the authors of pro-ana sites responded by either moving the sites to password-protected areas or developing disclaimers (or trigger warnings) that urged potential viewers to "click at their own risk." In previous scholarship, I have argued that these disclaimers can be read as a feminist response to the call that these spaces should not exist. By keeping the sites up—but providing disclaimers—pro-ana website authors recognized that young women needed a space in which they could build an identity that included their eating disorder.

Many people believe pro-ana sites are dangerous to women. However, I believe these sites can (and have in a number of particular cases) enable young women to transition over time from fully identifying as radically pro-ana to adopting an alternative identity. Some of these sites encourage readers to understand that disordered eating/disordered thinking can be a part of one's being, but it does not have to constitute one's entire identity.

House of Thin speaks to an interesting generational shift in the purpose of pro-ana sites. The author Mandi Faux recounts the purposes of pro-ana sites by generation, calling forth alliance with waves of feminism. She links her own approach to second-wave feminism in an attempt to emphasize the evolution of pro-ana sites as a modification of the separatist movement (if you are not pro-ana, you are against pro-ana) in early pro-ana sites toward a second wave in which there is a greater acceptance of the variations within the pro-ana population.

HOUSE OF THIN WEBMISTRESS

Mandi Faux is the author of multiple online spaces. Her Facebook, YouTube channel, and website describe her as: "TS *Mandi Faux* worlds [*sic*] premier transsexual escort model entertainer official website forum with pictures, poems, radio show, links, club." In her role as House of Thin webmistress, Faux seeks to establish her credibility, her ethos, within the pro-ana community in a couple of ways. On her "About Me" page, she lists not only her name and a link to the other websites she authors but also her height, weight, body mass index, and goal weight. As a member of the community, Faux as author must recognize the importance of establishing relative body size as a precursor to permission to speak as an authority or an insider. On the "About House of Thin" page, the author describes her own evolution as a person living with an eating disorder. As a part of that evolution, she describes the first iteration of the website as ThinVision, a "hard core pro-ana forum." She goes on to explain the difficulties she experienced trying to keep the forum online as she saw the purpose of the website transitioning from a "hard core" pro-ana site to a site that, if not welcomed recovery, at least admitted it. She writes,

> It's been a battle thus far and we've changed so much through it all. From full on hard core to the now one of kind support forum that's beyond what any other out there is today. Total change, isn't it? Yup . . . you have just entered into the Evolution of Pro-Ana. Constantly perfecting the way we support each other and making our lives better. People change, pro-ana changes . . . change is good. To improve you must change, right? Viva La Evolution!

As webmistress, she defines the kind of spaces that viewers will see in the House of Thin in opposition to other pro-ana websites:

> This is not the typical proana sites & promia websites you may have been use to seeing, but instead a truly pro-active eating disorder support group. The foundation of this pro-ana community web site is built to be supportive towards the eating disordered individual, and to focus

on the root causes of eating disorders in order to bring about positive change in attitudes.

She makes it clear on the introductory page that viewers will not find the "tips and tricks" or "thinspiration" images, but rather, that viewers can expect to find information about eating disorders and community support. The site is "pro-recovery," and she claims that "this is the first pro mia pro ana website of the second wave," mirroring the language of feminism. She concludes, "We've come a long way, baby."

AUDIENCE

The intended audience for House of Thin is primarily (young) women who identify as pro–eating disorder. In many ways, the intended audience is someone like me: a recovering anorectic. In other spaces, I have written about my own experiences with anorexia and my struggle to maintain a feminist identity while acknowledging my eating disorder. While third-wave feminist writings often claim that overcoming eating disorders is being feminist, I understand that my attempts at self-definition as a feminist must include my ambivalence about my relationship with food. For me, recovery is not a "one and done" experience but rather a series of daily choices about identification. The author of House of Thin recognizes that recovery is difficult, ongoing, and requires support from other people who identify more like me:

/ 217

> Also if you are part of a pro-recovery group that isn't doing you any good, this is also the proana web site for you. We don't focus on the disorder itself, but instead focus on the individual and possible reasons as to why disordered eating happened, and offer solutions to these root causes (done through the forums online journals).

Faux relays values and experiences shared by many who are ambivalent about the status of their relationship with anorexia. There is an expectation, however, that there will be other types of visitors to the site, including those who still identify as "hard core pro-ana." Members of this audience will not find what they are expecting, but the author makes repeated overtures to invite them into the space. Faux deliberately reaches out to a second-person you—"you will find"; "you suffer from"; "you do take"—so that readers choose to stay in the space. The author is also coaching the reader to consider recovery as an option: "If you do take that step towards recovery and an area triggers you too much, just leave that part of the group and you can still take part in the community without worries of being triggered." Another expected audience is observers/outsiders, some of whom in the past may have been responsible for the removal of pro-ana sites from ISPs. Reminding this potential audience that there is information "on various eating disorders, plus BMI, BMR and metric calculators and news articles," and not thinspiration and tips and tricks, limits that audiences' reasons for complaint against the website. For many outsiders who called for the removal of sites, the goal was to provide access to treatment information instead, and Faux provides that information in her "ED-ucation Library."

In providing what she calls "a safe, stable online home for those who are eating disordered," the author appeals to the viewers' emotions, drawing on feelings of alienation and chaotic relationships that frequently characterize those who self-identify as pro-ana. By developing a stable online home, the author creates a sense of space or place that can serve as respite from the audience's less hospitable physical environment.

DESIGN OF HOUSE OF THIN

The websites for which Faux serves as webmistress all have the same look and feel, and by 2014 web standards, that look and feel is dated. The pink type against a maroon background is difficult to read without carefully concentrating on the text. There are occasional spelling, grammar, and mechanics errors. However, rather than disrupting the author's ethos, these errors and colloquialisms signal to readers that this site is authentic. The author is, like "me" the hypothetical reader, more interested in communicating community than correctness. One of the primary missions of the site is to provide an interactive forum community, a place in which members can engage one another in conversation as they deal with daily iterations of their disorder.

However, links to both the pro-ana forum and the pro-mia forum are inactive, resulting in "a page not found" error message. This is not particularly surprising given that most pro-ana webmistresses, especially those who begin a path to recovery, eventually reach an identity of "mostly recovered." These sites, then, fall into neglect and disuse. House of Thin has a 2006–16 copyright notice, but its last visible update, on a page about "renovations" to the House, was January 15, 2007.[1] Despite the inactivity of the website and the unavailability of the forum, the mere existence of a space that suggests recovery is important. House of Thin serves as an artifact of the evolution of pro-ana from a volitional space to a space that can support recovery.

INVITATION TO RECOVERY

In an article about the "hidden anorectic," communications scholars Grace Lager and Brian McGee describe how, in magazines geared to girls and women, there are stories that showcase the extreme or ultimate anorectic, ignoring the many girls and women who are eating disordered but that fall into more normalized weight ranges—in particular, those not under one hundred pounds. These hidden anorectics, they argue, seek recognition of their disordered eating, an awareness that their relationships to food and to others are not "normal" but "disordered." It is for this group of people that a pro-ana space like House of Thin is most effective because the emphasis is not so much on how to be eating disordered but rather on the community of those who have similar experiences. I am not thin enough, the thinking goes, when one views the extreme anorectic, but I am still different. House of Thin appeals to this "hidden" audience in a space that suggests that you can be in recovery, or not; you can be actively pro-disorder.[2] Faux writes,

> We are still very much pro ana mia, in that using the words ana mia to describe anorexia bulimia allows for a friendlier atmosphere. We don't encourage nor push ed behaviors, but we do encourage personal development towards a better future.

/ 219

The expectation is that, through being in community with others who have similar experiences, viewers of this site will evolve toward "a better future," which often means recovery. This move toward recovery through developing supportive relationships is borne out in the scholarship on treating eating disorders:

> Because there is no universally effective treatment for AN [anorexia nervosa], it is useful to investigate which therapeutic and life experiences play the most important roles in the outcome from the perspective of the patients. In our sample, relationships (either with a partner or a therapist) played a major role in recovery. Patients said that a supportive relationship was the driving force that assisted them in recovery. (Tozzi et al. 150–51)

As Federica Tozzi and his colleagues suggest, "a supportive relationship" is crucial to recovery, and pro-ana spaces that respect the ambivalence of definition—of identity—provide spaces for developing a new sense of self, a self open to the process of recovery.

Faux uses a form of invitational rhetoric, supporting and encouraging her audience in a respectful way. Jennifer Bone, Cindy Griffin, and T. M. Linda Scholz provide an updated definition of invitational rhetoric:

> To engage in invitational rhetoric is to exchange ideas from positions of mutual respect and equality. Although this mutual respect and equality may be present in persuasive exchanges (e.g., Wood), from an invitational stance, rhetors explore and examine different views, not to advocate the adoption of another person's worldview or reality but, instead, to come away from the exchange with a richer and more comprehensive understanding of that worldview. (437)

This definition advocates for a "richer and more comprehensive understanding" of particular, often juxtaposed, worldviews. House of Thin seeks repeatedly to establish "positions of mutual respect and equality" that provide a space that invites recovery without demanding it or demeaning those who have not started that process.

Notes

1. Although the website was available in late November 2016, it was no longer accessible by mid-December.

2. A subset of the scholarship on pro-ana and pro-mia sites explores the ways in which language use and modification (dis-ease versus disease, dis-order versus disorder) communicates identities separate from medicalized discourse.

Works Cited

Bone, Jennifer Emerling, Cindy L. Griffin, and T. M. Linda Scholz. "Beyond Traditional Conceptualizations of Rhetoric: Invitational Rhetoric and a Move toward Civility." *Western Journal of Communication* 72.4 (2008): 434–62.

Cognard-Black, Jennifer, and Melissa A. Goldthwaite. "Books That Cook: Teaching Food and Food Literature in the English Classroom." *College English* 70.4 (2008): 421–36.

"The Dangers of Pro-ana Communities." *Futures of Palm Beach*. Accessed 23 September 2014.

Fox, Nick, Katie Ward, and Alan O'Rourke. "Pro-anorexia, Weight-Loss Drugs, and the Internet: An 'Anti-recovery' Explanatory Model of Anorexia." *Sociology of Health and Illness* 27.7 (2005): 944–71.

"House of Thin: Evolution of Pro-ana." *House of Thin*. Accessed 1 September 2014.

Lager, E. Grace, and Brian R. McGee. "Hiding the Anorectic: A Rhetorical Analysis of Popular Discourse Concerning Anorexia." *Women's Studies in Communication* 26.2 (2003): 266–95.

Lyons, Elizabeth J., Matthias R. Mehl, and James W. Pennebaker. "Pro-anorexics and Recovering Anorexics Differ in Their Linguistic Internet Self-Presentation." *Journal of Psychosomatic Research* 60.3 (2006): 253–56.

Reaves, Jessica. "Anorexia Goes High Tech." *Time* 31 July 2001.

"Totally in Control." *Social Issues Research Center.* Accessed 11 August 2014.

Tozzi, Federica, et al. "Causes and Recovery in Anorexia Nervosa: The Patient's Perspective." *International Journal of Eating Disorders* 33.2 (2003): 143–54.

16. RECONSTRUCTING THE FEMALE FOOD-BODY: PROFANITY, PURITY, AND THE BAKHTINIAN GROTESQUE IN *SKINNY BITCH*

Rebecca Ingalls

Rory Freedman and Kim Barnouin's *Skinny Bitch* is a diet book, one in a long line of texts trying to persuade women to change their lives by making healthier eating decisions that will help them to lose weight, find their inner sensuality, and develop confidence. The book was released in 2005, and sales boomed in 2007, which many media sources credited to Victoria Beckham, who was seen carrying the book in the summer of 2007 (Rich). Today, the book's sales have exceeded 1.5 million copies ("Full Details"), and the *Skinny Bitch* enterprise has grown to include a book for pregnant women (*Skinny Bitch: Bun in the Oven*), a book for men (*Skinny Bastard*), a daily "motivational" calendar, and even a recent series of *Skinny Bitch* novels based on a character called Clementine Cooper. With the original *Skinny Bitch*'s caricature of a well-proportioned female in a little black dress holding trendy sunglasses, its cover suggests that this text might be a member of the chicklit family, a story of a forlorn female who has not yet found love, who is recovering from loss of it, or who is on the brink of wedded bliss (in fact, the novels address those very issues). But a reader has only to crack it open to find that it becomes very obvious very soon that the authors, whose nutrition credentials are less than impressive, have a much grander conversion in mind than a healthier diet for the fashion-forward and lovelorn female.

Skinny Bitch is, in part, an argument for veganism. But it's not the compulsion toward veganism that is under scrutiny in this chapter. Rather, it's

the compelling, groundbreaking rhetorical construction of the grotesque female body that Freedman and Barnouin use to convey their argument for a pure, contained, controlled female body—specifically, the body that desires and consumes food—what I will call the "food-body." In contrast to the slew of new and timeless "feel good," forgiving dieting books on the market today—for example, *The Feel-Good Diet* (Hart and Grossman), *You: Losing Weight—the Owner's Manual to Simple and Healthy Weight Loss* (Roizen and Oz), *The Hungry Girl Diet: Big Portions, Big Results* (Lillien), and the famous *Breaking Free from Compulsive Eating* (Roth)—*Skinny Bitch* is unforgiving in its message. From the very first chapter, the authors subvert the familiar one-day-at-a-time rhetoric of fighting obesity as they employ liberal doses of profanity to guilt women out of their eating habits—as in, "it's no wonder you eat shit and garbage" (12). After they use toilet-speak to deprive readers of their favorite "satanic" vices, like caffeine, smoking, alcohol, and sugar, the authors depict scene after bloody scene of animals being slaughtered, condemn meat products as "rotting, decomposing flesh" that will contaminate and constipate the body, and accuse the federal government of maintaining monstrous food regulations. When they have saturated readers with the grotesque, Freedman and Barnouin spin their rhetoric back to the delicious and sensual as they   / 223
resuscitate the ultimate goal of thinness, which includes finding enjoyment in the delectable purity of vegan recipes, and becoming "worth" the expense of organic food shopping and fitting into high-end couture.

In the context of this important discussion of "food, feminisms, and rhetorics," Freedman and Barnouin's rhetorical approach is remarkable. As I will argue, *Skinny Bitch* seems to offer a modern-day reconstruction of the Bakhtinian sense of "grotesque realism," which refers, in part, to the excessive corporeality illustrated in artifacts depicting the carnival tradition but meant to be repressed in high culture (Bakhtin). Bakhtin emphasizes in his analysis that, despite many depictions of the grotesque as categorically dismal and sardonic, the fundamental elements of grotesque realism include *both* decay *and* rebirth, both shame and merriment, both filth and purity. As such, the Bakhtinian model of grotesque realism becomes markedly significant in Freedman and Barnouin's book as it carves a path from an image of the shameful female glutton and the repulsive foods she eats toward a revitalized, idealized image of the "Skinny Bitch." In its reconstructed form, the authors' use of grotesque realism becomes the rhetorical strategy of an agenda meant to steer readers away from "crap" like sugar and animal products, and toward "a way of life" that is "healthy, clean, energized and pure," one that will inspire a reader to "strut [her] skinny ass down the street" (10).

And it becomes a rhetorical tool to disgust, frighten, and strip female readers and their appetites down to the skin and bones of the authors' depiction of "truth" and sensuality and to cleanse the female food-body for good.

DEGRADATION AND REBIRTH: THE AMBIVALENCE OF GROTESQUE REALISM

Bakhtin's discussion of grotesque realism is grounded in the "mass literature" of sixteenth-century French writer François Rabelais. Author of the Gargantua and Pantagruel series, Rabelais details the lives of giants Pantagruel and his father, Gargantua, whose adventures take them through the fairs and marketplaces of France. Drawn from his own experience with the festivities of carnival culture, Rabelais's novels celebrate the subversion of religious and moral standards of the day through the feasting and unbridled merriment of carnival tradition, a celebration that was considered heretical by many in the church, the government, and academia. Rabelais's novels are important to an understanding of Renaissance culture, in part, because they capture the cultural values, the discourse, and the desires shared across classes during that time. Furthermore, Rabelais's focus on the grotesque sheds light on how we may view modern-day cultural depictions of corporeality and consumption.

Bakhtin's goal with *Rabelais and His World* is to clarify and extend Rabelais's discussion of grotesque realism. According to Bakhtin, myriad theorists have tried to analyze the carnivalesque tradition as depicted by Rabelais, but all have gravely missed the mark on the "ambivalence" embedded in it. He spotlights G. Schneegans, nineteenth-century German scholar and author of *The History of Grotesque Satire*, criticizing his work as representative of so many others' misguided depictions of the grotesque:

> [Schneegans's] mistakes are typical; they are repeated in the majority of works devoted to this subject, preceding, or especially, following his own. Schneegans ignores the deep ambivalence of the grotesque and sees it merely as a negation, an exaggeration pursuing narrowly satirical claims. (304)

Bakhtin's explanation of the "ambivalence" that other scholarly work on the grotesque has missed is this: where others deem depictions of the grotesque absolutely negative in their satire—that is, condemning gluttony, corporeality, and sexuality depicted in hyperbolic ways—grotesque realism, when examined more closely, reveals a degradation and a *rebirth*, an abuse and a *celebration*, a fusion with earthliness that recognizes the "low" and basely *while* it praises that connection to earth. To see only the negative in the grotesque, he argues, is to neglect the complex ambivalence of the world that Rabelais was trying to illustrate.

This ambivalence, this "combining in one image both the positive and the negative poles" (308) is what, according to Bakhtin, empowered the sociopolitical rhetoric of grotesque imagery—namely, the pursuit of liberation and the equalizing of societal classes. In his criticism of Wolfgang Kayser's 1957 book *The Grotesque in Painting and Poetry*, Bakhtin notes that Kayser's emphasis on the "gloomy, terrifying tone of the grotesque world" is shortsighted and that he fails to recognize the celebration inherent in the grotesque, "the spirit of carnival [that] liberates the world from all that is dark and terrifying; it takes away all fears and is therefore completely gay and bright" (46–47). According to Bakhtin, grotesque realism depicts an urge for freedom, a humorous perspective on "all that was frightening in ordinary life" that allows its participants to view these social horrors (poverty, filth, abuse of power, social constraint, disease) as "amusing or ludicrous monstrosities" (47). Furthermore, he asserts that the audience of the "marketplace" to which Rabelais directs his message, the laughing participants themselves, represent all corners of society; Rabelais's message is meant not to point out the corruption brought on by their differences but rather to bring them together. Bakhtin writes, "Rabelais creates that special marketplace atmosphere in which the exalted and the lowly, the sacred and the profane are leveled and are all drawn into the same dance" (160). Surely it is easy to see why such seditious ideas might be poorly received by those for whom class distinctions were critical.

In addition, Bakhtin's interpretation is not just meant to correct the scholars who have come before him but also to serve as a word of caution for those to come:

> The problem of the grotesque and of its aesthetic nature can be correctly posed and solved only in relation to medieval folk culture and Renaissance literature. The depth, variety, and power of separate themes can be understood only within the unity of folk and carnival spirit. If examined outside of this unity, they become one-sided, flat, and stripped of their rich content. (51–52)

Does he mean that grotesque realism could only exist during the Renaissance? No, I do not believe that is what he is telling us. Rather, he is concerned that modern interpretations of the Renaissance grotesque are misguided because they apply a modern lens to it; they conflate different styles of grotesque

Rebecca Ingalls

(for instance, Renaissance, Romantic, and modern), when they should be able to see that Renaissance grotesque realism was quite different and that "the unofficial folk culture of the Middle Ages and even of the Renaissance had its own territory and its own particular time, the time of fairs and feasts" (154).

Certainly, we can see how and why modern analyses of grotesque realism—particularly in the context of food consumption—might forego an awareness or appreciation of the ambivalence that Bakhtin defends. We have seen in industrial and modern depictions of food culture in America an absolutely bleak perspective on the relationship between food commerce and consumption. Consider Upton Sinclair's 1906 *The Jungle*, in which he details the gory conditions of Chicago slaughterhouses at the beginning of the twentieth century. With its focus on the relationship between the human immigrant poor and the beasts they killed and sold, and the degrading conditions that both had to suffer, Sinclair offers little celebration in his imagery: "old and crippled and diseased cattle . . . covered with boils," which would "burst and splash foul-smelling stuff into your face" when killed (96). Although Sinclair's narrative ends with some hope for a socialist revolution in America, the novel's graphic scenes are in no way celebratory or humorous. His goal is not to capture the grotesque in a carnivalesque fashion; rather, it is to show the utter bleakness of the meatpacking industry.

Consider, too, Eric Schlosser's more recent 2001 perspective on this same issue, *Fast Food Nation: The Dark Side of the All-American Meal*, in which he picks up the story of American meatpacking just a few decades after Sinclair's novel takes place. Appealing to readers through a romantic history of America's growing "car culture" of the 1940s, the changes in food culture that resulted, and the "founding fathers" of fast food, Schlosser details the story of some of America's favorite food giants: McDonald's, Burger King, Dunkin' Donuts, Kentucky Fried Chicken. However, this nostalgic look back in time does not remain dreamy for long, as Schlosser slowly dismantles the ethos of the masterminds behind fast food, taking his reader "behind the counter" and into the realities of corrupt fast food labor practices, into the technology of fast food composition, and into depictions of the gruesome depths of the meatpacking industry that rival those of Sinclair. Schlosser describes feedlot sanitary conditions that led to the spread of *Escherichia coli* 0157:H7, ones comparable—according to an unnamed official—"to those in a crowded European city during the Middle Ages, when people dumped their chamber pots out the window, raw sewage ran in the streets, and epidemics raged" (201). While it is especially intriguing in the context of this discussion on Renaissance grotesque realism to note "the official's" comparison

226 /

between the meatpacking industry of today and that of the Middle Ages, it is critical to note that Schlosser's goal is not to offer both darkness and light, a combination that, Bakhtin argues, can always be found in the grotesque imagery of Rabelais (Bakhtin 41). Rather, Schlosser's rhetorical agenda is to present only the grim aspects of cattle slaughter and commerce. There is no doubt that his final few chapters build up to a grand plea to his audience to rally against the fast food industry; and perhaps, as with *The Jungle*, the hope lies there in the possibility for social transformation. However, like Sinclair, Schlosser's rhetoric is not shaped around the kind of ambivalence we see in the folk culture of the Renaissance. For both of these authors, who work hard to use repulsion as a rhetorical tool, the message could not be less ambivalent.

And yet do such constructions of the grotesque mean that we cannot find forms of grotesque realism *today*, as it was intended in such works as those of Rabelais? No. In fact, I argue that we can see grotesque realism working hard as a rhetorical tool in Freedman and Barnouin's *Skinny Bitch*. It's the authors' use of the grotesque that makes it a particularly innovative rhetorical approach to food culture. As I explore in this chapter, *Skinny Bitch* utilizes profanity and humor, depictions of feasting, emphasis on the "lower stratum" of the body, and images of sexuality to envision a degradation *and* rejuvenation of the female body and of female food culture. For Freedman and Barnouin, the gluttonous woman who has wasted herself on the poverty of unhealthy eating is laughable, but there is hope for her. However, it is not the rejuvenation that Bakhtin had in mind, for *Skinny Bitch* spins the rhetoric of the grotesque toward a certain transformation that aims to do away with the grotesque altogether.

/ 227

TOUGH LOVE: PROFANITY, HUMOR, AND PERSUASION

The description on the cover of *Skinny Bitch* reads, in script letters, "A no-nonsense, tough-love guide for savvy girls who want to stop eating crap and start looking fabulous." The cover illustration is of a woman with a tiny waist in a sexy little black dress that emphasizes her curves, and she holds her sunglasses as she looks at the reader from behind her impossibly long eyelashes. It's an inviting image—sensuality and self-control—that the authors use to lure their audience. From the outset, the book might seem like a refreshing respite from the rhetoric of self-esteem and self-nurturing that has accompanied other diet books with similar aims. *Skinny Bitch* takes advantage of the plight of the woman who has already hit rock bottom in a cycle of fad diets and weight gain and loss; what has she to lose with a little cut-to-the-chase advice about how she has failed to change her food habits?

Part of the authors' rhetorical strategy is their use of profanity and name calling, which we also find in the culture of grotesque realism. Bakhtin explains, for example, that in the marketplace of Rabelais's narrative there was an

> atmosphere of frankness [that] inspired certain attitudes, a certain unofficial view of the world. These liberties were fully revealed in the festive square when all hierarchic barriers between men were lifted and a true familiar contact was established. Here all men became conscious participants in that one world of laughter. (188)

This blunt exchange of words and abuses involved both insult and praise, as seen in the prologue of *Pantagruel*, which begins, "O most illustrious and most valorous champions, gentlemen and all others who delight in honest entertainment and wit. I address this book to you" (qtd. in Bakhtin 159), and proceeds to insult any audience member who doubts the text:

> "May St. Anthony sear you with his erysipelatous fire . . . may Mahomet's disease whirl you in epileptic jitters . . . may the festers, ulcers and chancres of every purulent pox infect, scathe, mangle, and rend you, entering your bumgut as tenuously as mercurialized cow's hair." (qtd. in Bakhtin 164)

The praise and "billingsgate abuse" that accompany one another in the marketplace, argues Bakhtin, is representative of the core ambivalence of grotesque realism. While the language flatters its audience, it also degrades them. Bakhtin urges us to see the "affection" in the insult and to understand why the combination might inspire both the triviality of laughter and the power of transformation (164–65).

Today, as the cover of *Skinny Bitch* suggests, we might call this mix of exaltation and insult "tough love," and it gets its psychological power, in part, because it utilizes a "frankness" that aims to surprise and sharpen its audience (more than 1.5 million of them, apparently) to its message. To be sure, the tone and language of *Skinny Bitch* are somewhat shocking in the first few pages, and it is not entirely clear where the abuse ends and the endearment begins:

> Are you sick and tired of being fat? Good. . . . It's time to prance around in a thong like you rule the world. . . . You cannot keep eating the same shit and expect to get skinny. . . . So don't even try some pathetic excuse. . . . No one wants to hear it. . . . It's no wonder you eat shit and garbage. (10–12)

Freedman claims that the language used in the book is derived from her own native slang: "I'm from New Jersey, and as much as I hate to admit it, it's pretty much how I talk" (Rich). However, the combination of praise and insult becomes more critical to the authors' argument than mere dialect: they aim to address females who have pitifully let themselves go, but they also seem to suggest that those women have the potential to be sexy and powerful if they radically change their diet. The very use of the term "bitch" in the title of the text could be read as an example of Foucault's "reverse discourse," in which a marginalized population (in Foucault's analysis, homosexuality; in *Skinny Bitch*, women) "speak[s] in its own behalf, to demand that its legitimacy or 'naturality' be acknowledged, often in the same vocabulary" (Foucault 101). One might argue, too, as Kirsty Fairclough does about Freedman and Barnouin's text, that "the term [bitch] is used in a celebratory way to describe women who are confident, self-assured and focussed [*sic*]." In the context of grotesque realism, the reversal of language here lends to the notion of ambivalence: while the derogatory terms might be used in celebration, their original derogatory meanings are no farther away than the other side of the same coin. In the context of *Skinny Bitch*, however, that ambivalence becomes a kind of subtle threat: the underlying argument is that there's really only one way to be a "bitch," and not following the rules of the text could easily land a female reader back in the original, less appealing category of insult. / 229

Freedman and Barnouin also use vulgar language to employ humor in ways similar to that used by Rabelais in his prologue. There is a humorous irony in the fact that these two female authors are pushing against soft, restrained, nurturing female stereotypes in order to use words like "shit" and "farty"; while their tactics may offend some, their guile may entertain— and persuade—others, namely those women who have read and been disappointed by those dieting books that adopt a much more gentle approach. Similar to Bakhtin's suggestion about the language of Rabelais, the "liberties" taken in the discourse of *Skinny Bitch* invite women to laugh with the authors. But this laughing requires a certain courage; if they cannot laugh, will they not just continue to fall prey to the "fat-pig syndrome" (12) that the authors describe? Will there be no redemption for them? It is as if Freedman and Barnouin were suggesting that the first step to becoming a "Skinny Bitch" is to be able to see the humor in one's own gruesomeness. Thus, the use of the grotesque in *Skinny Bitch* is particularly compelling because it does not simply and only depict negativity and hopelessness, as many have argued about grotesque realism. Rather, it suggests that seeing the grotesque in oneself can make rebirth possible.

However, Freedman and Barnouin's hope for their readers is only conditionally celebratory. While their use of grotesque realism is in many ways reflective of Bakhtin's interpretation, there is a critical difference in the rhetoric of *Skinny Bitch* that distinguishes its argumentative goal from that of Rabelais. In his defense of the "ambivalence" of the grotesque, Bakhtin describes a constant reciprocal relationship between the body and the earth in a perpetual and celebratory process of decay and rebirth that subverts a dominant, rule-bound culture. For Freedman and Barnouin, however, the grotesque body is only worth celebrating if the recognition and the laughter leads to rebirth; there is no praise for a next cycle of degradation. Their use of pejorative words to spark humor and self-loathing is not to redeem women's food choices, nor is it to subvert a system that encourages women to cut way back on their indulgences. Rather, their goal is to inspire a kind of self-ridicule that encourages women to laugh ashamedly on their way to the rock bottom of their own self-image. When the authors poke fun at their readers, as in, "your junk food has a shelf life of twenty-two years and will probably outlive your fat, sorry ass" (17), it's humorous because it undercuts the onslaught of feel-good self-help texts. And it spotlights the proverbial elephant in the very large room that has become dieting discourse: sure, it's about self-esteem and self-control, but culture also nurtures the desire for women to want to be skinny and sexually appealing to other men and women. But there is no challenge to the system here; Freedman and Barnouin are laughing at women and their "pathetic" subservience to their own gastronomical weaknesses, not at their longing to be thin. Indeed, it is that very longing for thinness that the authors are trying to resuscitate. While Freedman and Barnouin seem to recognize the ambivalence of the grotesque, they also use the grotesque to try to persuade women to see how they have failed and to give them hope that there is an ideal body, an ideal life that awaits them if they are willing to recognize their own misery.

THE FEAST AND THE LOWER STRATUM: OR, "THE DEAD, ROTTING, DECOMPOSING FLESH DIET"

Similar to the rhetorical path of *Fast Food Nation*, *Skinny Bitch* eases its way into a discussion about meat so as not to lose its meat-loving audience right away. Freedman and Barnouin execute a slow drain of "gross vices" (11), starting with cigarettes and alcohol, then moving to soda ("liquid Satan" [13]) and coffee ("coffee is for pussies" [15]), then to junk food and over-the-counter medications, and finally to "shitty simple carbohydrates" (23) and artificial sweeteners ("because we're having so much fun, let's bash the shit out of Splenda" [35]). In a steady stream of condemnation, the authors draw from a well of moral and technical reasons for women to withdraw from these substances and foods: "Do you really think sugar or hydrogenated oils or eggs or milk won't make you fat? Sober up, asshole" (18). In this insult, we see a flicker of the core argument for a vegan diet that is to come, and we also see Freedman and Barnouin's own version of "you are what you eat": in constituting the aforementioned foodstuffs as poisonous, they simultaneously constitute their consumers as poisoned, "bad," addicted, and immoral for partaking in an industry that produces such foods. The symbiosis they describe flirts with what Bakhtin refers to in the grotesque realism of Rabelais but is rhetorically distinct in ways that move toward a very different ideal for their female readers.

This ideal develops more clearly in the belly of the book, when the authors enter the heart of their argument for veganism. Particularly striking in both Bakhtin's reading of Rabelais and in Freedman and Barnouin's *Skinny Bitch* is the analysis of meat consumption, decomposition, and relationship to the human body. Bakhtin describes and interprets in detail Rabelais's depiction of the "feast of cattle slaughter" and the birth of Gargantua (220). Focusing on the intimate connection between meat consumption, excrement, and birth in grotesque realism, Bakhtin asserts that these three themes rely on one another in Rabelais's grotesque representation of "a devoured and devouring world" (221). Specifically, Bakhtin describes the double meaning embedded in the consumption of tripe, or ox intestines, during the feast. After Gargantua's mother, Gargamelle, consumes far too much tripe—"sixteen quarters, two bushels, and six pecks" (223)—her own intestine begins to dislodge from her body, and simultaneously she goes into labor with her son. The concurrence of these events, argues Bakhtin, serves to connect "eating, the falling-out of intestines, [and] childbirth" (221–22). Bakhtin contends that regeneration may be found in the "essential" nature of excrement, which is symbolic of "man's vivid awareness of his materiality, of his bodily nature, closely related to the life of the earth" (224). Where there is waste matter, there is the reminder that life decays, reconnects to the earth, and is reborn.

Bakhtin argues that this unbreakable link between consumer and consumed exemplifies and makes fun of the religious rhetoric of the time. He writes, "The merry, abundant and victorious bodily element opposes the serious medieval world of fear and oppression with all its intimidating and intimidated ideology" (226). The hope in the medieval image of the grotesque, then, is in the rhetoric embedded in its core ambivalence, as if to say, "the world is in decay, but we all know it, we are all to blame, and we will rise above it." In their own argument, Freedman and Barnouin seem to adopt a similar rhetorical stance; although the authors seem to point ridiculing fingers at the toxic ideology of government authorities, they constitute the consumer and consumed as one and the same. However, as we will see, embedded in their reconstruction of the grotesque is a shaming of the "victim" that we do not find in Rabelais. Bakhtin emphasizes Rabelais's unique celebration of the corporeality of binging and waste, his "invitation to drink and be merry[, in which] we find abuses, but they have an affectionate tone" (170). But Freedman and Barnouin's rhetorical goal is not to inspire celebration, and their "abuses" are only conditionally affectionate.

The chapter "The Dead, Rotting, Decomposing Flesh Diet" begins Freed-man and Barnouin's seventy-five-page attack on the meat and dairy industries and on their female consumers. The authors begin with an argument against high-protein diets like Atkins, stating plainly to their audience: "You will be a fat, unhealthy, bloated pig if you live this way" (40). While it may be true that an imbalanced diet is not healthy, we see just a page later that it is not simply this imbalance that the authors berate but also the consumption of animal products entirely. Referring to meat products as "flesh" and "carcasses," Freedman and Barnouin unwind their logos from a critique of Atkins to the claim that humans are not physically built to hunt and consume meat; they then provide a *Fast Food Nation*–like depiction of the gore of animals abused, fed antibiotics to keep them from succumbing to the diseases common to their conditions, and exposed to the toxicity of pesticides used by farmers (44–48). Strikingly similar to Sinclair and Schlosser, Freedman and Barnouin draw connections between the chemicals used in the meat industry and the diseases that surface in the human body that consumes that meat. They also rebuke the dairy industry for its marketing rhetoric, drawing on sources like MilkSucks.com (an affiliate of PETA) to argue against the need for cow's milk in the human diet and making the case that milk (and eggs) is actually toxic because it contains the same kinds of chemical contaminants as factory-produced meats (57–62).

At this point in their argument, and in ways similar to Rabelais's use of grotesque realism to undermine the ideological tyranny of the time, Freed-man and Barnouin employ the grotesque to blame the government and de-fend the doctors and scientists who seem to know what the government won't tell us. They deconstruct the ethos of the FDA, warning their readers, "Do not be lulled into a false sense of security that our government keeps food safe" (50). Blaming the US government for its poor restrictions, Freedman and Barnouin call attention to the FDA's approval of "drugs approved for use in animal feed," salmonella found in chicken, and contaminated water that poisons fish. The authors constitute all meat as "decomposing, rotting animal carcasses" and harshly confront readers:

> You don't want to see it, but you'll *eat* it? So, yeah, if you want to get skinny, you've got to be a vegetarian—someone who doesn't eat dead animals or seafood. Quit whining.... [S]hut the fuck up, look at an inspirational picture of a skinny bitch, and clean out your freezer. (52–53)

And their provegan, pure consumption, pure body, pure being campaign continues into the heart of the book.

After they condemn meat and dairy products and censure the US government, the authors' rhetoric takes a turn both toward and away from the consumer-consumed argument that Bakhtin discusses in Rabelais's grotesque realism. Bakhtin asserts that consumption, birth, and excrement are symbiotic in an ambivalent system meant to illustrate a degenerating society as it opens up the possibility for positive change, and Freedman and Barnouin's chapter "You Are What You Eat" hints at a similar cycle of ambivalence:

> You are what you eat. You are a human body comprised of organs, blood and guts, and other shit. The food you put into your body works its way through your organs and bloodstream and is actually part of who you are. So every time you put crap in your body, you are crap. (65)

/ 233

Certainly, the argument here can be compared to Bakhtin's argument about the feast preceding Gargantua's birth. However, the rhetorical purposes of these two texts are significantly different. Delving once again into the monstrosities of the meat industry, Freedman and Barnouin emphasize the transfer of toxins from contaminated food products to the human body that consumes them, but there is no hope to be found in the remnants of excrement in the "tripe" that their female readers eat. Furthermore, the guilt belongs not just to government officials but also, and perhaps even more, to consumers. It's not a kindly reminder that we be more food-conscious; it's an absolute threat that introduces a kind of logos, a transitive sort of reasoning that is critical to the core argument of *Skinny Bitch*: *if* you don't stop eating meat and dairy products *completely, then* you will be "crap." The authors write,

> Animals...know they are about to be killed and they are panic-stricken. ... You are eating fear, grief, and rage. You are eating suffering, horror, and murder. You are eating cruelty. You are what you eat. You cannot be thin and beautiful with a glowing complexion when you eat fear, grief, and rage. (75–76)

It might appear that the goal of Freedman and Barnouin is to use this logic to persuade their audience to take an ethical stand against animal cruelty. But the emotionally wrenching language they use to make an argument for aesthetic beauty swallows that call for social change. Indeed, pathos is a powerful tool here in this passage: persuading a female reader to desire and achieve physical beauty means first convincing her that she is emotionally vacuous and cruel.

Moving back into the body, the authors turn their attention to what Bakhtin calls the "lower stratum" of the body. In Rabelais's novel, Bakhtin claims, the mouth and the digestive organs of the body are closely connected: The mouth "is the open gate leading downward into the bodily underworld. The gaping mouth is related to the image of swallowing, this most ancient symbol of death and destruction" (325). It is, he describes, "the gaping mouth of Satan, the 'jaws of hell.'" However, he also explains, "birth and death are the gaping jaws of the earth and the mother's open womb," which constitutes the "jaws" and the "lower stratum" as *both* destructive and regenerating (329). For Freedman and Barnouin, however, there is no regeneration in swallowing foods that are evil—soda is "liquid Satan," and women's consumption of meat products is toxic and morally wrong, even associated with murder (13). In a chapter rightly called "Pooping," they stress the importance of excrement, relying on potty humor and profanity to raise the subject. But a healthy bowel, they claim, is one that only non-animal-based products are passing through. Embracing the notion that "fear relieves constipation" (174), Freedman and Barnouin warn readers that the meat-eater will find that her regular diet will "clog up [the] ass" and perpetuate a "shithead" identity (90–91). Again, the celebration of the grotesque is conditional: only the body cleansed of its old food identity will reach a higher ideal, never to return to its old ways. If the reader chooses not to adopt the vegan diet, she is confined to her own grotesque identity through which she will continue to be a piece of shit.

ERADICATING THE GROTESQUE, RECONSTRUCTING THE FEMALE FOOD-BODY

The preceding analysis brings us to an important question about how the rhetorical goal of Rabelais is reconstituted in Freedman and Barnouin's argument. If grotesque realism depicted in the medieval work of Rabelais is a prayer for freedom, then what freedom is *Skinny Bitch* trying to present to its readers? Bakhtin describes the grotesque body as "a body in the act of becoming. It is never finished, never completed; it is continually built, created, and builds and creates another body. Moreover, the body swallows the world and is itself swallowed by the world" (317). In this constant act of (re)creation, he points out, "the artistic logic of the grotesque image ignores the closed, smooth, and impenetrable surface of the body and retains only its excrescences (sprouts, buds) and orifices, only that which leads beyond the body's limited space or into the body's depths" (318). Indeed, Freedman and Barnouin's grotesque body is in the act of becoming, but their logic is not geared toward the body's redegradation once it has been sanitized. The "freedom" that they present to their readers is not in the earth-bound, universal cycle of human death and rebirth. Rather, it is a celebration of a permanently "closed, smooth, and impenetrable" female food-body—restrained, restricted, purified. "Freedom" for the "Skinny Bitch" means that she can see clearly what she used to be and "bitch-slap" her old self when it wants to stray toward old cravings for satanic "vices" (124) like junk food and animal products. And as for the closing of orifices and a certain impenetrability, Freedman and Barnouin promote the closing of the "gaping mouth" by suggesting that a woman who wants to challenge herself to change even further in this life "can earn extra credit by fasting. Yeah, fasting—willfully abstaining from food," for which they provide instructions (131–35).

The "Skinny Bitch" is not the slobbering, overflowing, profane body of the grotesque. After all, Freedman and Barnouin's use of profanity serves as a rhetorical tool in this text, not as a model for behavior. Their goal for the "Skinny Bitch" is for her to program her mind through absolute affirmations, which they list at the close of their text:

/ 235

> Every day in every way my ass is getting smaller.
> Every day in every way my thighs are getting thinner.
> Every day in every way my stomach is getting flatter.
> Every day in every way I'm losing more and more weight.
> Every day in every way I'm loving my body more.
> Every day in every way I'm getting healthier and healthier.

We must note the logical progression of their mantras: it is only after a woman sees the evidence of the purification of her body, and her own weight loss, that she can begin to love that body. The morality-laden rhetoric of food-consciousness that we saw flickering earlier in the book is barely visible now, as the authors place their final emphasis on the wearing of sexy clothes:

> You worked hard for this body and you should be proud of it. . . . So don't be afraid of wearing high-fashion, revealing clothes. . . . But please keep in mind that looking cheap or cheesy doesn't accomplish anything. (191)

A flair, a sensuality, a subtle flaunting is okay. But a girl must know when she has stepped back over the line and into her grotesque form.

With a closing plea to their female readers that they remember not to judge themselves by how much "attention or validation [they] get from men," that they continue to follow the rules of the book, that they have faith that this new lifestyle will get them the man they desire, and that they really do have power, Freedman and Barnouin sign off with a terse, "Use your head, lose your ass" (191). But we know by now that it's not just the reader's ass that has been indicted here; it is the reader's grotesque identity, intolerable and disgusting in the eyes of the authors and, they hope, now intolerable and disgusting in the eyes of the readers themselves. In the light of this ideal, we find at the close of the text that the "Skinny Bitch" is merely the palimpsest for what used to be the grotesque body, barely recognizable now in her thinness, her self-control, and her refined tastes. And therein lies the freedom that Freedman and Barnouin promise. The "Skinny Bitch" is meant to be celebrated but only if she is willing to leave the feast for good.

Works Cited

Bakhtin, Mikhail. *Rabelais and His World*. Trans. Hélène Iswolsky. Indiana UP, 1984.

Fairclough, Kirsty. "Fame Is a Losing Game: Celebrity Gossip Blogging, Bitch Culture, and Postfeminism." *Genders* 48 (2008): n. pag. Accessed 25 June 2014.

Foucault, Michel. *The History of Sexuality*. Vol. 1. *An Introduction*. 1978. Vintage Books, 1990.

Freedman, Rory, and Kim Barnouin. *Skinny Bitch*. Running P, 2005.

"Full Details: *Skinny Bitch*." *Running Press Book Publishers* 2014. Accessed 28 November 2016.

Hart, Cheryle B., and Mary Kay Grossman. *The Feel-Good Diet: The Weight-Loss Plan That Boosts Serotonin, Improves Your Mood, and Keeps Pounds Off for Good*. McGraw-Hill, 2008.

Lillien, Lisa. *The Hungry Girl Diet: Big Portions, Big Results*. St. Martin's/Griffin, 2014.

Rich, Motoko. "A Diet Book Serves Up a Side Order of Attitude." *New York Times* 1 August 2007. Accessed 25 June 2014.

Roizen, Michael F., and Mehmet C. Oz. *You: Losing Weight—the Owner's Manual to Simple and Healthy Weight Loss*. Free Press/Simon and Schuster, 2011.

Roth, Geneen. *Breaking Free from Compulsive Eating*. Plume, 1993.

Schlosser, Eric. *Fast Food Nation: The Dark Side of the All-American Meal*. Harper Perennial, 2001.

Sinclair, Upton. *The Jungle*. 1906. Bantam Books, 1981.

17. GUSTO AND GRACE: *TWO FAT LADIES* AND THE RHETORICAL CONSTRUCTION OF A FAT CULINARY ETHOS

Sara Hillin

Jennifer Paterson and Clarissa Dickson Wright burst onto the culinary scene in a thirty-minute BBC2 cooking show entitled *Two Fat Ladies*, which aired from 1996–99. Their opening jingle declared, "Fasten your tastebuds for a gastronomic ride! / 'Cause us two fat ladies are hitchin' up to get into your kitchen." Journalists, who presumably felt they were given carte blanche to make weight-related jokes, since the two had *agreed* to be known as the two "fat ladies," practically fell over themselves with endless quips, calling the two hosts "telly-tubbies" and "corpulent dames" (Dam 50) and "two chubby foodies" (D'Arminio 57) and using descriptions such as "think Posh and Ginger Spice with 40 years—and 150 more pounds—under their belt" (Dam 50). Through four seasons on television and in several cookbooks, the two stars occupied a unique rhetorical space, showcasing dishes such as "Gigot of Monkfish," "Roasted Conger Eel," and "Duntreath Roast Grouse"—esoteric but hearty dishes presumably unknown to most US viewers. Their knowledge of complex and obscure British dishes was formidable, as were their personalities. Both offered unfiltered opinions of healthy eating, vegetarianism, and dieting that went decidedly against the grain of the mid-to-late 1990s health consciousness trend in both culinary shows and magazines targeted toward women. They also "came out" as fat, as evidenced by their embracing the show's title and their seeming comfort with a term that often makes others uncomfortable.[1]

In "Finding the F Word for It," Marilyn Wann alludes to the power inherent in owning and saying the word "fat." "My first liberation," she states, "was in large part lexical. I started using the dread[ed] F-word . . . 'fat'" (23). This simple act of naming, Wann argues, "changes the power dynamic for the better" (24). Melinda Young also confronts the "F" word, commenting that "fat is a powerful, dangerous, slippery word, concept, and discourse" (250). She argues that the narratives "encircling fat women's bodies promoted by magazines are under-achievement, unrealized potential, failure, and the body as an incomplete project" (250). All of this adds up, she asserts, to a detrimental illustration of femininity (250). And fatness, indeed, as Robyn Longhurst explains, "is thought to reflect poorly on individuals, communities, and nations" (871). The two fat ladies, however, turned every aspect of this negativity on its head; both were wildly successful culinary experts and television personalities who took the opportunity to argue against an ignorant allegiance to slimming and vegetarian diets (particularly those aimed at women). Their mission was to disrupt the dominant weight-normative discourse that exalted thin bodies—the bodies that Longhurst describes as ones that "exercise and deny themselves food in the pursuit of an aesthetic ideal" (877). Furthermore, both remained unmarried and childless by choice until their deaths, a double whammy to the traditional notions of a woman's "realized" potential.

As Patricia Boling argues in "On Learning to Teach Fat Feminism," scholarship supporting fat feminism must "let fat feminists explain their own positions, letting *their* words and arguments do the speaking" (120). Following Boling's call, in this chapter, I highlight the ladies' *own* words, culled from the four seasons, interviews with Wright and Paterson, Paterson's columns for *The Spectator*, and the texts of the two fat ladies' cookbooks. I argue that Wright and Paterson cleverly exploited strategic essentialism and invitational rhetoric to open a space for feminists, women and men alike, to embrace the "F" word and eschew the oppression of diet-obsessed culture. I borrow the methodology for analysis from Sarah Hallenbeck's concepts of actor-network theory and feminist-materialist methodology, which can help us to "collapse the artificial distance we often construct between a coherent, preexisting 'context' and the subjects of our research" (21). Hallenbeck advocates a fresh perspective in feminist rhetorical research that analyzes "how gender differences are reproduced, naturalized, and resisted through the spaces and injunctions surrounding oratorical practices that could be considered 'everyday'" (10). In this case, cooking and related activities (such as food writing, demonstrations, and cooking on television) represent the everyday context from which the two fat ladies produced a complex rhetorical power—one that allowed them to exploit several of the more negative cultural connotations of fatness and somehow build a positive ethos through that very act. The project Hallenbeck advocates in feminist rhetorical analyses is to "commit to undertaking broader, more widely distributed considerations of how gender differences and norms become naturalized, enhanced, or diminished" (25). Through my analysis, I show how the ladies exposed such naturalized norms about female diet and thinness and sought to counter them by combating fat phobia and promoting a different type of culinary "health consciousness" through their image *as* fat women. Further, with bold confidence, they used their writing to make other public arguments, expanding options for women rhetors.

The genesis of the show is worth mentioning, as it was producer Patricia Llewellyn who had first envisioned a culinary series featuring fat women. (Wright and Paterson had only met once before through happenstance at a banquet promoting another British cooking show.) In an interview with Elizabeth Winkler in 1997, Paterson explains that although the two did not know one another until Llewellyn invited them to lunch, they had a "natural affinity," sharing a sense of humor, "the same feelings about food," and similar religious beliefs, as both were "practicing Roman Catholics." Despite the fact that the show was her idea, Llewellyn admits a bit of trepidation concerning the first few private screenings of *Two Fat Ladies.* "There was little doubt," she writes, "that our two fat ladies were enormously entertaining" (Wright and Paterson, *Cooking With* 9). However, she also asked herself, "How would they [BBC producers] react to Jennifer and Clarissa's militant anti-vegetarianism? What would be made of their constant ridicule of all the recent press reports of what constitutes a healthy diet?" (9). Indeed, Wright and Paterson took opportunities to openly distance themselves from healthy-eating experts, such as in their book *Cooking with the Two Fat Ladies,* where Wright states, "Neither of us much believe the pronouncements of soi-disant health experts" (12). In the same volume, Wright conjures up an image of the pair's mutual love for meat dishes, writing of a yearning "for roasted marrow bones wrapped in a napkin, served with a silver marrow scoop" and a desire for "rare barons of beef or kidneys cooked in their own caul or fat" (42). The almost sexualized language she uses ("eyes go dreamy" at the mention of meat) may seem repulsive to some audience members, yet it embodies the women's unfettered and genuine antihealth-craze stance, and it uses the damaging assumption about the connection between fatness and a loss of control or uninhibited appetite to their advantage. The sincerity of their campaign to exalt cooking with meat, fat, lard, and sugar is undeniable.

Though much was made of the ladies' criticisms of certain "healthful" eating conventions (which allowed journalists to hyperbolize a kind of gluttonous lack of self-control and knowledge about eating healthy that is often attributed to fat women), their concern with practicality (both in the purchasing and preparing of food) is also an underrepresented and important facet of their rhetoric. In a 2011 interview for the *Scotsman*, Wright advocated purchasing meat from butcher shops and farmers' markets, explaining that those venues offered meats that would keep longer, thus saving customers money and resulting in less "cash in the trash" ("Interview" 19). She also added the following, which spoke to an attitude of moderation in eating meat: "We eat far too much meat, and bad quality meat at that. I love meat, but even I don't feel the need to eat it every day, and certainly not twice a day" (19). Journalists willfully ignored the complexity of Wright and Paterson's views on meat buying and consumption; rather, they continually crafted the easily digestible and culturally expected narrative of two fat women who prepared food with a wanton disregard for its nutritive content.

In celebrating a love of food and their own bodies and presenting this love as a form of healthful living, the women were forerunners in the movement to combat fat oppression. They could also be considered fat activists, advancing the ideas of size acceptance and being comfortable in one's own skin and with one's own political views, which seemed to go hand in hand for both of the ladies. As Abigail Saguy and Kevin Riley explain, fat activism, a movement that "has reclaimed the word fat," has not joined the cause to eradicate obesity; rather, it has "countered such claims [that weight adversely affects one's health] by saying that one can be healthy at any size and that claims about obesity being a health risk are simply overblown" (870). As outsiders from the United Kingdom, the ladies were free to comment directly on what they saw as a uniquely American obsession with food deprivation and the quest for thinness. In one interview, Paterson posited that Americans are not used to decent food and that "there are these teeeerrrrible [*sic*] women's magazines telling them everything ought to be low-fat . . . then they die of anorexia" (Dam 50). Additionally, Paterson claimed that the pair routinely did things culinarily that Americans would not dare to try and that audiences were shocked at such admonishments as "'yogurt is no substitute for cream'" (50). The fact that they cited Americans specifically as *failing* to live by healthful standards is a cheeky but sobering blow to the country's self-professed concern with mindful food consumption, as evidenced by such popular mid-to-late 1990s diets such as Atkins, Sugar Busters, "Eat Right for Your Blood Type," South Beach, and others. But Paterson's comment about the media lends another poignant angle to their agenda, tersely but accurately identifying dieting as a ruse or front to keep women in a submissive state through fat shaming and controlling body image. Comments such as these help us to further see the ladies' importance as feminist activists[2] who used cooking as a platform from which to share their polemic.

Though Wright did the majority of the writing for the ladies' cookbooks, Paterson's writing style is also noteworthy due to its rhetorical force—often in the form of a soliloquy. Once in a while, she took a confrontational tone in her *Spectator* articles on a specific social issue and then abruptly shifted her written voice to offer the details of that particular piece's actual culinary focus. Possibly the best example of her unique style can be seen in her October 29, 1988, column, in which she opened by attacking those who criticized the Duchess of York for leaving the infant Princess Beatrice home while she "is covering the Antipodes with her husband." "You may or may not fancy the Yorks," Paterson states, "but one thing is for sure, they have a perfectly good home, well trained staff and I suspect a better than average nanny to look after their little one" ("Diary" 7). For the following two paragraphs, Paterson rails against those who apparently saw Fergie's travels as a dereliction of motherhood. In closing her polemic, Paterson does her trademark, dramatic rhetorical quick change (though technically an unacceptable disruption of purpose, form, and genre by most Western standards of composition) by concluding with her strongest point and launching straightaway into a cheerful description of tea at the Ritz:

/ *241*

> During the late unpleasantness, many mothers sent their children to America and Canada to get them out of the war. The ones I knew, Milo Cripps, David Queensbury and Michael Bishop all thought of it as a great adventure, no tears, no fuss, and on returning were devoted to their mothers until their deaths, though the late Lady Bishop did remark on seeing her Canadianised son, "Can this be anything to do with us?" So let's just leave "Fergie and Bea" to their own devices. Tea at the Ritz has always been considered an excellent treat for visiting children or foreigners, and so it is, in that prettiest of hotels; but to my mind breakfast is even better. (7)

Paterson disrupts rhetorical expectations—she *demands* that her audience consider her position, and she is attempting to shift the discourse on motherhood from one that is judgmental to one that is accepting of a wider array of responsibilities and types of care. This is the same tactic that the ladies would use decades later in their cookbooks and on screen.

In another October 1988 column, Paterson took on a perceived tendency in the courts to side with women rather than men in divorce cases, regardless of a woman's destructive behavior that might have led up to the split. "Surely," she proclaimed, "the baddie should be the one to be punished whether male or female? I feel for Mike Tyson even though he is in quite a different category" ("Diary" 7). In the next sentence, which begins a new paragraph, she shifts without any transition to describing a recent gala to celebrate the twenty-fifth anniversary of the founding of the Department of Special Collections and its archives at Boston University. One can see in Paterson's words an example of a feminist using the platform she had gained through food writing in order to make arguments about other pressing issues, such as the "mommy wars," fairness in divorce cases, and food safety.

Concerning the latter, Paterson's November 1988 column directly entreated her audience to mobilize with her and persuade the Ministry of Agriculture, Fisheries, and Food to deal with a virulent strain of salmonella "coming from any egg yolk that has not been cooked through and through like a hard boiled egg" ("Diary" 7). Left unchecked, Paterson warned, the detriment to egg-related cuisine could be ruinous:

> It will be farewell to all the hollandaise, bearnaise, mayonnaise sauces, all soufflés and chocolate mousses and all the other mousses . . . So Ag. and Fish, what have you to say? I am still eating eggs, but for how long? (7)

Paterson's passion for preserving both public health and also a chef's right to continue to make an array of dishes with the necessary ingredient is clear here, but so is her forthright style of argumentation. She employed a technique of offering opinions and having the last word in one fell swoop, punctuating her resoluteness by shifting back into a less political voice more fitting for discussing, for example, a recipe for asparagus and smoked salmon tarts.

Paterson's direct, bold style was also evident when she wrote about food that others prepared. She did not mince words if she found a dish not to her liking, and several restaurants were the subject of her ire. Concerning her visit to Deals restaurant in 1999, she wrote that her dining companion was given "a steak plate with a humdrum collection of various fishy morsels, scattered with bits of shredded mixed salad and covered with that white-goo dressing to be found on bought potato salad or coleslaw—abysmal" ("Deals" 42). The dessert (something called "chocolate mud") also did not escape her biting criticism: "Ho bloody ho! This was a slice of something so disgusting as to make you retch. A gelatinous sweet middle covered with a dark topping and the smarties, not tasting of chocolate, more like neat instant coffee" (42). The Stafford hotel restaurant did not fare much better, with Paterson bemoaning "a terrible piece of cold felt masquerading as a Yorkshire pudding" and stating bluntly that "if only the kitchen could get its act together," the hotel would be a "wonderful meeting place" ("Stafford" 54). Such forthrightness would also appear in each cookbook Wright and Paterson later produced; in the introduction to the "Real Scotch Egg" recipe, the authors state, "This is a very different object from those revolting things to be found in British pubs and on supermarket shelves" (*Cooking With* 58). The gusto with which they damned bad food (whether the result of poor cooking technique, shoddy ingredients, or the attempt to cut corners with more "healthy options") and praised good food to the heavens can be seen as an aspect of their fat ethos—big, bold, and unapologetic. But more importantly, this ethos was rooted in experiential knowledge and decades of training in cooking traditional British food—food rooted in tradition that was often at unfortunate odds with influential but rootless (and sometimes ridiculous) trends in cooking that were essentially based on depriving oneself of something (carbohydrates, sugar, fat, and so on).[3]

In terms of the ladies' targeted television audience and appeal, they were initially considered anomalous among a slew of shows hosted by chefs whose agenda was based on healthy eating. Jack Neff explains that awareness of the Food Network began to "soar" in 1997, climbing to thirty-three million viewers by 1998, with women composing roughly 60 percent of that number. At that time, a typical daily lineup would have included *Emeril Live* and several other shows that touted low fat or low carb cooking or easy, quick recipes, such as *How to Boil Water*. Neff also proclaims *Two Fat Ladies* to be the "most offbeat" Food Network show offered to date, citing as apparent evidence the episode where the ladies cook for a girls' school and "grouse that all the girls are probably vegetarians these days, then decide they look too healthy to be herbivores as they whip up meatloaf with mincemeat and chicken livers" (10).

/ 243

Often, the ladies were dismissed as an eccentric pair, with journalists making a caricature of them, labeling them as "campy," emphasizing the motorcycle and sidecar they rode in from one seaside meat market or butcher shop to the next, focusing on their wisecracks and, of course, their featured cuisine, which was heavy on hearty meat dishes incorporating anything from rabbit to bull penis. Using hyperbole to bemoan the latter fact, a comment from Aubry D'Arminio from *Entertainment Weekly* encapsulates this view perfectly, stating that "the grub could kill you . . . But the banter was delicious, as when Clarissa talked smack about pheasants ('They have gang bangs!')" (57).

Such commentary subtly reflects the cultural message that we are given repeatedly, according to Boling, that "if we're fat, we're weak, unable to exercise control, continually caving into the insistent demands of our bodies and appetites" (111). Additionally, though facetious, this kind of comment belied the ladies' political concerns, especially those related to food. In their book *Two Fat Ladies: Full Throttle*, for example, Wright advocates political activism to address food safety, pleading that "in this age of activists I wish you would all go out and protest for fresher, safer products rather than just not buying what is available" (41). And in a chapter simply entitled "Meat," Wright argues that protests are preferable to turning to vegetarianism in improving the manner in which animals are raised and prepared for consumption:

> I have never understood the reasoning that if you don't like the way meat is reared or killed you should turn vegetarian. Surely you should stand up and fight for changes and support the organic trade rather than risk your life with a paraquat-fed Third World Carrot. (71)

Their pleas for their fans' participation in reforming the treatment of animals in poultry and beef farming and supporting organic farming again illustrate their shrewd navigation of various media to instigate change or at the very least invite their audiences to interrogate their own beliefs about food and decide whether they could, in fact, help change the practices they opposed.

Wright also sought to dispel the notion that their recipes were composed of "all that fat stuff, all those artery cloggers" (Lawley) in countering with the following theory: "You know, the only thing that stimulates serotonin in the body is animal fat. And I'm quite certain that the increase in antidepressants is directly relatable to the decrease in eating fat" (Lawley). Regardless of the truth behind Wright's adamantly stated conviction that eating animal fat is a legitimate means of increasing serotonin (and her claim about the rise in antidepressant use verges on self-parody), she uses this idea to promote the claim that the consumption of meat and fat is of some benefit to us.

The ladies were, of course, not the first female chefs to champion meat eating. Julia Child had famously attributed her longevity and health to eating red meat and drinking gin. But what is rhetorically noteworthy about the two ladies' campaign to restore people's faith in meat quality and consumption is that they truly seemed to have the general public's best interests at heart, becoming champions for more informed eating rather than basing one's consumption on misguided cultural norms that particularly bedeviled women. And they also enacted a brilliant move advocated by Marilyn Wann, who argues that it is a rather "measly" goal to simply embrace size-acceptance as an individual, and a better one is to "repurpose the stereotype of gluttony/ sloth by exercising for our protest and telling other people how to eat for a change!" (25). The two ladies found their niche in doing just that—telling others how and what to eat and how to best prepare it and, not only that, but what to fight for in the ongoing battle to maintain integrity in the production and sale of meat.

The ladies capitalized on their fame as other celebrity chefs do, offering several cookbooks (such as *Cooking with the Two Fat Ladies* and *Two Fat Ladies: Full Throttle*) and doing interviews and book tours. Unlike most typical mainstream cookbooks, though, which offered bland commentary (if any commentary) along with recipes, the two fat ladies' volumes were replete with a good dose of explanation for why each dish was so satisfying. Meat, and particularly red meat, had come under attack in the 1990s, which the ladies found unacceptable and addressed in *Cooking with the Two Fat Ladies*:

> In this year of grace 1996, meat is a very important issue. More and more, the media are attacking the nutritional quality of meat without spelling out the actualities of the situation . . . The other threat to the meat industry is the rise of the vegetarian. (40)

Wright, in particular, did not want to sit idly by while a public remained in the dark about what they were consuming and their rights to quality foods, often advocating activism to stir the powers that be into addressing such issues. In *The Two Fat Ladies Ride Again*, she admonished her readers to "clamor for the wider availability of the bloater [ungutted herring] (I remember when you could only buy olive oil in chemists' shops—public demand is a great mover of mountains)" (104).

Their rhetoric was both public and private in the sense that they exploited television and print media for feminist ends but also offered some of their most poignant comments in conversation with each other, with viewers as the "eavesdropping audience." Such banter may not have been directly intended to effect change in the increasingly intense quest for body perfection, but at the same time, their desire to promote size acceptance *did* reach millions of female viewers internationally. In the first season, we see Wright make a subtle argument to stick with a recipe rather than caving to the need to substitute low fat ingredients for high fat ones. In the episode entitled "Fruit and Vegetables," Wright demonstrates making a meal called "Bubble and Squeak," which involves several ounces of lard or beef dripping. She adamantly claims that only two types of fat are acceptable in this dish:

> You *must* use either lard or beef dripping. They're the only fats you can really get to sufficiently high temperatures to make this dish properly. If you don't, for some reason, use either of these, then go and cook something else. ("Fruit and Vegetables")

Wright's blunt end comment punctuates the conversation with certainty: there simply is no substitute, and any argument to ameliorate the recipe's cardinal sin of including this ingredient would be futile. Paterson, who is off in the corner preparing a tomato pudding, concurs immediately with Wright, chiming in with, "They're so much better with beef dripping, aren't they?"

The ladies found a way to use their ethos as fat women to validate their (seeming) excesses. As Karen Ross and Sujata Moorti explain, "issues of body size . . . have been dominant thematics in media discourse for some time, often discussed in the context of poor health and diet but more insidiously framed within a rhetoric of excess and loss of control" (83). But the ladies thwarted those marginalizing representations. True, they did not offer dishes that took into account moderation of fats and carbohydrates, but they had much to say concerning food quality and condemned depriving oneself of necessary energy and nutrition in the name of sticking to a diet driven either by ignorance or the desire for thinness. Wright championed the eating of a healthy breakfast every morning, lamenting in *The Two Fat Ladies Ride Again* that

> we stagger downstairs, grab a cup of something hot and probably instant and if we eat at all, it is probably cereal—with semi-skimmed milk even though the body cannot absorb the calcium in the milk without the fat, and osteoporosis is on the increase. (88)

Paterson, who smoked cigarettes conspicuously on the show, was constantly portrayed as "scathingly contemptuous of 'healthy' eating" (Owen), though in reality what goes under the umbrella of "healthy eating" is a wide spectrum of practices, some of which (such as avoiding animal fats) the ladies sought to expose as decidedly *unhealthy*.

The two fat ladies' appeal was widespread, despite criticism from the British press that they negatively influenced British diet. In fact, as Jamie Wilson comments in a 1999 *Guardian* article, they "developed a following . . . where they were hailed by viewers as heroines leading the fight against 'body fascism' as promoted by Hollywood and TV programmes" (20). The ladies controlled their own media image though the rhetorical device of strategic essentialism, which is the "process of making an identity ingredient the core part of one's persona that legitimizes the right to speak" (Palczewski, Ice, and Fritch 162). As fat ladies, Wright and Paterson were not required to work within the lines of delicate or submissive femininity and self-control, attributes that tend to be associated with thin women. Thus unburdened by such cultural shackles, Wright and Patterson, perhaps ironically, made fatness and its misguided connotations (that heaviness indicates a "larger than life" personality) their rhetorical platform. In other words, they harnessed the power that could be obtained from their stature and wielded it to rhetorical ends.

Despite the ladies' following, not all responses were kind. Some audiences were not receptive to fat women speaking with authority, and one particular comment that surfaced in 1996 enraged both the ladies and their following. Writing for the *London Evening Standard*, Victor Lewis-Smith declared that the ladies exuded "uncompromising physical ugliness" and "thoroughly ugly personalities" (n. pag.). Though widely demonized (and rightly so) for his offensive ad hominem attack, Smith's comment does hint at something deeper—a typical, visceral reaction that some have to fat women exhibiting acceptance of and even great pride in their bodies and their sharp wit and independence.[4] This attitude may have stemmed from discomfort with how   / 247
easily the ladies transgressed the dichotomies that placed the body as separate from the mind. As Boling argues, "not only have traditional dichotomies read bodies, the flesh, carnality, and nature as feminine and opposed to mind, intellect, self-control, discipline, and culture, which are read as masculine, but female bodies are held up to different standards than male ones" (111). Wright and Paterson, armed with a formidable knowledge of cuisine and excellent written styles, trampled the binary and expectations that they should be languid, ignorant, and ashamed as fat women, cowering under criticism that their food was unhealthy and their banter and manner of dress too bold or unattractive. Instead, they sought to mobilize and rally others to take up their causes: promoting more ethical manufacturing and sale of meats, educating oneself about health claims related to diet, and ending gender-based size discrimination.

Though its focal point was cooking, the ladies' project (their articles, books, interviews, and television series) in a feminist rhetorical sense encompassed much more, promoting size acceptance and dispelling widely publicized half truths about eating (particularly the consumption of meat) that sought to shame fat women and men and impoverish their diets. Additionally, they worked to help others join their ranks, offering audiences food for thought on what the pressing issues were in the area of meat production, as well as what was worthy of protest. They battled against what Melinda Young describes as women's shared "common consciousness in the fear of fat" (251) and worked tirelessly as fat activists to argue for an increase in public awareness of and backlash against limited access to certain foods and misinformation about their consumption. They also transgressed binaries to repair the damaging and condescending image of fat women, using both their gusto and their grace to impact the "problematic representation of femininity" (Young 249) that decades of fat-phobic media and attitudes had fostered. Their continued relevance as feminists, then, lies in this very transgression and its apparent success.

Notes

1. In a 1999 BBC Radio 4 interview, Wright offered the following response to Sue Lawley's question about whether they minded the show's title:

> Well, people used to say, like journalists hate the word "fat," especially American journalists, and they used to say "Don't you object to the title?" And I said . . . "which bit do you object to, you know? Are you saying I'm thin?" And they get terribly embarrassed, and there was actually one journalist who couldn't say the word fat, we had to sort of re-educate him to say it.

2. It seems likely that Paterson and Wright were culinary experts first and foremost and accidental spokeswomen for the anti–fat shaming movement secondarily. A quick look at their careers bears this out. Paterson contributed recipes, restaurant reviews, and descriptions of culinary events (often also peppered with commentary on social or political issues) to the British magazine *The Spectator* from 1986 to 1992 (twelve articles in all). She was also the head cook for *The Spectator* beginning in 1978. Wright, on the other hand, had extensive experience cooking for illustrious figures and groups of people. She had, in fact, been a barrister prior to pursuing success in the culinary world, and so she would have likely had a powerful foundation in rhetorical techniques, particularly those related to forensic discourse. Both were largely self-taught chefs, and neither found their niche on television until they were in their sixties.

3. On this note, Paterson also displayed a great enjoyment in watching *others* enjoy good cuisine, and this characteristic is exemplified in her awe of Olga Deterding, who often dined at the Ritz:

> I once saw her eat an entire leg of lamb and a Dundee cake at a sitting, but that was nothing to a little feast she once ordered to be sent to her Ritz suite. Feeling peckish and having no companion that evening, she ordered dinner for four with grouse as the main course . . . then wheeled [the trolley] in herself and scoffed the lot, washed down with several bottles of claret. Now that's what I call guts, real guts. ("Diary" 7)

In this passage from October 29, 1988, she simply celebrates a woman's carnality and voraciousness, praising it as fortitude, whereas other writers would probably consider it deeply taboo to report on (let alone praise) a woman's ability to consume a large amount of food.

4. Commenting further on this type of rancor, Ross and Moorti explain that the fat woman who is public about her self-acceptance and/or sexuality "has sinned against patriarchy's cultural expectations of femininity and must be disciplined back into line, reinforcing the social standards of gender performance" (89). Additionally, this attitude has been identified by Saguy and Riley as "fat phobia" or the "fear and hatred of body fat and fat people" (882). Probably much to Smith's chagrin, however, the ladies were internationally valued and adored for their brusque and forthright personalities as much as for their immense influence on the culinary world. As Owen commented in her 1999 article, just after Jennifer's death from lung cancer, their show "won unsurpassed ratings for a food programme, was sold to Australia, Japan, Israel, Canada, South Africa and the United States."

Works Cited

Boling, Patricia. "On Learning to Teach Fat Feminism." *Feminist Teacher* 21.2 (2011): 110–23.

Dam, Julie. "Telly-Tubbies." *Entertainment Weekly* 17 July 1998: 50.

D'Arminio, Aubry. "Dish of the Week." *Entertainment Weekly* 1 August 2008: 57.

"Fruit and Vegetables." Dir. Patricia Llewellyn. *Two Fat Ladies*. BBC2. Optomen Television, 23 October 1996.

Hallenbeck, Sarah. "Toward a Posthuman Perspective: Feminist Rhetorical Methodologies and Everyday Practices." *Advances in the History of Rhetoric* 15 (2012): 9–27.

"Interview: Clarissa Dickson Wright, Chef." *The Scotsman* 11 March 2011: 19.

Lawley, Sue. "Clarissa Dickson Wright Interview." *Desert Island Discs*. BBC Radio 4. 21 November 1999.

Lewis-Smith, Victor. "Two Fat Ladies." *TV Reviews*. Kindle ed. Badastral Books, 2012.

Longhurst, Robyn. "Becoming Smaller: Autobiographical Spaces of Weight Loss." *Antipode* 44.3 (2011): 871–83.

Neff, Jack. "'More Butter!' Food Network Makes Shows Great Theater." *Advertising Age* April 1998: 10–12.

Owen, Emma. "Jennifer Paterson." *The Guardian* 10 August 1999. Accessed 30 November 2016.

Palczewski, Catherine Helen, Richard Ice, and John Fritch. *Rhetoric in Civic Life*. Strata Publishing, 2012.

Paterson, Jennifer. "Deals: Pontevecchio." *The Spectator* 1 July 1988: 42.

———. "Diary." *The Spectator* 21 October 1988: 7.

———. "Diary." *The Spectator* 29 October 1988: 7.

———. "Diary." *The Spectator* 15 November 1988: 7.

———. "The Stafford: La Chanterelle." *The Spectator* 23 September 1988: 54.

Ross, Karen, and Sujata Moorti. "Is Fat Still a Feminist Issue? Gender and the Plus Size Body." *Feminist Media Studies* 5.1 (2005): 83–104.

Saguy, Abigail C., and Kevin W. Riley. "Weighing Both Sides: Morality, Mortality, and Framing Contests over Obesity." *Journal of Health Politics, Policy, and Law* 30.5 (2005): 869–921.

Wann, Marilyn. "Finding the F Word for It." *Off Our Backs* 34.11/12 (2004): 23–26.

Wilson, Jamie. "'Fat Lady' TV Chef Dies." *The Guardian* 10 August 1999: 20.

Winkler, Elizabeth. "How We Met: Clarissa Dickson Wright and Jennifer Paterson." *The Independent* 19 January 1997. Accessed 30 November 2016.

Wright, Clarissa Dickson, and Jennifer Paterson. *Cooking with the Two Fat Ladies.* Clarkson Potter Publishers, 1996.

———. *Two Fat Ladies: Full Throttle.* Clarkson Potter Publishers, 1998.

———. *The Two Fat Ladies Ride Again.* Ebury P, 1997.

Young, Melinda. "One Size Fits All: Disrupting the Consumerized, Pathologized, Fat Female Form." *Feminist Media Studies* 5.2 (2005): 249–52.

18. DECONSTRUCTING THE PLUS-SIZE FEMALE SLEUTH: FAT POSITIVE DISCOURSE, RHETORICAL EXCESS, AND CULTURAL CONSTRUCTIONS OF FEMININITY IN COZY CRIME FICTION

Elizabeth Lowry

Ever since feminism's second wave—a movement emphasizing the relationship between the personal and the political—fat positive discourse has come to be embedded within broader feminist thought. Amy Farrell writes, "While fat denigration was a mainstay of first-wave feminism, within second-wave feminism fat women found a place that encouraged new bodily perspectives by challenging the valorization of the thin body" (140). Although Farrell links fat activism to feminism and describes how fat activism is culturally reflected in discourses of second-wave feminism, other cultural theorists present conflicting narratives. For instance, Priscilla Walton and Manina Jones describe how in the late 1970s, female novelists began to challenge the highly masculinist genre of detective noir by creating new detective stories involving tough female protagonists who were professional (not amateur) sleuths. Rather than embrace diverse body types, these novels of the 1970s and 1980s promoted the "valorization of the thin body." Female detectives were portrayed as being in excellent physical condition. Wiry and fit, they were presented as models of modern feminism—and, by extension—as formidable rivals to their male counterparts. The female detective could not be fat—nor could any woman who wanted to be taken seriously as a feminist: "Fatness, a powerful cultural sign of degeneracy, threatened to undo all the difficult work feminists had done to prove their worthiness" (Farrell 113). Hence, in order to be seen as worthy competitors in a patriarchal society, women could not allow themselves to be seen as too female. Here, I draw an essential distinction between femaleness and femininity. Kirsten Bell and Darlene McNaughton draw on extensive scholarship to argue that fatness has long been considered to be a "female" trait and that, in contrast to men, women are far more likely to be identified as "fat" (111). Fatness and femaleness are inextricably bound in feminist discourse suggesting that patriarchal values conflate slenderness with femininity but fatness with an undesirably cumbersome "femaleness." Considering the postfeminist cultural landscape, I conceptualize contradictory representations of the female body in genre literature as being emblematic of cultural discourses that emerged from second-wave feminism. In other words, I examine ways in which the postfeminist stance seems to undermine the second-wave feminist agenda by embracing behaviors and attitudes toward femaleness and femininity that might be interpreted as disempowering women. Further, given competing representations of the female body in feminist discourses, how can fat positive discourse be reconciled with the athletic, tomboyish physique of the female private investigator (PI)?

In this chapter, I discuss the relationship between feminism, fat positive discourse, and the detective novel. I do this by exploring the realm of dessert-themed detective "chicklit" populated by fat female protagonists. While skinny chicklit protagonists' lives revolve around fashion, shopping, and the acquisition of shoes, the audience of fat positive women's fiction experience the vicarious pleasures of dessert: instead of salivating over the prospect of new stiletto heels, readers of fat positive detective fiction are tantalized by buttercream frosting. Typically, these novels include the name of a dessert in their titles, and their covers are adorned with brightly colored pictures of sweet treats. Examples of these would be Jessica Beck's donut-themed mysteries; Joanne Fluke's Lake Eden novels, which are packed with dessert recipes; and G. A. McKevett's Savannah Reid Mysteries, in which a female PI and her assistant solve crimes precipitated by the consumption of various desserts. Using examples from these works, I consider the relationship between fat positive discourse and the detective novel within varying feminist contexts, arguing that social attitudes toward fat women may be changing in ways that also cause us to consider sociocultural relationships between constructions of femaleness and femininity.

As a traditionally masculinist genre, detective novels make a particularly interesting study when discussing corporeality because of how they are culturally situated with respect to feminism. Detective novels that are specifically coded as "chicklit" invariably provide "cozy" mysteries, ones that are not graphically violent and that often feature a romantic subplot. Further, the term chicklit is controversial both because there is disagreement as to whether or not the chicklit supports or undermines a feminist agenda and because no one can quite agree on what chicklit is. In this chapter, I work with Stephanie Harzewski's definition, which pinpoints the following features: Chicklit is lighthearted, often funny. The protagonist is single and self-sufficient. She is interested in men but finding a husband is not her only objective—she is also looking to find herself and excel in her career. Significantly, chicklit also places an emphasis on consumerism (3). In recent years, a popular subgenre of detective chicklit has involved baking. Often, these novels combine recipes with sleuthing, presumably so that readers can try their hand at making characters' meals. But cookery is only one of many detective chicklit subgenres: over the past ten years we have seen romance, sci-fi, paranormal ghost-themed chicklit, vampire and werewolf chicklit, craft and hobby chicklit, and pizzeria and coffeehouse chicklit.

It is worth exploring the detective subgenre, with respect to fat positive discourse, because chicklit involving overweight protagonists is still relatively rare and mysteries involving overweight protagonists are rarer still. Specifically, I look at how fat positive discourse, or "fatness," is used as a form of agency in detective novels written for women. How does a fondness for high calorie food convey the agency necessary to solve a mystery? How is the protagonist of a fat positive women's detective novel represented, and how does that representation speak to feminine empowerment? In what ways do these novels support as well as undercut fat positive discourse? How do these novels undermine or reinforce an assumed feminist agenda? And finally, how successful are these novels at redefining femininity for a twenty-first-century audience?

A FONDNESS FOR FATTENING FOOD AS AGENCY

The fatness of the mystery novel protagonists and their fondness for food ultimately provide the agency that helps them to solve the crime. Food, particularly that which is forbidden, becomes a vehicle by which knowledge is gained, discoveries are made, action is taken, and problems are solved. These food-driven narratives are used to carve out a rhetorical space to challenge harmful assumptions about fat people as being lazy, stupid, and libidinous.

Before there were fat female detectives in popular American detective literature, there were Rex Stout's Nero Wolfe novels. Penned in the mid-twentieth century, the Nero Wolfe mysteries may offer the first examples of fat positive discourse in the detective genre. Wolfe is an obese middle-aged PI living in Manhattan, but he is treated with deference unusual for a genre in which only comic characters (usually bumbling mentally deficient policemen) are fat. Wolfe's fat is offset by his brilliance and the fact that he is highly cultured: he has a penchant for rare orchids and fine European cuisine. For Wolfe, eating is a creative and sophisticated act akin to an appreciation for fine art. By virtue of these qualities, Wolfe is effectively "excused" for being fat—and the fact that he is fat actually becomes the means by which he solves mysteries. Wolfe's meals and the meditative process of eating seem to fuel his brain, helping him to solve crimes. Further, Wolfe's formidable size unnerves suspects, causing them to reveal crucial information.

The notion of consumption as a form of agency is reenacted in fat positive women's detective novels. For example, in Fluke's Lake Eden novels, Hannah Swensen, an amateur sleuth, owns a bakery named the Cookie Jar. Not only are Hannah's baked goods a vehicle by which the crimes occur (her cookies are always present at the scene of the crime), they are also the means by which the mysteries are solved: Hannah trades fresh-baked cookies for information, and the Cookie Jar becomes a place where the townsfolk congregate so that Hannah and her assistant, Lisa, can eavesdrop on customers' conversations to pick up vital clues. Beck's donut shop mysteries—highly derivative of Fluke's work—operate according to the same principles of baking and community. The idea that these protagonists create recipes and produce as well as consume their baked goods are important details in that they counter long-standing negative stereotypes about fatness: These women are neither lazy nor passive; they are hardworking and are as much producers as they are consumers. Just as Nero Wolfe's conspicuous consumption (that no doubt leads to his girth) is framed as a creative act, so too is the consumption enacted by the women who run bakeries (their own businesses) in town. Nonetheless, dessert-themed detective novels are driven by a reader's fantasies of excess: instead of the self-sacrifice and asceticism of the female PI, the reader lives vicariously through the chicklit protagonist who can literally have her cake and eat it, too.

CORPOREAL EXPERIENCE AND THE FAT (FEMALE) PROTAGONIST'S SELF-PERCEPTION

The detective narrative is a genre well suited to an abandonment of corporeal experience (female or otherwise) because its protagonist is usually preoccupied with the cerebral task of mystery solving. Since the protagonist's mind is thus engaged, the author can avoid attending to her body. Here, it is important to note that the Nero Wolfe mysteries are told by Archie, Wolfe's assistant. The reader has no access to Wolfe's inner life, and so his experience of inhabiting a fat body is never illuminated. Similarly, female sleuths before the 1970s (for example, Miss Marple and Nancy Drew) avoided the notion of feminine corporeality altogether. We know that Nancy Drew is slender and attractive and that Miss Marple's age renders her virtually invisible to those around her—but beyond that, readers are given little sense of how these women inhabit their bodies.

Mystery writers of the 1970s and 1980s reintroduced the issue of corpo-reality but jettisoned any troublesome "excesses" of femaleness like men-struation—and fat. According to Farrell, second-wave feminist discourse held "that in order to compete in the newly structured public world, women needed to eliminate signs of inferiority, including the marks of primitiveness and impulsivity that fatness symbolized" (113). Being ostentatiously female was clearly considered a mark of inferiority and seems to explain why the female PI of the 1970s was lean and tomboyish. The female PI's physical strength and stamina was underscored in an effort to create a female char-acter with whom male readers could identify—that is, a female protagonist who could effectively become mainstream (Walton and Jones 11). / *255*

While the quintessential female PI almost always engages in a fitness reg-imen and watches her caloric intake, McKevett's, Fluke's, and Beck's charac-ters do not necessarily do so. In these novels, exercise and dieting are rarely entertained as being worthwhile. In fact, dieting tends to signify insecurity and neediness. Savannah, McKevett's protagonist, mentions that dieting was something she used to do before she learned to accept her body, concluding: "Girls have to get smart about weight" (*Cereal Killer* loc. 1601). Hannah, from Fluke's novels, feels much the same way about dieting as Savannah and has a particular loathing for exercise. When Hannah considers going on a diet in *Cream Puff Murder*, she looks at herself in the mirror thinking: "There was no escaping the truth. She was stout, like her Grandma Swensen" (14). However, in the same novel, Hannah does end up losing weight in order to fit into an expensive Regency dress her mother has bought her for a book launch. After all options are explored—including ordering an entirely new dress—Hannah realizes that she has no choice. Her diet and exercise regi-men is markedly unpleasant, but more importantly, she learns which of her two suitors really cares about her. One encourages her to lose more weight, but the other tells her that it makes no difference to him: "She didn't have to lose weight to attract Norman. He loved her just the way she was" (153).

McKevett's *Cereal Killer* offers a critique of the diet industry in which myths about feminine beauty are perpetrated mainly for corporate profit. In this novel, plus-size models are coerced into dieting to meet unrealistic and psychologically damaging cultural standards. One, Caitlin Connor, dies from an overzealous weight-loss program. Addressing Caitlin's agent, the deceased's husband shouts: "She's responsible . . . Her and that damned ad company and the Wentworths. They were willing to let Cait kill herself just to sell cereal" (loc. 473). In McKevett's work, skinny women (for example, the protagonist Savannah's assistant, Tammy) are sometimes seen as objects of pity trapped in cycles of compulsion and pointless self-denial. In a similar vein, Fluke suggests that the benefits that Hannah gains from her lifestyle are more important than whatever temporary satisfaction she might gain from weight loss. Further, when Hannah does in fact lose weight, there is no significant positive change in her life. She continues to find love, a supportive community, and pleasure in her career—minus only the pleasure of eating sweets. Readers relate to Hannah and Savannah in distinct ways. Hannah and Savannah are no less attractive because of their weight: in fact, their size is what makes them who they are. Hannah is constantly undergoing a process of trying to feel more comfortable with herself, and readers can join her in that process. Savannah has already reached self-acceptance, and readers can aspire to be more like her. Most importantly perhaps, these protagonists are all constructed as being attractive in their own right, with or without the "extra" pounds.

In her critique of fat positive discourse, Samantha Murray problematizes how we read the fat female body. While the fat positive movement compels people—particularly women—to embrace their bodies, it rarely takes into account the realities of life as fat person. For instance, learning to embrace one's body type is presented as a matter of simply accepting oneself as fat—but, as Murray points out, "the ways in which I live in my fat body are *always* multiple, contradictory, and eminently ambiguous . . . the idea of a unified unambiguous identity is untenable" (270). Conceiving of her own fat identity as being unambiguous causes Murray to feel disconnected from her body:

> It seemed to me that while the fat body was afforded visibility via the fat pride movement, the centrality of the body to identity and the concept of embodied subjectivity was lost. It was as if to accept my body and identify as fat . . . I had to simply *forget* the dominant discourses that shaped my understanding of my body. (270)

In other words, fat positive discourse is useful in that it encourages fat people to feel good about themselves, but what Murray refers to the as the "fat pride" movement does not necessarily account for the material conditions that fat people must contend with and how they are treated by others. In this sense, fat affirmation means ignoring the realities of having a fat body within a fat-hating culture: "It seemed I had to forget my own fat body, to 'rise above it' somehow. I had to locate my 'fat identity' in my consciousness. I didn't feel I was living it out as an embodied subject" (270). Adhering to a phenomenological model that separates mind from body does not account for the lived experiences of fat people because in actuality, the mind and body are interconnected. As Murray puts it, there is a "complex relationship between the body as it is lived and the body as it is imagined/perceived by others" (271). Fat positive novels can reimagine more positive models of mediation between the individual (fat) body and the social collective, but ultimately, those models are based on fantasy.

Beck's writing is particularly indicative of the problem of "living from the neck up" as it glosses over the issue of corporeality almost entirely. Near the beginning of each novel, the protagonist usually makes a brief reference to her ample size—then states that she is comfortable with her weight. Typically, then, the matter is dispensed with and little mention is made of it for the rest of the book. We do not learn how Beck's Suzanne feels within her body and how she engages with the world as a fat woman. We are invited to like Suzanne because she makes delicious donuts and has a flair for solving mysteries. The fatness (with which she apparently feels so comfortable) is something that readers are primed to more or less overlook. On the other hand, Fluke and McKevett do take up the matter of weight—attending to corporeality very deliberately. Unlike Beck's protagonist Suzanne, Fluke's Hannah and McKevett's Savannah live in their bodies, not just their minds. / 257

McKevett's Savannah is described as being a "voluptuous" woman. Notably, she is a full-fledged PI (rather than an amateur sleuth), and she is in excellent physical condition. Savannah's weight never seems to impede her movements, and she is capable of moving quickly—even though she apparently doesn't work out. Savannah is active, quick on her feet, and aggressive when she needs to be. When an arsonist shoves her, he soon finds himself "lying on the ground at her feet, curled into a ball, holding his head and moaning . . . a small trickle of blood running down his forehead" (*Buried* 10). In her ability to fell a male opponent, Savannah defies assumptions about fat people not being fit. Size is considered only to be an advantage for Savannah, who sees her girth as giving her a certain power of presence. Therefore, in Savannah's mind, the fat female body is always positive— although of course there is the occasional snide remark to contend with. For example, when Savannah tells her wedding planner that she would like to be married in a white dress, the planner is horrified: "'Really? White?' She glanced quickly up and down Savannah's figure, which was without a doubt considerably more . . . ample . . . than her own teeny-tiny bod. 'White isn't exactly slenderizing'" (*Buried* 44). While men seem to find Savannah's curves attractive, women project their insecurities onto her and find fault with her physique. Savannah takes this in stride: "She had always loved her body. Overly voluptuous though it was—according to the weight/height charts. What were a few pounds here and a few there? This body was uniquely, wonderfully hers" (*Buried* 107). Here, the use of the word "overly" intimates excess, but McKevett makes it clear that the perception of excess is a social construct. Savannah does not consider the "few pounds here and a few there" to be "extra." She considers them to be normal and natural. As such, McKevett sends a fat positive message: fat women can and should be regarded as fit and beautiful. Savannah is never directly described as being fat, but the author does provide hints that Savannah is more than simply voluptuous; for example, a police officer refers to her as being "chunky," and Savannah's niece says that her aunt's body is "soft" like a "big cushy pillow" (*Buried* 38). Savannah, well aware that she is considered overweight, admits that she's "too hefty to be a plus-sized model" (*Cereal Killer* loc. 1283).

Further, Savannah's experience is distinctly corporeal. Her body is often described, and she enjoys all of the sensations that come with it—from her attraction to her boyfriend to the pleasures of chocolate and bubble baths. However, Savannah's pleasures are handled delicately. She eats sweets but does not gorge herself and is not compulsive about food. McKevett's work is never sexually explicit, but it is distinctly sensual as Savannah challenges stereotypes of fat people either as being asexual or overly libidinous. McKevett attempts to create more positive models of mediation between the fat individual and a fat negative social collective. For the most part, Savannah's fatness is admired rather than reviled. Further, Savannah herself does not balk from "owning" her fatness and living in her fat body.

In contrast to McKevett's Savannah, Fluke's Hannah is nowhere near as comfortable with her body or her sexuality. Hannah is ambivalent about her weight, sometimes seeming to accept it as a fundamental part of her identity and at other times wishing that she were otherwise. In virtually every novel, Hannah notices the difference between herself and her "beautiful, petite mother and sisters" as well as her "unfortunate tendency to put on extra pounds" (*Red Velvet* 44). But despite these occasional feelings of inadequacy, Hannah's weight is constructed as an integral part of her identity and the locus of the qualities that make her approachable. In this sense, Fluke appears to be engaging and perhaps even perpetuating stereotypes about women—that they are naturally nurturing and enjoy feeding and caring for others. Further, Hannah's discomfort with her body and her awareness of being overweight appear to be perpetuating a stereotype specifically about fat women, that they are excessively grateful for male attention.

Moreover, Hannah's sexual desires are hinted at, but never quite fulfilled, and her ambivalence about her own body is clear. Fluke mentions that Hannah "tingles" when hugged or kissed by either of her two suitors, but other than those exchanges, her relationship with both men remains surprisingly chaste. While Hannah questions her own attractiveness, others apparently do not— indicating that she is more attractive than she believes she is. In fact, the two most eligible bachelors in Lake Eden are apparently in love with her: "There was nothing like having two men vying for her affections. It kept them both on their toes and it made her feel much younger, more beautiful, and much thinner than she actually was" (*Red Velvet* 63). However, despite Hannah's insistence on not dressing or dieting to please men, many of her insecurities stem from her awareness that her suitors could easily be lured away by thinner women. While Hannah seems to recognize the folly of dieting and a problem- / 259 atic cultural focus on women's weight, she never quite succeeds in embracing her size. Instead, she simply tries to divert her attention from it, choosing to focus on other things. In this regard, Hannah's discomfort expresses what Murray claims is the fat positive movement's lack of attention to the lived experience of individual fat bodies. But Hannah does inhabit her body—she simply isn't comfortable in it all the time—an issue that Fluke invites the reader to interpret as being more of a sociocultural problem than a genuine personal problem that Hannah needs to attend to. Fluke's work depicts the ambiguity that Murray mentions—at times, Hannah feels attractive, but she also suffers pangs of regret that she is not petite and pretty like the other women in her family. Although Hannah is mostly able to accept her body as it is, she seems happier when she is not thinking about it at all. There is no real attempt at fat positive discourse here—simply a sense of resignation. Fat does not matter if one is able to achieve what Murray refers to as the "time-honored fat girl thing, which is 'living from the neck up'" (270).

RECLAIMING AND REDEFINING FEMININITY?

Walton and Jones suggest that the "feminist" female PI novels of the late twentieth century were deemed successful because they became mainstream

—that is, they found male as well as female audiences. The fact that these novels gained such a widespread readership meant a triumph for feminism, in that novels with a female protagonist could sidestep what was considered to be the undesirable label of "women's fiction." However, the twenty-first-century proliferation of detective novels written deliberately as chicklit (often including love interests or romantic subplots) have been criticized for turning back the clock on feminism: women are amateur sleuths again, dilettantes who solve mysteries and eat dessert. Savannah, Hannah, and Suzanne all enjoy baking and spend a great deal of time in the kitchen. People turn to them to be consoled and nurtured. Hannah is constantly feeding and caring for her two suitors, Mike and Norman. Savannah enjoys cooking and caring for her boyfriend, Dirk. By second-wave standards, these women are depicted as relishing feminine roles that appear to subjugate rather than empower them.

In turn, late twentieth-century representations of the tomboyish female PI could be accused of advocating a rejection of femininity. Indeed, the female PIs portrayed in what Walton and Jones conceive as being feminist works are constructed as being as similar to their male counterparts as possible. They are unsentimental and tough. They do not keep house or cook. They are typically single and certainly childfree. They are wily, keen on fitness, crisp, and to the point. It is assumed that these qualities, along with an implied rejection of essentialized feminine attributes help to make these women effective detectives. In contrast, chicklit detective novels, particularly those that feature fat protagonists, highlight all qualities previously rejected as being excessively womanly: affection for children, cooking, housekeeping, nurturing, and maintaining a voluptuous figure.

Arguably, one cannot attain gender equality by taking on more masculine traits and habits, but neither can gender equality be attained by women who are overly accepting of passive domestic roles in which women are presented primarily as nurturers. The question is, are essentialized feminine attributes, such as the desire to nurture and a love for cooking, in chicklit helping to empower women or merely reinscribing pernicious nineteenth-century-era discourses of feminine domesticity? Plenty of chicklit involves slender female protagonists who feed, nurture, and behave in feminine ways, but what are the implications for the fat protagonist who engages in similar behavior? Both models appear to be problematic. But beyond embracing domesticity, the fat female protagonist is more vulnerable in that she is, perhaps, seen to be engaging in these servile activities to offset her negative association with femaleness in favor of a more positive association with femininity. Is fat positive chicklit reifying harmful stereotypes about constructions of femaleness and femininity, or is it challenging those stereotypes? Stephanie Harzewski writes, "Chick lit should not be considered 'antifeminist' but a selective, half-utopian amalgamation of earlier feminist tenets" (181). Harzewski's emphasis on the idea of selection suggests that we should not see feminism as a monolithic discourse and that it can mean different things to different people. Often chicklit is unabashedly escapist, playing on fantasy and wish fulfillment—but more substantially, it could be argued that fat positive chicklit, particularly in the detective genre, suggests that women do not have to distance themselves from "female" qualities in order to be successful. As mentioned earlier, fatness is not a feminine quality, but it is culturally coded as a "female" quality. Stereotypical female qualities, such as nurturing and feeding others, are now celebrated, but they are also frequently conflated with excessive consumption: a voracious appetite for shopping, sex, or food. Ironically, however, writers of fat positive chicklit cannot fully realize the excesses of their protagonists because there is still a need to avoid perpetuating pernicious stereotypes about fat people. For this reason, a fat protagonist must not be graphically engaged in sex nor must she over-indulge. Enjoyment and pleasure are encouraged but kept "palatable." Audiences may want to indulge their own fantasies of excess vicariously, but since this excess is always already implicated in the body of the fat female protagonist, it must eventually reach its limit.

CONCLUSION

The texts I have discussed here are significant because they situate discourses of fat positive femininity historically and reveal complex differences between postfeminism and second-wave feminism. Second-wave feminism saw two competing constructions of female corporeality: fat positive discourse and the lean tomboy protagonist reflected in feminist appropriations of a masculinist literary tradition. In order to be taken seriously by men, women were to reject their "femaleness." Simultaneously, however, women were to embrace their bodies and celebrate a diversity of body types. In postfeminism, a movement sometimes accused of resubjugating women to patriarchal norms, the fat female body is recoded in order to disrupt common cultural assumptions about fat people. However, these assumptions can only be disrupted up to a certain point because there are limits on the degree of excess permitted a fat protagonist. Excess is indeed celebrated, but excess itself cannot be taken too far because prejudices against fat people are so culturally engrained.

At its most radical, fat positive chicklit in the detective genre counters the status quo by placing the fat woman, including her (socially unacceptable) appetites, at the very center of the narrative and of social life. Fatness is a resource—a benefit rather than a liability—and cultural beliefs about fat people are challenged and overturned. McKevett, in particular, seems to be working consciously to dismantle harmful standards of body image, appropriating and recoding perceptions of empowered femininity by attending specifically to the fat female body.

The writers of genre fiction featuring plus-size women ask readers to identify with fat protagonists, to be inspired by them, and to empathize with them. These writers also attempt to reclaim discourses of both femininity and femaleness, suggesting that their protagonists need no longer abide by prescriptive notions of femininity. Further, so-called feminine behaviors (based on both positive and negative stereotypes) no longer need to be deemed antifeminist: negative feminine traits, such as a focus on frivolity or consumption, can be recoded, as can positive feminine traits, such as nurturing and offering comfort. Most importantly, fat positive genre fiction suggests that in order to be taken seriously as professionals, women no longer have to repudiate a negatively coded excess of femaleness—that is, fat.

Works Cited

Bell, Kirsten, and Darlene McNaughton. "Feminism and the Invisible Fat Man." *Body and Society* 13 (2007): 107–31.

Farrell, Amy Erdman. *Fat Shame: Stigma and the Fat Body in American Culture.* New York UP, 2011.

Fluke, Joanne. *Cream Puff Murder.* Kensington, 2011.

———. *Red Velvet Cupcake Murder.* Kensington, 2014.

Harzewski, Stephanie. *Chick Lit and Postfeminism.* U of Virginia P, 2011.

McKevett, G. A. *Buried in Buttercream.* Kensington, 2012.

———. *Cereal Killer.* Kensington, 2004.

Murray, Samantha. "Doing Politics or Selling Out? Living the Fat Body." *Women's Studies* 34 (2005): 265–77.

Walton, Priscilla L., and Manina Jones. *Detective Agency: Women Rewriting the Hard-Boiled Tradition.* U of California P, 1999.

CONTRIBUTORS

INDEX

CONTRIBUTORS

ARLENE VOSKI AVAKIAN is a professor emerita of women, gender, and sexuality studies at the University of Massachusetts Amherst. Her books include *Lion Woman's Legacy: An Armenian-American Memoir*; *Through the Kitchen Window: Women Explore the Intimate Meanings of Food and Cooking*; *From Betty Crocker to Feminist Food Studies: Critical Perspectives on Women and Food*; and *African American Women and the Vote, 1837–1965*.

ALEXIS BAKER is an assistant professor of English at Anne Arundel Community College in Arnold, Maryland. Her chapter was inspired by her dissertation on the representation of women's identity in Holocaust narratives and art. This is her first publication.

LYNN Z. BLOOM is a Board of Trustees Distinguished Professor Emerita at the University of Connecticut. She learned the essentials of writing from Dr. Seuss, fun; Strunk and White, elegant simplicity; Art Eastman, nitpicking revision; and Benjamin Spock, "If you don't write clearly, someone could die." Her books include *Doctor Spock: Biography of a Conservative Radical*; *Writers without Borders: Writing and Teaching Writing in Troubled Times*; and *The Seven Deadly Virtues and Other Lively Essays*.

ERIN BRANCH is an associate teaching professor at Wake Forest University, where she teaches courses in writing and rhetoric. Her work has appeared in *Rhetoric Society Quarterly*, and her book *Transforming Tastes* is forthcoming from the University of Nebraska Press.

JENNIFER COGNARD-BLACK is a professor of English at St. Mary's College of Maryland, where she teaches literature, theory, and writing. Her short stories, essays, and criticism have appeared in a number of journals and magazines, including *College English* and *Feminist Studies*, and she's the author or coeditor of five books, including *Books That Cook: The Making of a Literary Meal* (with Melissa Goldthwaite).

JENNIFER E. COURTNEY is an associate professor of writing arts at Rowan University, where she teaches undergraduate and graduate courses in writing. Her work has appeared in *Rhetoric Review, Composition Forum*, and *What We Are Becoming: Developments in Undergraduate Writing Majors*.

ABBY DUBISAR is an assistant professor of English and an affiliate faculty member in women's and gender studies at Iowa State University, where she teaches classes on women's and feminist rhetoric, gender and communication, and popular culture analysis. Her research analyzes the rhetorical strategies of women peace activists in a wide variety of contexts, from archival holdings to YouTube.

MELISSA A. GOLDTHWAITE, a professor of English, teaches writing at Saint Joseph's University. She's the editor, coauthor, or coeditor of *Books That Cook: The Making of a Literary Meal; The Little Norton Reader; The St. Martin's Guide to Teaching Writing; The Norton Reader; Surveying the Literary Landscapes of Terry Tempest Williams*; and *The Norton Pocket Book of Writing by Students*.

MORGAN GRESHAM is an associate professor of English at the University of South Florida St. Petersburg, where she serves as the coordinator of first-year composition and writing studies. Her research interests include feminism, computers and composition, and writing program administration.

SARA HILLIN is an associate professor of English at Lamar University, where she also serves as the writing director and teaches courses in rhetoric and pedagogy. Her essays have appeared in *Writing and Pedagogy* and *Computers and Composition Online*.

REBECCA INGALLS is a former associate professor and a former director of first-year writing at Drexel University. Her work has appeared in *Inventio; Academe; POROI; Harlot*; the *Journal of Teaching Writing*; the *Journal of Popular Culture*; the *Review of Education, Pedagogy, and Cultural Studies*; and *Writing and Pedagogy*. She coedited *Critical Conversations about Plagiarism*. She is currently studying to be a nurse-midwife.

TAMMIE M. KENNEDY is an associate professor at the University of Nebraska Omaha. She is a coeditor of *Rhetorics of Whiteness: Postracial Hauntings in Popular Culture, Social Media, and Education*. Her essays have appeared in *Composition Studies, Feminist Formations, Rhetoric Review, JAC,* the *Journal of Religion and Popular Culture*, the *English Journal*, *Brevity*, the *Journal of Lesbian Studies*, and in numerous books.

WINONA LANDIS is a PhD candidate in English literature at Miami University of Ohio, where she focuses on Asian American studies, critical race and feminist theory, and popular culture studies. She is the assistant editor of the *Journal of Asian American Studies*. She is working on her dissertation, which focuses on race and readership in comics and graphic novels.

ELIZABETH LOWRY received her PhD in rhetoric and composition from Arizona State University, where she now holds a lecturer position in rhetoric and composition. Her research interests include public spheres, material culture, and nineteenth-century women's rhetorics. Her work has been published in *Rhetoric Review*, *Aries*, *Word and Text*, and in edited collections.

SYLVIA A. PAMBOUKIAN is a professor of English at Robert Morris University, where she teaches nineteenth-century literature with a focus on the medical humanities. She is the author of *Doctoring the Novel: Medicine and Quackery from Shelley to Doyle*.

CONSUELO CARR SALAS is a doctoral candidate in rhetoric and composition at the University of Texas at El Paso. She is working on her dissertation "Commodified Perceptions of Culture: A Rhetorical Inquiry of Food Advertisement Narratives." She coedited *Latin@s' Presence in the Food Industry: Changing How We Think about Food*. Her work has also appeared in the *Community Literacy Journal*.

CARRIE HELMS TIPPEN is an assistant professor of English at Chatham University, where she teaches courses in writing and literature. Her work has appeared in *Food and Foodways*; *Southern Quarterly*; and *Food, Culture, and Society*. Her ongoing book project, *Stories of Southern Cooking: Defining Authentic New Southern Identity in Recipe Origin Narratives*, examines rhetorical strategies for proving authenticity in contemporary cookbooks.

ABBY WILKERSON is a philosopher and an associate professor of writing at the George Washington University, where she teaches a first-year seminar on food justice. Her publications include the forthcoming *The Thin Contract: Social Justice and the Political Rhetoric of Obesity*; *Diagnosis: Difference—the Moral Authority of Medicine*; articles in *Food, Culture, and Society*; *Radical Philosophy Review*; and anthologies.

KRISTIN WINET is an assistant professor of English at Rollins College in Winter Park, Florida, where she also directs the first-year writing program. Her scholarship has been published in *Kairos*, the *English Journal*, and a number of edited collections. She is also an award-winning travel writer and photographer.

INDEX

Italicized page numbers indicate figures.

Abarca, Meredith E., 190, 194–95
Abileah, Rae, 60
Abu-Jaber, Diana, 7, 132–41
accountability logic, 110–11
activists, 60; rhetorical communication, 64–65. *See also* fat activism; peace activism
Adichie, Chimamanda, 194
affective identification, 143–45, 149–52
African Americans, 16, 62, 151; erasure by, for African American audiences, 24–25. *See also* Great Migration; *Sweets: Soul Food Desserts and Memories* (Pinner)
Against Race (Gilroy), 24–25
agency, 111, 121, 253–54; rhetorical, 56–57, 210
Ahmed, Leila, 134
Ahmed, Sara, 151, 175, 176, 181, 182
Alcott, Louisa May, 159
alternative agrarian rhetoric, 121–22, 126, 130
American Frugal Housewife, The (Child), 49, 52–54

American Woman's Home, The (Beecher and Stowe), 48
"angel in the house" ideology, 155, 167n4
animal cruelty, 233–34, 244
Animal, Vegetable, Miracle: A Year of Food Life (Kingsolver), 90, 96–98
Anne of Green Gables (Montgomery), 161–63
anorexia. *See* pro-ana websites
"antiracist" language, 24–25
Appadurai, Arjun, 196, 197
Appetites (Knapp), 182
appliances, 10n1, 37
Arab Americans: contested categories, 135–36; food imagery as accommodation, 134; gender relations, 138–39; identity construction, 135–39; patriarchal past, 133, 138; stereotypes, 7, 132–33
Arab cuisine, 132–42
Arabian Jazz (Abu-Jaber), 132
Art of Eating, The (Fisher), 87n2, 112–13
Atlantic, The (magazine), 86
Auden, W. H., 78–79

authenticity, 8, 10, 22–23, 194, 195–97
autobiographies, 6, 89–99; cookbooks as, 17; Fussell, 90, 91–92; Hamilton, 90, 92–96; Kingsolver, 90, 96–98; major kitchen chapters, 94–96. *See also* Fisher, M. F. K.
Avakian, Arlene Voski, 1, 3, 7, 10n2, 79

Baker, Alexis, 8–9
Bakhtin, Mikhail, 223–27, 230; body in act of becoming, 234–35; consumer-consumed argument, 231–33
baking: as cultural capital, 25–26; southern African American rituals, 22–23, 25
balance, 71–72, 81, 86
Balicki, Dana, 60
Barnouin, Kim, 9, 222–24, 227–36
Bartner, Ashley, 106–7
Bartner, Jason, 106–7
Baudrillard, Jean, 197
Bauer, Jan, 179
Bechdel test, 172, 183n4
Beck, Jessica, 252, 254, 257
Beecher, Catharine, 48
Bell, David, 102
Bell, Kirsten, 252
"Beyond Persuasion: A Proposal for an Invitational Rhetoric" (Foss and Griffin), 63
biculturality, 139–40, 143
Bilston, Sarah, 158, 159
Birdsell, David, 204, 205
Bitch Magazine, 174
Black Exodus: The Great Migration from the American South (Harrison), 20
Blackford, Holly, 158
Blankenhorn, David, 50–51
blogs and websites, 7, 9–10, 31, 49, 56, 174; culinary tourism, 103–4, 108, 110–11; kitchen thrift, 49, 52, 56. *See also* pro-ana websites
Blood, Bones, and Butter: The Inadvertent Education of a Reluctant Chef (Hamilton), 90, 92–96

Bloom, Lynn Z., 6, 44
Boling, Patricia, 238, 244, 247
Bone, Jennifer, 220
"Borderland" (Fisher), 81
Boston Cooking-School Cook Book (Farmer), 33
Botticelli, 89
Bourdain, Anthony, 98–99n2, 104
Bower, Anne, 15, 38, 62
Brain Games (television show), 192–93
Branch, Erin, 6
brand names, 34, 35, 36, 37
Brave (film), 164–65
Brightmoor Farmway, 119–20, 128–29
Brophy-Warren, Sorcha, 50–51
Brown, Leanne, 52
Bruner, Michael S., 4
Buchanan, Lindal, 49
Building Houses Out of Chicken Legs (Williams-Forson), 15, 16, 25
Buried in Buttercream (McKevett), 257–58
Burke, Kenneth, 4, 62–63, 121
Burnett, Frances Hodgson, 156–57
Bush, Laura, 133
"Butterhorn Rolls" recipe, 42–44, *43*
Buxbaum, Yitzhak, 202

California, Hmong immigrant farms in, 125–26
Campbell, Karlyn Kohrs, 61, 79, 80–81
Cannon, Poppy, 78
Can Opener Cookbooks (Cannon), 78
capitalism, 128
Capps, Lisa, 200
Carnell, Susan, 192–93
carnival tradition, 223, 224–25
Carruth, Allison, 143
Cereal Killer (McKevett), 255, 256
Cheng, Emily, 144
"chicklit" novels, 252–53, 260–61
Child, Julia, 90, 98n1, 244
Child, Lydia Maria, 49, 52–54
children's literature, 8; comic tone, 159, 160; food sharing, 155–56, 165–66. *See also* girl poisoner, figure of

Chiu, Monica, 152
chronology, in cookbooks and recipes, 17, 27, 32, 66
church social activities, 23, 44
citizenship, 123, 133
Claiborne, Sybil, 63–64
Clarke, Mary, 66, 69
Code Pink, 60, 72
Cognard, Peg, 30–31, 33–37, 39; "Incidents in My Life" memoir, 37, 40–41
Cognard-Black, Jennifer, 5–6, 212
Cohen, Devorah, 202–3
collaboration, 97; recipe sharing, 36, 37, 42–43
College English food issue, 61
colonizing attitudes, tourism and, 101–5, 109, 112–13
commodified perception of culture (CPC), 194–95
commodity fetishism, 103, 104–5
commune living, 63–64
community, 97; African American, 21–27; of cooking women, 31–32, 36, 38, 42, 45
community cookbooks, 38, 45
Complete Tightwad Gazette, The (Dacyczyn), 49, 54–55
compulsory able-bodiedness, 123, 127
compulsory heterosexuality, 123
consumer cannibalism, 103
consumer-consumed argument, 231–33
consumerism, 50, 53–54, 143
Consuming Geographies (Bell and Valentine), 102
"Consuming Nations" (Peckham), 107–8
contemplation, strategic, 57
convenience foods, 36–37
conviviality, 129–30
Cook, Ian, 103, 105–7
cookbooks, 5; community, 38; epideictic rhetoric, 23–24; as feminist historiography, 15–17, 27; primary sources, 18; as storytelling, 38; as wedding gifts, 30; by women in

concentration camps, 203, 206. *See also* recipes
cooking equipment, 10n1, 19, 22, 37, 55
Cooking with the Two Fat Ladies (Wright and Paterson), 239, 245
cosmopolitanism, 102–5, 113
Costa Rica, 100–101
Cotton, Mary Ann, 157–58
Cougar Town (television show), 175
Courtney, Jennifer E., 6
Crang, Philip, 103
Cream Puff Murder (Fluke), 255
Crescent (Abu-Jaber), 7, 132–41
critical literacy studies, 121, 130
cucina povera, 106
cultural logic, 193, 196–97
cultures, rhetorical representations of, 8–10
"Cutting Expenses When You Think You Have Nothing Left to Cut" (Simper), 56

Dacyczyn, Amy, 49, 54–55
Dane, Barbara, 70
d'Arabian, Melissa, 49, 55
D'Arminio, Aubry, 243
"Date a Girl Who Eats" (Dawson), 104
Dávila, Arlene, 196
Dawson, Valen, 103–4
Dean, Velia, 60, 61, 65, 70–71
Decoding Advertisements (Williamson), 193
decontextualization, 102, 105–7
Del Gandio, Jason, 61, 63, 64–65, 69, 71
De Los Santos, Penny, 106
desires, 85–86, 143
detective novels, dessert-themed, 9–10, 251–62; agency and fondness for fattening food, 253–54; corporeal experience and self-perception, 254–59
detective novels, 1970s and 1980s, 251, 255
Detroit, 119–20, 128–29
Detroit Black Community Food Security Network, 130

devouring, 102, 107–9
Dickinson, Greg, 190, 192
didactic materials, 32, 61
diet books, 9, 222–36
differences, acknowledgment of, 114, 138
Dinner Roles (Inness), 78
disability studies, 122–23
Dobbernationloves (Dobson), 108–9
Dobson, Andrew, 108–9
documentary medium, 144, 152
domestic revolution, 66–71
domestic sphere, as public space, 22–23, 25
Donati, Kelly, 109
Dow, George, 133
Drink (Johnston), 174, 179
drinking, 8, 92, 171–86; emotion work, 8, 173, 175–80; gendered ideologies, 182; normalization of, 182; prevalence, 171–72; temperance rhetorics, 171, 172, 182; women's practices, 173–75
Dubisar, Abby, 6
Duruz, Jean, 109

"Eat for 40 Cents a Day" (Simper), 56
Eating the Globe (Dawson), 103–4
"eating the globe," 103
Eat My Words: Reading Women's Lives through the Cookbooks They Wrote (Theophano), 17–18, 45n1
economy, concept of, 53
Edelman, Lee, 149
Eisenhower, Dwight D., 71
embodied rhetoric, 5–6, 8–10, 30–47; handwritten recipes, 30–31, 45n2; logos of recipes, 32–34; of recipes, 38–40. *See also* gastronomical kairos
emotional meaning of food, 77, 79
emotional responses, 142–44
emotion work, 8, 173, 175–80, 182
empowerment, 42
Enchanted Broccoli Forest, The (Katzen), 30

Eng, David, 146, 147
Engelhardt, Elizabeth, 15–16
Enoch, Jessica, 202
Enos, Theresa, 79
epideictic rhetoric, 23–24
ersatz nostalgia, 198
escapism, 102, 109–11
essentialism, 105, 107–8
ethos, 4, 200–201, 210
Ettenberg, Jodi, 110, 113–14
Eucharistic imagery, 84, 85, 87n3
everyday practices, 190, 192, 238–39
everyday rhetors, 49, 56–57
Eves, Rosalyn Collings, 62
excrement, 230, 234
executives, feminist, 90
Extravagant Hunger, An: The Passionate Years of M. F. K. Fisher (Zimmerman), 77

faculty wives, 92–93
Faigley, Lester, 193
failure, 149
Fairclough, Kirsty, 229
family: heteronormative, 123–24, 127–28; hiring within, 26; judgment by, 41
family meal, 127, 130
family rhetoric, 7, 120–21; family values in the kitchen, 126–30; Hmong immigrant farms and, 125–26; indirect forms of exclusion, 125–26; in kitchen, 126–30. *See also* sustainability
Farmer, Fannie Merritt, 33, 45n4
farmers' market, 123–24, 128
Farrell, Amy, 251, 255
fast food, 226–27
Fast Food Nation: The Dark Side of the All-American Meal (Schlosser), 226–27, 232
fat, as term, 238
fat activism, 240, 244–45, 248n2, 251; material conditions and, 256–57, 259; reclaiming and redefining

femininity, 259–61. *See also* detective novels, dessert-themed

fatness, 9, 40; fat positive discourse, 256–57; as female trait, 252, 261

fat shaming, 241, 247–48, 249n4, 251

Faux, Mandi (webmistress), 10, 216–18, 220

feel-good diet books, 223, 230

feminine style, 6, 18, 79, 80–82, 86

feminism: fat feminism, 238; influence on rhetoric, 61–63; postfeminism, 98; rhetorics, 3–5; second-wave, 62, 72, 97, 251, 255; social drinking and, 173–74; third-wave, 174, 217; transnational, 113

"Feminist Food Studies: A Brief History," 79

Feminist Mystique (Friedan), 92

Feminist Rhetorical Practices: New Horizons for Rhetoric, Composition, and Literacy Studies (Royster and Kirsch), 4

Ferguson, Roderick, 127

Fertel, Rien, 18

fetishizing domestic tasks, 61

"Fifty Most Important Women in Food, The" (Sekules), 77

financial hardship, 56

"Finding the F Word for It" (Wann), 238

Fisher, Al, 77, 81

Fisher, M. F. K., 6, 7, 77–88, 89, 98, 100, 107; *The Art of Eating*, 87n2, 112–13; emotional meaning of food, 77, 79; feminine style, 79, 80–82, 86; gastronomical kairos, 79, 80, 82–85; *The Gastronomical Me*, 81, 89–90; *How to Cook a Wolf*, 78–79, 86; *Serve It Forth*, 6, 78, 81; "A Thing Shared," 82

Fix, Nick, 214

Fleitz, Elizabeth, 62

Fluke, Joanne, 252, 254, 255, 258

food-body, 223, 234–36

food commentators, 44

food culture, 127

Food for Our Grandmothers: Writings by Arab-American and Arab-Canadian Feminists (Kadi), 134

food insecurity, 130

food justice, 7, 121–23

Food Network, 55, 243

food preservation, 54

food-related messages, 1–3

food-related practices, 7–8

food safety, 9, 242, 244

food sharing, 155–56, 165–66

Food Traveler's Handbook, The (Ettenberg), 110, 113–14

Foss, Sonja K., 61, 63–64

Foucault, Michel, 229

Franklin, Ben, 51

Freedman, Rory, 9, 222–24, 227–36

freedom, 182; food-body and, 234–35

Friedan, Betty, 92

From Betty Crocker to Feminist Food Studies (Avakian and Haber), 79

Fromer, Julie E., 161

frugality discourses, 50–51

Frye, Joshua J., 4

Fussell, Betty, 90, 91–92

Fussell, Paul, 92

Gallo, Stephanie, 175

Gargantua and Pantagruel series (Rabelais), 224–34

gastronomical identity, 83, 136–37

gastronomical kairos, 79, 80, 82–85

Gastronomical Me, The (Fisher), 81, 89–90

Gaytán, Marie Sarita, 194

"Gender Bender" (Morris), 173–74

gender subversion, 66–71

Gerhardt, Cornelia, 33–34

Giard, Luce, 28

Gilroy, Paul, 24

Girardelli, Davide, 192

girl poisoner, figure of, 8, 155–70; age conventions, 8, 158–59; *Anne of Green Gables*, 161–63; *Brave*, 164–65; gender norms and, 156–57;

girl poisoner, figure of (*continued*)
Harry Potter and the Chamber of Se-crets, 163–64; *Little Women*, 159–61;
marginalized, protection of, 163–64;
naiveté of, 158–59, 166; noxious food
and transgression, 159–60, 167n6;
The Secret Garden, 155–57, 167n3
Glaser, Gabrielle, 171, 174
Glenn, Cheryl, 3, 15, 16, 28
global economic exchange networks,
143–44
global memoryscapes, 195, 197
Goldthwaite, Melissa A., 212
Good and Cheap (Brown), 52
Good Wife, The (*TGW*) (television
show), 8, 171, 172, 175–86
Gopnik, Adam, 90
Gourmet (magazine), 77
Grafton County, New Hampshire, 120,
130
Grape Leaves: A Century of Ar-ab-American Poetry (Orfalea and
Elmusa), 134
Great Day Cookbook, The (Dean and
Zimmerman), 60, 61, 65, 70–71
Great Migration, 19–29; "the ancestor"
and "the stranger," 22–23; conditions
in the South, 20–21, 28; violence,
20–21, 23–25; violence and work as
impetus for, 20–21; women's inter-state travel, 22–23, 24
green thrift, 51, 54
Greenwich Village Peace Center, 61,
63–64, 69–70
Gresham, Morgan, 9
Griffin, Cindy L., 61, 63–64, 220
Griffin, Farah Jasmine, 21, 23
Groarke, Leo, 204, 205
grocery stores, Mexican aisle, 189–90
Grose, Jessica, 174
grotesque female body, 222–23
Grotesque in Painting and Poetry, The
(Bakhtin), 225
grotesque realism, 9, 223–27; ambiva-lence of, 224–25, 227–28, 229, 230–33

Haber, Barbara, 3, 79
Halberstam, Judith, 127, 149
Hall, Stuart, 136, 193
Hallenbeck, Sarah, 238–39
Hallock, Whitney, 60
Hamblin, James, 86
Hamilton, Gabrielle, 90, 92–96,
98–99n2
Hannerz, Ulf, 102–3
Hardman, Kay, 66, 67
Harrison, Alferdteen, 20, 23
Harry Potter and the Chamber of Se-crets (Rowling), 163–64
Harry Potter series (Rowling), 163
Harzewski, Stephanie, 253
Hassan, Salah D., 134
heirlooms, cookbooks as, 17–18, 39,
46n10
Heldke, Lisa, 106, 109–10, 113
Her Best-Kept Secret (Glaser), 174
Hesford, Wendy, 113, 146
Hess, Marta, 62
Hillin, Sara, 9
historiography, 5–6; cookbooks as,
15–19, 27; (re)writing Great Migra-tion in cookbooks, 19–28
History of Grotesque Satire, The
(Schneegans), 224
Hmong immigrant farmers, 125–26
Hochschild, Arlie, 173, 175, 180
Holocaust: Auschwitz, 202–3; cook-books written in camps, 203, 206;
cultural and spiritual identity in
writings, 210; female survivor stories,
201–2; noble representations, 202
Holocaust art by women, 8–9, 200–211;
analysis, 204–9; historical and schol-arly background, 201–4; nutrition as
theme in, *205*, 205–8, *207*
homemaking, professionalization of,
32–33
hooks, bell, 102, 103, 105
Hopp, Stephen, 97
Horowitz, Sara, 201
House of Thin (website), 9, 214, 217–18

How to Cook a Wolf (Fisher), 78–79, 86
Hum, Sue, 196
hunger, desires and, 85–86, 89
Hunter, James, 50, 51

identity construction, 8–9, 10n2, 22, 25; American, family rhetoric and, 124–25, 130; Arab Americans, 135–36, 135–39; control of eating, 166nn1–2; foods from home, 135–37; in Holocaust art, 201, 203–11; Junior League cookbooks, 62; physical body not foundation, 202–3, 207–8; pre-Holocaust selves, 201; on pro-ana websites, 213
if/then structure, 32
I Hate to Cook Book (Bracken), 92
imagined nostalgia, 196–97
"Incidents in My Life" (Cognard), 37, 40–41
Ingalls, Rebecca, 9
ingredient list, 32–33, 38
Inness, Sherrie, 3–4, 36, 62, 78
instructions, written, 31; logos of recipes, 32–34
intersectionality, 65, 102, 142
invitational rhetoric, 9, 61, 63–66, 213, 217, 219–20

Japan, 143
Jezebel (website), 174
Johnston, Ann Dowsett, 174, 179
Jones, Manina, 251, 259–60
Joy of Cooking (Rombauers), 30
Jungle, The (Sinclair), 226, 227
Junior League cookbooks, 62
"just deserts" or denouement, 39

kairos, gastronomical. *See* gastronomical kairos
Kasper, Lynne Rossetto, 106
Katz, Wendy, 155, 168nn9–10
Katzen, Mollie, 30
Kennedy, Mary Frances. *See* Fisher, M. F. K.

Kennedy, Tammie M., 8
Kingsolver, Barbara, 90, 96–98
Kirsch, Gesa E., 4, 5, 56, 57–58, 172, 175
kitchen thrift, 6, 48–59; defined, 51; as gendered genre, 49; positioning women rhetors, 56–58; prescriptive texts, 48–49; texts, 51–56
Knapp, Caroline, 182
Knelman, Judith, 157
Knoepflmacher, U. C., 158–59
Knopf-Newman, Marcy Jane, 134
Kovner, Jean, 66, 67
Kueny, Kathryn, 173

"Ladies! Liquor! Ladies and Liquor!" (McCurdy), 174
Lager, Grace, 219
Lake Eden novels (Fluke), 252, 254, 255, 256
Landis, Winona, 7
Lean In: Women, Work, and the Will to Lead (Sandberg), 98
Left ideology, food and, 126
Legal Nomads: Telling Stories through Food (Ettenberg), 110
Leonardi, Susan, 18, 38
Lewin, Esther, 66, 67, 68
Lewis-Smith, Victor, 247
Liberman, Judith, 208–10, *209*
literacy, recipe, 34, 45n1
Little Women (Alcott), 159–61
lived experience, 80–81, 257, 259
Llewellyn, Patricia, 239
localism, 119–20
locavore philosophy, 96–98
logos of recipes, 32–34
Long Ago in France (Fisher), 77
Longhurst, Robyn, 238
Lorde, Audre, 114
Los Angeles, and Women Strike for Peace, 60–61, 62–63, 66–69
love, 85–86, 89
Lowry, Elizabeth, 9–10
Lunsford, Andrea, 15, 16–17, 28
Lupton, Deborah, 136

Malaysia, 2
male-centered narratives, 16–17; activ-
    ist movements, 66; Great Migration,
    21; rhetoric field, 61–62
Maltz Museum of Jewish Heritage
    (Beachwood, Ohio), 200
Marx, Karl, 103
masculine style, 80
mass production, 194–95
Mastering the Art of French Cooking
    (Child), 90
Matchar, Emily, 61, 72
material world, 39, 42
Mattingly, Carol, 172
Maybrick, Florence, 157
McCurdy, Christen, 174
McEntee, Jesse, 120
McGee, Brian, 219
McKevett, G. A., 252, 255, 256, 262
McKuen, Rod, 71
McNaughton, Darlene, 252
McRuer, Robert, 123
Measured Meals (Mudry), 80
meat industry, 142–43, 226–27, 232–34,
    244
MELUS (journal), 134
memoirs, 19–20, 37, 40–41
memories, 19, 32, 201
Mess of Greens, A (Engelhardt), 15–16
Mexican food packaging, 8, 189–99;
    authenticity, 195–97; cultural logic,
    196–97; grocery stores, Mexican
    aisle, 189–90; images of Mexican
    women, 190–99, *191*, *195*; stereotypes
    of women, 194; women commodi-
    fied, 194
middle-class affluence, 36–37, 57, 103,
    173
Minkoff-Zern, Laura-Anne, 125
mixed-race characters, 143–44
Molz, Jennie Germann, 102, 103, 104
money-making ventures, 26–27
monster, figure of, 157–58
Monteverde, Costa Rica, 100–101
Montgomery, Lucy Maud, 161

Moorti, Sujata, 246, 249n4
Morris, Alex, 174
Mother and Child (Olomucki), *205*,
    205–6
motherhood, 144, 149, 241; Jewish
    woman's identity and, 204–5
Mudry, Jessica, 80, 86
multiculturalism, 114, 144–45, 151–52
Murray, Samantha, 256–57, 259
My Kitchen Wars (Fussell), 90, 91–92
My Year of Meats (Ozeki), 7, 142–54;
    diversity and biodiversity in, 143–44;
    global economic exchange networks,
    rejection of, 143–44; pathos in, 143;
    same-sex couples, 147–49

namesakes for recipes, 19
narrative, 5; alternative, cookbooks
    as, 17–18; migration, 21; traditional
    historical, 16–17
narrative, recipes as, 18, 32, 38–39
Nasser, Gamal Abdel, 134
National Council of Negro Women
    cookbooks, 62
*Nefesh Chaya: The Unique Avodas
    Hashem of the Jewish Woman* (Pin-
    cus), 204
Neff, Jack, 243
neoliberalism, 121, 122, 143, 144–45
Nericcio, William Anthony, 193–94
Nero Wolfe mysteries (Stout), 253–54
Neuhaus, Jessamyn, 62
"new domesticity" movement, 72
New York Magazine, 174–75
No Future (Edelman), 149
nostalgia, 196–97
"Nourishing Arts, The" (Giard), 28

Obama, Barack, 126
obesity, 122–23
objects of feeling, 176–77
Ochs, Elinor, 200
Oishi, Eve, 152
Olbrechts-Tyteca, Lucie, 192
Olomucki, Halina, *205*, 205–6

O'Neill, Molly, 77
"On Learning to Teach Fat Feminism" (Boling), 238
orientalism, 133, 146
Origin (Abu-Jaber), 132
O'Rourke, Alan, 214
Other, culinary tourism and, 101–3, 105, 107, 109, 111–12
Owen, Emma, 246, 249n4
Ozeki, Ruth, 7, 142–54

packaging: single-story stereotypes, 194; as symbolic, 192–93. *See also* Mexican food packaging
Paley, Grace, 60–70
Parts Unknown (television show), 104
Paterson, Jennifer, 9, 237–50
pathologies, 85
pathos, 7, 143, 234; of recipes, 34–37
peace activism, 6, 60–74; bake sales, 65, 71; gender subversion and domestic revolution, 66–71; international cuisine linked, 67–68
Peace de Resistance (Los Angeles's Women Strike for Peace), 60–61, 62–63, 64, 66–69
Peacemeal (Greenwich Village Peace Center), 61, 63–64, 69–70
Peace Never Tasted So Sweet (Abileah and Hallock), 60
Peckham, Shannon, 107–8
Perelman, Chaim, 192
persuasion, rhetoric of, 60, 63–64, 79, 121, 227–30
Phillips, Kendall, 197
Pilcher, Jeffrey, 192
Pilgeram, Ryanne, 123–25, 128
Pincus, Rav Shimshon Dovid, 204, 208
Pinner, Patty, 17–28
Planet Taco (Pilcher), 192
Plastas, Melinda, 65
pleasure, 6, 85, 92
plus-size models, 256
poison, 8
Pollan, Michael, 126–27

positive feeling, 7, 9, 143, 144–45, 149; multicultural assimilation, 151–52
poverty, 2, 119, 130; thrift advice, 52–53, 56
power, 5, 80, 182
Practice of Everyday Life, The (de Certeau, Giard, and Mayol), 28
prescriptive texts, 48–49
"presence," 192
presentation, 193, 194, 196–97
Primavera (Botticelli), 89
private property, 128–29
pro-ana websites, 9, 10, 212; evolution of, 214, 216; "hidden anorectic" and, 219; history, 214–16; House of Thin, 9, 214, 217–18; invitational rhetoric, 9, 213, 217, 219–20
Proust, Marcel, 136
Prudent Homemaker, The (Simper), 49, 56
public space, domestic sphere as, 22–23, 25

qualitative rhetoric of food, 80
quantification, discourse of, 86
Queer Art of Failure, The (Halberstam), 149
queer theory, 122–23, 149

Rabelais, François, 224–34; degradation and rebirth in, 224–25, 227; insult and praise in, 228; misreading of, 225–26
Rabelais and His World (Bakhtin), 224–27
racialization, 151, 196
radical rhetoric, 63–66
Ratcliffe, Krista, 4, 110–11
"Ravensbruck Women's Concentration Camp" (Saidel), 203
readers, 39, 44, 46n9, 79–80
"Reader's Digest" Great Recipes for Good Health, 30
Real Housewives franchise (television show), 175

recipe cards, 28, 30–31
recipes: credit lines, *34*, 35; "Date Puffed Rice Balls," *34*, 34–40; embodied rhetoric of, 38–40; as generic form, 5–6; literacy, 34, 45n1; logos of, 32–34; namesakes, 19; as narratives, 18, 32, 38–39; pathos of, 34–37; rhetoric of, 31–40; as scientific genre, 32–33; "standard two-part format," 32, 35. *See also* cookbooks
Recipes for Reading (Bower), 15
Reclaiming Rhetorica (Lunsford), 15, 16–17
Red Velvet Cupcake Murder (Fluke), 258–59
regulations, farm, 125–26
rehabilitation, 122–23, 126, 129–30
rehabilitative consumption, 122–23, 126–27
relatability, 106
Renaissance traditions, 224–26
representations, 132–33, 193–94, 196–97
reproduction, 143–44, 146–47
responsibility for cooking, 62, 64, 66–71
reverse discourse, 229
"'Revising the Menu to Fit the Budget': Grocery Lists and Other Rhetorical Heirlooms" (White-Farnham), 18
Reyes, Mitchell, 197
rhetorical agency, 56–57, 210
rhetorical analysis, 3–5, 49, 79
rhetorical listening, 4, 110–11
rhetorical strategies, 5, 6–7, 9–10; culinary tourism, 101–2
Rhetoric for Radicals: A Handbook for Twenty First Century Activists (Del Gandio), 63, 64–65, 71
Rhetoric of Food, The: Discourse, Materiality, and Power (Frye and Bruner), 4
Rhetoric Retold (Glenn), 15, 16
Rich, Adrienne, 123
Riley, Kevin, 240
Ritchie, Joy, 201
Rivkin, Jay, 66, 68

"romantic fantasy of the 'primitive,'" 105
Ronald, Kate, 61, 201
Ross, Karen, 245, 249n4
Rowling, J. K., 163–64
Royster, Jacqueline Jones, 4, 5, 56, 57–58, 61, 172, 175
Rumsey, Suzanne, 46n10
rural communities, 15–16, 120–21. *See also* family rhetoric
Rural Literacies (Schell), 121–22
Ruskin, John, 156, 157–58
Ryan, Kathleen, 49

Saguy, Abigail, 240
Saidel, Rochelle, 203
Salas, Consuelo Carr, 8
same-sex couples, 124, 147–49
Sandberg, Sheryl, 98
Saxton, Gene, 78
Scandal (television show), 172, 175
Sceats, Sarah, 42
Schell, Eileen, 121–22, 125, 126, 130
Schlib, John, 61
Schlosser, Eric, 226–27
Schneegans, G., 224
Scholz, T. M. Linda, 220
Schumack, Riet, 119–20, 128–29
scientific genre, recipes as, 32–33
second-wave feminism, 62, 72, 97; competing constructions of female corporeality, 251, 255, 261
Secret Garden, The (Burnett), 155–57, 167n3
self, 200–201, 210
self-awareness, 57, 144
self-denial, 85
self-perception, 254–59
self-sacrifice, 156–57, 166
Selzer, Jack, 49
sensory descriptions, 80
Serve It Forth (Fisher), 6, 78, 81
Sesame and Lilies (Ruskin), 156
shaming, 9, 27, 232; fat shaming, 241, 247–48, 249n4, 251
Sheraton, Mimi, 136

Shi, David, 50
Shoemaker, Leslie Cory, 136–37
silencing, 15, 16, 24–25, 28
Simper, Brandy, 49, 56
simplicity, 32, 50, 84–85
simulacra/simulation, 197
Sinclair, Upton, 226, 227
single-story stereotypes, 194
Skinny Bitch (Freedman and Barn-
    ouin), 9, 222–36; grotesque realism
    in, 223–24, 227–30; profanity, use of,
    227–30; rebirth, 230; reconstruction
    of food-body, 234–36; veganism,
    230–34
Slow Food movements, 106, 109
Smart-Grosvenor, Vertamae, 10n1
social circulation, 5, 172–73, 175
social networks, 18, 25
Sokolov, Raymond, 79
southern foodways, 15–16; African
    American women recreate, 21–28
Spectator, The (magazine), 238, 241–42,
    248n2
"standard two-part format," 32, 35
Stanley, Alessandra, 175
Steinem, Gloria, 171
Steingarten, Jeffrey, 52
Stern, Rebecca, 158, 160
Stewart, Pamela, 179
Stolen Years (Zyskind), 202
storytelling, 38–39
Stout, Rex, 253–54
Stowe, Harriet Beecher, 48
strategic essentialism, 246–47
subversion, 6, 60. *See also* girl poisoner,
    figure of
Supplemental Nutrition Assistance
    Program (SNAP), 52
sustainability, 7, 119–20; alternative
    agrarian rhetoric, 121–22, 126, 130;
    reciprocal exchange, 120. *See also*
    family rhetoric
Sutton, David, 136
*Sweets: Soul Food Desserts and Mem-
    ories* (Pinner), 17–29; epideictic

rhetoric, 23–24; origins of recipes,
    18–19; rewriting Great Migration in
    recipes, 19–28

*Table Comes First, The: Family, France,
    and the Meaning of Food* (Gopnik),
    90
Taboclaon, Aleah, 104
tea rituals, 161
technologies, 36–37, 46n8
television shows, 9, 49, 55
temperance rhetorics, 171, 172, 182
temporality, 39–40, 144; heteronorma-
    tive, 127–29
Ten Dollar Dinners (television show),
    49, 55
Terezín concentration camp, 137
Tex[t]-Mex (Nericcio), 193–94
Theophano, Janet, 17–18, 45n1
thrift: as discursive tradition, 49–50;
    as thriving, 50, 51, 52–53. *See also*
    kitchen thrift
thriving, 50, 51, 52–53, 56
Time cover (1993), 144
Tippen, Carrie Helms, 5
Today (television show), 175
Tomlinson, Graham, 32
"tough love," 228
tourism, culinary, 7, 100–115; armchair
    travel, 106–7; colonizing attitudes,
    101–5, 109, 112–13; cosmopolitanism,
    102–5, 113; decontextualization, 102,
    105–7; devouring, 102, 107–9; escap-
    ism, 102, 109–11; feminist perspec-
    tive, 111–14; masculinist gaze, 109
"tourist gaze," 107
Tozzi, Federica, 219
traditional concepts, 5
traditional historical narratives, 16–17
transgression, noxious food and,
    159–60, 167n6
travel journalism, 101
travel writing, 7
"Truth, Lies, and Method: Revisiting
    Feminist Historiography" (Glenn), 16

Tuscan tourism, 106
Two Fat Ladies (television show), 9, 237–50; antihealth-craze stance, 239; restaurant criticism, 242–43; *Spectator* articles, 238, 241–42, 248n2
Two Fat Ladies: Full Throttle (Wright and Paterson), 244, 245
Two Fat Ladies Ride Again, The (Wright and Paterson), 245, 246

United States Department of Agriculture, 51–52
Urry, John, 107

Valentine, Gill, 102
veganism, 9, 10, 222–23, 231–34
victimhood, rejection of, 25
Victorian era poisoning cases, 157–58
visual rhetoric, 8–9; commodified perception of culture, 194–95; metaphor, 204, 205; presence, 192; on recipe cards, 34, 39. *See also* Holocaust art by women

Walton, Priscilla, 251, 259–60
Wann, Marilyn, 238, 244–45
Ward, Katie, 214
Warmth of Other Suns, The: The Epic Story of America's Great Migration (Wilkerson), 20
Waxman, Zoë Vania, 202, 210
Weissová-Hošková, Helga, 206–8, *207*
Well-Tempered Women (Mattingly), 172
West, Isaac, 63–64
Whatever Happened to Thrift? (Wilcox), 50
White, Kate, 62
White-Farnham, Jamie, 18, 39, 46n10, 62
Whitehead, Barbara, 50–51
"Who Set You Flowin'?" (Griffin), 21

Wilcox, Ronald, 50
Wilkerson, Abby, 7
Wilkerson, Isabel, 20, 23
Williams-Forson, Psyche, 15, 16, 25, 27
Williamson, Judith, 193
Wilson, Jamie, 246
Winet, Kristin, 7
Winkler, Elizabeth, 239
witches, 155, 165
Witkowski, Terrence, 50
Woman's Home Companion (magazine), 78
Women and Children Being Sent on a Transport from the Terezin Ghetto (Weissová-Hošková), 206–8, *207*
Women and the Holocaust exhibit (Maltz Museum of Jewish Heritage), 200–201
Women in the Holocaust (Liberman), 208–10, *209*
women poisoners, 157–58, 165
Women's International League for Peace and Freedom (WILPF), 61, 65, 71
Women's Society of Christian Service, 35
women's studies classes, 142–43, 152
Women Strike for Peace (WSP), 60–61, 62–63, 65–66
Wright, Clarissa Dickson, 9, 237–50

Yakini, Malik, 130
Yates, Joshua, 50, 51
Young, Melinda, 238, 248
Youth Development Garden (Brightmoor Farmway), 119–20

Zimmerman, Anne, 77
Zimmerman, Barbara B. J., 60, 61, 65, 70–71
Zyskind, Sara, 202

Studies in Rhetorics and Feminisms

Studies in Rhetorics and Feminisms seeks to address the interdisciplinarity that rhetorics and feminisms represent. Rhetorical and feminist scholars want to connect rhetorical inquiry with contemporary academic and social concerns, exploring rhetoric's relevance to current issues of opportunity and diversity. This interdisciplinarity has already begun to transform the rhetorical tradition as we have known it (upper-class, agonistic, public, and male) into regendered, inclusionary rhetorics (democratic, dialogic, collaborative, cultural, and private). Our intellectual advancements depend on such ongoing transformation.

Rhetoric, whether ancient, contemporary, or futuristic, always inscribes the relation of language and power at a particular moment, indicating who may speak, who may listen, and what can be said. The only way we can displace the traditional rhetoric of masculine-only, public performance is to replace it with rhetorics that are recognized as being better suited to our present needs. We must understand more fully the rhetorics of the non-Western tradition, of women, of a variety of cultural and ethnic groups. Therefore, Studies in Rhetorics and Feminisms espouses a theoretical position of openness and expansion, a place for rhetorics to grow and thrive in a symbiotic relationship with all that feminisms have to offer, particularly when these two fields intersect with philosophical, sociological, religious, psychological, pedagogical, and literary issues.

The series seeks scholarly works that both examine and extend rhetoric, works that span the sexes, disciplines, cultures, ethnicities, and sociocultural practices as they intersect with the rhetorical tradition. After all, the recent resurgence of rhetorical studies has been not so much a discovery of new rhetorics as a recognition of existing rhetorical activities and practices, of our newfound ability and willingness to listen to previously untold stories.

The series editors seek both high-quality traditional and cutting-edge scholarly work that extends the significant relationship between rhetoric and feminism within various genres, cultural contexts, historical periods, methodologies, theoretical positions, and methods of delivery (e.g., film and hypertext to elocution and preaching).

Queries and submissions:
Professor Cheryl Glenn, Editor
   E-mail: cjg6@psu.edu
Professor Shirley Wilson Logan, Editor
   E-mail: slogan@umd.edu

Studies in Rhetorics and Feminisms
Department of English
142 South Burrowes Bldg.
Penn State University
University Park, PA 16802-6200

Other Books in the Studies in Rhetorics and Feminisms Series

A Feminist Legacy:
The Rhetoric and Pedagogy
of Gertrude Buck
Suzanne Bordelon

Regendering Delivery:
The Fifth Canon and
Antebellum Women
Rhetors
Lindal Buchanan

Rhetorics of Motherhood
Lindal Buchanan

Conversational Rhetoric:
The Rise and Fall of a
Women's Tradition,
1600–1900
Jane Donawerth

Feminism beyond
Modernism
Elizabeth A. Flynn

Women and Rhetoric
between the Wars
Edited by Ann George, M.
Elizabeth Weiser, and
Janet Zepernick

Educating the New
Southern Woman:
Speech, Writing, and Race
at the Public Women's
Colleges, 1884–1945
David Gold and
Catherine L. Hobbs

Women's Irony:
Rewriting Feminist
Rhetorical Histories
Tarez Samra Graban

Claiming the Bicycle:
Women, Rhetoric, and
Technology in Nine-
teenth-Century America
Sarah Hallenbeck

The Rhetoric of Rebel
Women:
Civil War Diaries and
Confederate Persuasion
Kimberly Harrison

Evolutionary Rhetoric:
Sex, Science, and Free Love
in Nineteenth-Century
Feminism
Wendy Hayden

Liberating Voices:
Writing at the Bryn Mawr
Summer School for Women
Workers
Karyn L. Hollis

Gender and Rhetorical
Space in American Life,
1866–1910
Nan Johnson

Antebellum American
Women's Poetry:
A Rhetoric of Sentiment
Wendy Dasler Johnson

Appropriate[ing] Dress:
Women's Rhetorical Style
in Nineteenth-Century
America
Carol Mattingly

The Gendered Pulpit:
Preaching in American
Protestant Spaces
Roxanne Mountford

Writing Childbirth:
Women's Rhetorical Agency
in Labor and Online
Kim Hensley Owens

Rhetorical Listening:
Identification, Gender,
Whiteness
Krista Ratcliffe

Feminist Rhetorical
Practices:
New Horizons for Rhetoric,
Composition, and Literacy
Studies
Jacqueline J. Royster and
Gesa E. Kirsch

Rethinking Ethos:
A Feminist Ecological
Approach to Rhetoric
Edited by Kathleen J. Ryan,
Nancy Myers, and
Rebecca Jones

Vote and Voice:
Women's Organizations
and Political Literacy,
1915–1930
Wendy B. Sharer

Women Physicians and
Professional Ethos in
Nineteenth-Century
America
Carolyn Skinner

Praising Girls:
The Rhetoric of Young
Women, 1895–1930
Henrietta Rix Wood